EMERGENCY
Planning and Management

Ensuring
Your Company's Survival
in the Event of a Disaster

Second Edition

William H. Stringfield

Government Institutes
An imprint of
The Scarecrow Press, Inc.
Lanham, Maryland • Toronto • Oxford
2005

 **Government
Institutes**

Published in the United States of America
by Government Institutes, an imprint of The Scarecrow Press, Inc.
A wholly owned subsidiary of
The Rowman & Littlefield Publishing Group, Inc.
4501 Forbes Boulevard, Suite 200
Lanham, Maryland 20706
http://govinst.scarecrowpress.com

PO Box 317
Oxford
OX2 9RU, UK

Library of Congress Cataloging-in-Publication Data

Stringfield, William H.
    Emergency planning and management: ensuring your company's survival in the event of a disaster—2nd ed.
       p. cm.
    Includes bibliographical references and index.

    ISBN: 0-86587-690-8 (pbk. : alk. paper)

    1. Emergency management. 2. Business planning.

HV551.2 .S77 2000
685.4'77—dc21   99-088949

Summary Contents

Contents

Preface to the Second Edition

Since the publishing of the first edition of *Emergency Planning and Management*, much has changed and much has remained the same concerning emergency preparedness and mitigation efforts. Disasters continue to happen frequently. We have been plagued by the concerns over Y2K and the potential computer issues it could have produced, El Nino and how it has played havoc on our weather, and let us not forget terrorism and workplace violence.

However, the basic question that I pose to you remains the same. Would your business be able to survive a catastrophic emergency situation and remain in business, or would you be forced to close your doors forever, as do more than 50 percent of businesses in the two years following a disaster? Over the past several years, the United States has been bombarded with a number of serious communitywide disasters that have impacted tens of thousands of businesses. Many of these businesses have either failed or suffered tremendous losses in the days and months following the disaster. What is unfortunate is that the majority of these businesses that suffered so greatly did so needlessly. Most businesses that failed following an emergency situation had one thing in common: they did not have an effective emergency response and business recovery plan in place at the time of the emergency.

Why is it that we continue to see such large numbers of businesses failing following emergencies? Why is it that so many businesses are not effectively prepared for emergencies? Possibly the answer lies in the fact that we do not address emergency planning in an effective manner in college programs designed to train business executives or in those training programs that are part of an executive's continuing education. If we don't inform business managers about the importance of disaster planning, how can we expect them to implement such programs?

This book is intended to provide you with the knowledge necessary to properly plan for and recover from workplace emergency situations. Emergency planning is not a simple topic, and effective plans typically take several months to develop and implement. However, the potential rewards certainly justify the time spent. It is time to take the necessary action to protect yourself, your assets, and your employees. Remember, if you don't prepare, nobody will.

*William H. Stringfield** *
Brewton, Alabama

---

* The author can be reached through the publisher (301-921-2355) and by email at wstringfield@bigfoot.com

About the Author

William H. Stringfield has over 20 years of experience dealing with the response to, and the planning and training for, emergency situations within industry and public safety organizations.

He is the author of three books: *Emergency Planning and Management, The Executive's Guide to Disaster Planning,* and *A Fire Department's Guide to Implementing Title III and the OSHA Hazardous Materials Standards.* In addition, he has written over two dozen articles on emergency planning, training, and response.

Chapter 1

An Emergency Planning Primer

Emergency planning is by no means a new concept or philosophy. Businesses and communities have conducted varying degrees of emergency planning and disaster preparation for decades. Industry and governmental agencies on the federal, state, and local levels all share in the responsibility for developing procedures and capabilities for handling hazards resulting from natural or technological causes. Every day thousands of businesses throughout the world suffer from emergency situations ranging from very minor (such as a medical emergency which may have no impact on the economic well-being of a business) to major (such as losses from fires or explosions). Whether you are a small business with ten employees or a large corporation employing thousands, you have a responsibility to provide a safe environment for your employees, preserve company facilities and equipment, and protect the community from the impact of an emergency at your business.

Businesses have for too many years put a tremendous reliance on the local community to handle problems at their facilities. Far too many executives have unrealistic expectations about capability of the local fire, police, and emergency medical services to handle emergencies at their facilities. We watch too many "true-to-life" action dramas on television and at the movies and when a real incident occurs at our facility and the emergency responders arrive, we are shocked that maybe they don't have all the tools and tricks that are depicted on television. Every business in this country must be prepared to handle those types of emergencies that may reasonably be expected to occur. If you are not prepared and are expecting the local fire department or emergency squad to handle the situation without your assistance, you had better get out the help wanted ads and look for new employment. The main emphasis of community emergency planning is to protect the community. Community emergency planning initiatives are concerned with life safety, the environment, and property—in that order. Property adjacent to your facility may have a higher priority than yours, in that a community is trying to minimize the spread of an incident to other properties.

An emergency action plan (EAP) is commonly defined as a well-thought-out document that details the who, what, when, how, and where, as well as standard operating procedures for handling emergency situations. When facilities develop emergency action plans, they typically develop a document that is intended to satisfy federal and/or state requirements for the development of emergency action plans and requirements of insurance carriers that underwrite the facility. Obviously it is a good idea to meet those regulations and requirements pertaining to emergency planning, but it should not be your primary motivation. When your primary emphasis is regulation compliance, you will write your plan with only that goal in mind. However, if you write your plan with the goal of protecting your employees and your company assets, you will find that you also will achieve your regulatory requirements.

An EAP is just as important to a business as having a business plan. One of the frequent causes of business failure is the absence of an effective business plan. You cannot expect your business to grow and survive if you do not have an effective business plan. The same holds true for your business as it relates to emergencies. If you do not have an effective emergency action plan, you cannot expect your business to survive an emergency situation.

An effective emergency action plan includes the following four components:

- **Assessment**
  The assessment component determines the types of hazards the facility may be vulnerable to and the potential level of risk to employees and facility assets.

- **Preparedness**
  The preparedness component determines the activities, programs, and systems that are developed prior to an emergency situation and that are used to support the facility response program.

- **Response**
  The response component determines activities that are intended to stabilize and control the emergency situation.

- **Recovery**
  The recovery component determines activities that are needed to return the facility to a functional status.

The remainder of this book is designed to help you develop the four components of an effective emergency plan.

Why Insurance Is Not Enough

Far too many business executives think that the proper way to protect a business from catastrophic loss is to carry extensive amounts of insurance. Ask an insurance agent what the best way to protect your business from loss is and the agent will probably suggest that you increase the value of your current insurance. You can have all the insurance in the world and your business can still fail following a major emergency. I am certainly not telling you not to have proper insurance coverage, but it is important for you to carefully select the proper type and amount of coverage for your facility. One of the most important factors in business survival following a disaster is the ability of a business to continue service to its customers during the recovery period. If you lose your customers, you will lose your business. Therefore, one of the major topics discussed throughout this book will be strategies that a business should employ to help maintain its customer base. Some of the concepts that I will present will go against everything you may have been taught in Business 101. My goal is to show you strategies that might allow you to remain in business following a major incident, and, in the process, I may have to ask you to change some of your thinking.

Case History—Turbo Widgets

For twenty years Turbo Widgets has been in the business of manufacturing specialized widgets used in the electronics industry. They are known as an industry leader and have a 20 percent market share. Turbo Widgets maintains one manufacturing facility and employs 300 workers. They have sufficient insurance, as recommended by their insurer, to protect their property, inventory, and equipment. They also carry a business interruption policy to cover lost income should a devastating incident curtail their ability to manufacture and distribute their product. In addition, their insurance carrier makes an annual safety inspection. They meet all of the fire and life safety code requirements mandated for their facility. The facility has an emergency action plan which was revised last year. They have never had a major incident at the facility.

How would you assess the ability of this facility to stay in business following an emergency? Let's create a catastrophic emergency at Turbo Widgets.

It is 2 am and the facility is closed for the night. The only personnel on site are two maintenance mechanics and a security guard. The fire alarm system activates, indicating a fire in the warehouse area. The security guard follows the procedures as outlined in the emergency action plan and calls 911 to report the fire alarm. By the time the fire department arrives, the fire involves a large portion of the warehouse. The fire department does its best to save the facility, but even then the facility is a total loss.

The next day Turbo Widgets contacts the insurance carrier and the process to rebuild the Turbo Widget plant begins. The company president is quoted in the local newspaper as say-

ing that Turbo Widgets was fully insured for the loss and that management is committed to rebuilding the plant. Sounds familiar doesn't it?

A week after the fire, the management of Turbo Widgets is forced to lay off all but ten of its management personnel. Their business interruption policy was designed to cover only the loss of net income, not the additional amount needed to cover payroll.

Would you be able to absorb your employee costs or would you have to lay off many of your career employees?

Turbo Widgets does begin to rebuild its facility, but it takes much longer than expected. Originally, management planned to be back in production within four months. However, it takes ten months. It seems that the city and state require that environmental and transportation impact studies be conducted, and these studies delay the rebuilding process by several months.

When the Turbo Widgets facility is finally close to completion, the company begins contacting many of the employees it had been forced to lay off after the fire. It is critical to rehire as many of these experienced personnel as possible, especially those who had been involved in product design and research. But Turbo Widgets is surprised to find that many of its former employees have since found other jobs and are not interested in changing jobs again. In addition, some of the key design personnel have found jobs with other electronics manufacturing companies and are earning salaries equal to or better than their Turbo Widgets salaries. Some former employees want to negotiate salaries that are much higher than those they had been prior to the fire. These problems in rehiring former employees were not planned for. Now many new employees must be hired and trained, and this will increase Turbo's startup costs.

How many of your employees do you think you would be able to rehire?

When Turbo Widgets goes back to its customers to inform them that Turbo is back in production, about 50 percent are not interested in purchasing from them. They have found new suppliers, and many are receiving a better price than they had with Turbo. To make matters even worse, the competition has hired many of Turbo's best salespersons who have the inside track on luring away Turbo's old customers.

What impact would your competition have on your business? If your competition had 10 months to wine and dine your customers while you were out of the picture, what percentage of your customers would you lose to them?

In order to get back its old customers and attract new ones, Turbo Widgets is forced to offer 45- and 60-day net terms instead of its customary 15- and 30-day terms. In addition, Turbo will have to cut its prices to win back its customers. Cutting prices and giving better terms was the last thing on the mind of Turbo's management at a time when the company needed as much cash flow as possible.

What strategies might you implement to get your customers back? Would you be required to offer better terms and better prices? What impact would this have on your business?

The Turbo Widgets case study illustrates a situation that occurs all too frequently. Many business executives maintain the "it can't happen to me" philosophy when preparing for emergencies. Keep in mind that it can happen to you and very likely will one day if you maintain this mindset. The key to survival following a disaster is to start with the attitude that a serious incident can occur at your facility and then to develop and implement strategies based on this assumption.

Direct and Indirect Losses from Incidents

When a business is hit by an emergency, it can suffer two kinds of loss. These losses can be classified as direct and indirect.

Direct losses are measured in terms of dollars that are directly lost as the result of an emergency. Direct losses are the most easily measured and include damage to property, equipment, and inventory.

The accurate measurement of direct losses requires that you maintain current records of equipment and inventory and keep them in a secure place. Lack of inventory information will make it difficult to collect insurance following an incident. If you carry business interruption insurance, it is important to realize exactly what is covered by the policy and what documentation your insurance carrier will require when making a claim.

Following the fire, Turbo Widgets files insurance claims for $14.5 million in equipment replacement and $8.7 million for lost inventory. Turbo Widgets was denied $3.4 million related to equipment and $1.3 million in inventory because the company had failed to update its offsite equipment and inventory records which were kept in a bank safe-deposit box. In filing its insurance claim, Turbo Widgets used documentation that was over 12 months old. All records concerning recent purchases and current inventory were maintained at the facility and were destroyed during the fire. Management was just too busy making widgets to think about updating offsite records.

Proper record management is one of those elements most critical to effectively surviving a loss. We will discuss record management strategies in great detail in Chapter 6.

Indirect losses are those losses from an incident that are much harder to measure in dollars, at least initially. Indirect costs cause many businesses to fail because the businesses do not anticipate the impact of these kinds of losses. It is important to note that most indirect costs are not covered by insurance. Indirect costs that are frequently overlooked include the following:

- **Replacements costs not adjusted for inflation**
  Often management will only consider the cost that was paid for a piece of equipment when insuring its replacement cost. Equipment replacement costs must be reassessed on a regular basis. The frequency will depend on the type of business you are in and how fast equipment is discontinued or replaced by new technology. I have found very few businesses that update their equipment replacement costs on a regular basis. This is a major mistake if you expect to have adequate insurance to cover replacement costs following an emergency.

- **Cost of temporary facilities and equipment**
  This can include many things like the rental or purchase of equipment, tools, office equipment, computers, and telephone systems. The real costs associated with temporary facilities is very frequently underestimated. Temporary facilities are generally more costly than permanent facilities. If you are trying to lease office or warehouse space on a month-to-month basis, you will generally pay a premium for such a lease. Then the costs associated with the establishment of telephone service and utilities must be added to this. Setting up a temporary facility is very similar to starting up a new business. Most people underestimate the costs associated with establishing a business and similarly underestimate the cost of establishing temporary facilities.

- **Loss of employees**
  Often major incidents that shut down a facility for any length of time require that many key employees be laid off since most employers do not have adequate cash reserves to maintain employees. This layoff creates a major problem when the facility goes back on line because many of these former employees will have found other jobs. The hiring of new personnel generally requires that additional costs be allocated for training and and also may necessitate a higher per unit cost until employees are adequately trained and comfortable with the process.

- **Increased insurance costs**
  Having a major incident at your facility may change your risk profile with your insurance carrier. Anticipate that your insurance rates will increase. It is also possible that your insurance may be canceled, requiring you to obtain policies from another carrier. You may very likely be placed in a high-risk category, which will add to your indirect costs. In some cases, an incident that does not even involve your facility may cause your insurance rates to increase or make the process of obtaining additional insurance very difficult. For example, it became very difficult

to obtain insurance in Florida following Hurricane Andrew in 1992. Not only have businesses seen their rates increase for certain types of coverage, but also many insurance companies have canceled existing insurance policies and will no longer issue new policies in Florida.

- **Loss of customers**
  If you were unable to deliver your product or service for one, three, or six months, what percentage of your market share would you lose? How many of your customers would come back to you when you reopened your doors? These are questions that are certainly easy to answer for most business executives. The key to a successful business is keeping your customers happy and having them return to you time and time again.

- **Fines and legal fees**
  A major incident at a business often brings many unexpected visitors such as inspectors from the U.S. Occupational Safety and Health Administration (OSHA).

Fines in the $100,000 to $1,000,000 range are becoming commonplace following major incidents, especially those that cause injuries and deaths to employees. OSHA proposed nearly $6.4 million in penalties for alleged safety violations following a fire and explosion at a Pasadena, Texas petrochemical plant in 1989.

Legal fees can be astronomical following a major emergency. Litigation can arise from employees, customers you are unable to deliver promised goods to, and businesses and communities near your facility that were impacted by your emergency.

Additional indirect costs that can never be fully measured often involve human suffering due to job loss, physical injuries, and psychological trauma.

Failure to properly anticipate indirect costs as part of your emergency planning could put your business in a dangerous financial position following the emergency. A comprehensive emergency action plan that includes survivability procedures will put you ahead of 98 percent of your competition.

Federal Requirements for Development of Emergency Action Plans

There are a number of federal regulations that require the development of emergency action plans by employers. In general, all employers with more then ten employees are required to develop a written emergency action plan that addresses basic emergency situations that could occur at the facility. Employers with ten or fewer employees may communicate their plans to employees orally and need not maintain a written emergency action plan.[1]

---

[1] OSHA 1910.38(a) Employee Emergency Action Plans.

Overview of Federal Requirements

To make matters very confusing, there are numerous federal and state regulations that require businesses to conduct some aspect of emergency planning.[2] Not all of these regulations will be applicable to all businesses but, at a minimum, all businesses are required to have an emergency action plan as outlined in OSHA 1910.38(a) Employee Emergency Action Plans.

The following paragraphs will provide a basic overview of the planning requirements of two federal regulations that impact a tremendous number of businesses.

OSHA 1910.38(a)—Employee Emergency Action Plans

Emergency action plans are specifically required by 1910.38, Employee Emergency Action Plans. Under this OSHA regulation each employer shall have a written emergency action plan that shall cover those designated actions employers and employees must take to ensure employee safety from fire and other emergencies.[3] Emergency action plans shall define exactly what constitutes an emergency and specifically what actions are to be taken. Examples of emergencies include personnel injuries, fire, chemical spills, severe weather, bomb threats, and civil disturbances.

The following elements, at a minimum, shall be included in the plan:

1. Emergency escape procedures and emergency escape route assignments

2. Procedures to be followed by employees who remain to operate critical plant operations before they evacuate

3. Procedures to account for all employees who remain to operate critical plant operations before they evacuate

4. Rescue and medical duties for those employees who are to perform them

5. The preferred means of reporting fires and other emergencies

6. Names or regular job titles of persons or departments who can be contacted for further information or explanation of duties under the plan

In addition, the employer shall establish an employee alarm system which complies with 1910.165.[4]

1. The employee alarm system shall provide warning for necessary emergency action as called for in the emergency action plan, or for reaction time for safe escape of employees from the workplace or the immediate work area, or both.

---

[2] A list of other federal regulations that require emergency planning is included in this section.

[3] For employers with ten or fewer employees, the emergency action plan may be communicated orally to employees.

[4] OSHA 1910.156 Employee Alarm Systems.

2. The employee alarm shall be capable of being perceived above ambient noise or light levels by all employees in the affected portions of the workplace. Tactile devices may be used to alert employees who would not otherwise be able to recognize an audible or visible alarm.

3. The employee alarm system shall be distinctive and recognizable as a signal to evacuate the work area or to perform actions designated under the emergency action plan.

4. The employer shall establish procedures for sounding emergency alarms in the workplace. For those employers with ten or fewer employees in a particular workplace, direct voice communication is an acceptable procedure for sounding the alarm provided all employees can hear the alarm. Such workplaces need not have a backup system.

5. If the employee alarm system is used for alerting fire brigade members, or for other purposes, a distinctive signal for each purpose shall be used.

6. The employer shall establish in the emergency action plan the types of evacuation to be used in emergency circumstances.

Before implementing the emergency action plan, the employer shall designate and train a sufficient number of persons to assist in the safe and orderly emergency evacuation of employees.

OSHA 1910.120—Hazardous Waste Operations and Emergency Response

This regulation requires that employers develop and implement a written emergency action plan that will allow their employees to handle or assist in the handling of hazardous substance releases. *Emergency response* means a response effort by employees from outside the immediate release area or by other designated responders to an occurrence which results in, or is likely to result in, an uncontrolled release of a hazardous substance. Responses to incidental releases of hazardous substances where the substance can be absorbed, neutralized, or otherwise controlled at the time of release by employees in the immediate release area, or by maintenance personnel, are not considered to be emergency responses within the scope of this standard. Responses to releases of hazardous substances where there is no potential safety or health hazard (i.e., fire, explosion, or chemical exposure) are also not considered to be emergency responses.

Under 1910.120(q) an emergency action plan shall be developed and implemented to handle anticipated emergencies prior to the commencement of emergency response operations. The plan shall be in writing and available for inspection and copying by employees, their representatives, and OSHA personnel. Employers who will evacuate their employees from the workplace when an emergency occurs, and who do not permit any of their employees to assist in handling the emergency, are exempt from these requirements if they provide an emergency action plan in accordance with 1910.38 (a).

The employer shall develop an emergency action plan for emergencies which shall address, as a minimum, the following to the extent that they are not addressed elsewhere:

1. Emergency planning and coordination with outside parties

2. Personnel roles, lines of authority, training, and communications

3. Emergency recognition and prevention

4. Safe distances and places of refuge

5. Site security and control

6. Evacuation routes and procedures

7. Decontamination

8. Emergency medical treatment and first aid

9. Emergency alerting and response procedures

10. Critique of response and follow-up

11. PPE and emergency equipment

12. Coordination of facility, local, and state emergency action plans to avoid duplication

Other federal regulations that require the development of emergency action plans are described in the next few paragraphs.

OSHA 1910.119—Process Safety Management of Highly Hazardous Substances

This OSHA regulation was promulgated as part of the Clean Air Act Amendments (CAAA) of 1990. The major objective of the process safety management (PSM) of highly hazardous chemicals regulation is to prevent unwanted releases of hazardous chemicals, especially into areas that could expose employees and others to serious hazards.

The PSM standard targets highly hazardous chemicals (approximately 135) that have the potential to cause a catastrophic incident. Within the PSM standard there are specific requirements pertaining to emergency planning.

Superfund Amendments and Reauthorization Act (SARA) Title III Emergency Planning and Community Right-to-Know Act of 1986

Establishes requirements for federal, state, and local governmental agencies, and many business facilities regarding emergency planning and the reporting of hazardous and toxic materials. This regulation is reviewed in detail in Chapter 3.

Oil Pollution Act of 1990 (OPA)

This regulation, which is commonly referred to as OPA, amended the federal Water Pollution Control Act. It covers both facilities and carriers of oil and related liquid products, including deep-water marine terminals, marine vessels, pipelines, and railcars. Requirements include the development of emergency response plans, regular training and exercise sessions, and verification of spill resources and contractor capabilities.

40 CFR Part 68 — Risk Management Programs for Chemical Accident Release Prevention

This Environmental Protection Agency (EPA) regulation was promulgated as part of the Clean Air Act Amendments (CAAA) of 1990. It is similar in scope to the OSHA Process Safety Management standard described above, but the primary focus is community safety rather than employee safety as in the OSHA standard. The regulation requires the development of an emergency response plan which includes protective actions for employees, procedures for responding to a hazardous materials release, descriptions of mitigation technologies, and procedures for informing the public and emergency response personnel about the release. What makes this regulation interesting is that EPA publishes on its website (http://www.epa.gov/swercepp) most of the information that a facility submits. The information that you submit concerning your emergency preparedness measures will be readily available to the public.

40 CFR Part 112—Spill Prevention Control and Countermeasures Plan

This regulation applies to facilities engaged in drilling, producing, gathering, storing, processing, refining, transferring, distributing, or consuming oil and oil products, which, due to their location, could reasonably be expected to discharge oil, in quantities that might be harmful, into or upon navigable waterways or adjoining shorelines, or upon the waters on the contiguous zone.

Facilities covered by the regulation must prepare a Spill Prevention, Control, and Countermeasures (SPCC) plan.

40 CFR 264.50 through 264.56, Subpart D—Contingency Plan and Emergency Procedures

These requirements fall under the Resource Conservation and Recovery Act (RCRA) administered by the EPA. This regulation deals with facilities having hazardous wastes as identified in the regulation. Facilities falling under this regulation must develop emergency procedures which include the following elements:

- Description of actions personnel are to take in response to fires, explosions, or any unplanned release, whether sudden or gradual, of hazardous waste

- Coordination agreements with local governmental agencies, hospitals, hazardous waste contractors, and local and state emergency response organizations for response to a facility emergency

- Designation of individuals who will function as emergency coordinators and alternate emergency coordinators

- Designation of emergency equipment and maintenance requirements for such equipment

- Evacuation and accountability procedures for site personnel

49 CFR Part 194—Response Plans for Onshore Oil Pipelines

This regulation contains requirements for the development of oil spill response plans to reduce the environmental impact of oil discharged from an onshore oil pipeline. This regulation applies to operators of an onshore oil pipeline that, because of its location, could reasonably be expected to cause substantial harm, or significant and substantial harm to the environment, by discharging oil into or on any navigable waters of the United States or adjoining shorelines.

National Fire Protection Association

The National Fire Protection Association (NFPA) has been a leader in the development of fire safety codes and standards since 1896. The mission of this international nonprofit organization is to reduce the burden of fire on the quality of life by advocating scientifically based consensus codes and standards, research, and education for fire and related safety issues.

The lifeblood of NFPA is its consensus standards-making system, which produces the National Fire Codes and over 300 codes and standards covering all areas of fire safety and used in nearly every country in the world. In some way, virtually every building, process, service, design, and installation in society today is affected by the codes and standards developed through this open system.

The following NFPA standards and recommended practices may be of interest to those involved in emergency planning and response.

NFPA 471—Recommended Practice for Responding to Hazardous Materials Incidents

The intent of this document is to outline minimum requirements that should be considered when responding to and dealing with hazardous materials incidents and to recommend standard operating guidelines for responding to such incidents. Topics covered within the document include the following:

- Incident Response Planning
- Response Levels
- Site Safety
- Personal Protective Equipment
- Incident Mitigation
- Decontamination

This document will help facilities comply with hazardous materials emergency response requirements as established in OSHA 1910.120(q), Hazardous Waste Operations and Emergency Response.

NFPA 472—Standard for Professional Competence of Responders to Hazardous Materials Incidents

The intent of this standard is to identify levels of competency that are required for personnel involved in the response to hazardous materials incidents, whether from public or private organizations. It identifies competencies required for the following responders:

- First Responder Awareness Level
- First Responder Operational Level
- Hazardous Materials Technician
- Incident Commander
- Private Sector Specialist Employees

This document will help facilities comply with hazardous materials emergency response requirements as established in OSHA 1910.120(q), Hazardous Waste Operations and Emergency Response.

NFPA 600—Standard on Industrial Fire Brigades

The intent of this standard is to provide minimum requirements for organizing, operating, training, and equipping industrial fire brigades. It deals with all levels of industrial fire brigade, from the incipient level to the advanced exterior and interior structural fire brigade level.

This document will be of assistance to any facility developing a compliance program to meet OSHA 1910, Subpart L for Fire Protection.

NFPA 1561—Standard on Fire Department Incident Management System

Although this document indicates that it is a "fire department incident management system" the concepts contained within the document are applicable to any organization, private or public, providing emergency response activities. The document includes the following major areas:

- Implementation of the incident management system
- Interagency coordination
- Command structure
- Training and qualifications
- System components
- Roles and responsibilities

This document help facilities comply with requirements pertaining to the use of an Incident Command System as established under OSHA 1910.120(q), Hazardous Waste Operations and Emergency Response.

NFPA 1600—Recommended Practice for Disaster Management

The intent of this document is to recommend minimum criteria for disaster management planning for private and public organizations. The document examines the following core areas of disaster planning:

- Assessment and mitigation
- Preparedness
- Response
- Recovery

This document will be of assistance to facilities in meeting the requirements of OSHA 1910.38, pertaining to emergency action plans.

Chapter 2

Assessment of Your Vulnerability

Could your business handle an emergency situation? I would hope that the answer is yes. However, experience has demonstrated time and time again that the majority of businesses do not have an effective plan in place for handling an emergency.

All businesses are vulnerable to emergencies. The extent of your vulnerability will in part depend on the type of business activity you are involved in and the degree of preparedness and level of training of your employees. An analysis of your business's vulnerability to particular hazards will provide the basis for developing a practical, workable emergency action plan.

What types of emergencies is your facility vulnerable to? Fires, medical emergencies, hazardous material spills, earthquakes, etc.? We can make a general assumption that almost all facilities will be vulnerable to fires and weather-related emergencies. But how do we determine the specific types of emergencies that might threaten our business in particular?

There has been a considerable effort at the federal and state levels to identify hazards such as earthquakes, hurricanes, and dam failures. Information on these types of hazards should be available for your community. Check with your local office of emergency management or civil defense and ask for a copy of the government-perceived threats for your community.

In analyzing and assessing the vulnerability of your business, you must consider environmental, indigenous, and economic factors. These factors are the basis for:

1. Estimating the likelihood of damage, either by direct effects on your facility or by indirect effects resulting from your business's dependency on a facility damaged elsewhere

2. Making plans for protective measures within individual facilities or complexes of facilities to minimize damage and casualties

3. Reviewing insurance policies for liability and coverage

As an example of an environmental factor in determining vulnerability, an industrial facility may be endangered because of proximity to the following:

1. A flood plain

2. Facilities that manufacture, use, or store hazardous materials

3. Nuclear target facilities such as military facilities and defense contractors
   Although in recent years with the ending of the Cold War this threat has become less critical in emergency planning, this topic could become a concern at any time and should be considered as part of your plan.

4. An area prone to forest fires

Business facilities may also be vulnerable to the following:

1. Indigenous factors

2. Lightweight materials used in the construction of the facility
   Businesses tend to build facilities as cheaply as possible. This is especially true of manufacturing and distribution facilities. Lightweight materials such as aluminum and steel prefab are generally very good but tend not to hold up well in extreme weather situations, such as hurricanes and tornadoes.

3. Process materials that in themselves are hazardous or might generate hazardous by-products in the event of a release or a fire

4. Stored combustible materials such as paper goods, plastics, and lumber that might increase the fire load potential

5. Floor layout and arrangements of equipment and inventory that might hinder the evacuation of employees and restrict the access of emergency personnel to the problem area

6. Critical equipment such as machinery and tools
   Some businesses utilize very specialized production machinery that has been custom designed for them and their process. Should this equipment be damaged or destroyed during an emergency it could have severe consequences on the facility while custom machinery is made or repaired.

7. Inadequate exits for rapid evacuation of the building
   Most businesses only have the absolute minimum number of exits as required by the local fire code. Keep in mind that the formulas used to determine type, number, and size of exits are based on nationally determined standards. Your particular facility, because of its design, processes utilized, or other factors, may require additional exits.

8. Improperly maintained fire protection systems
   Each year facilities with well-designed fire protection systems suffer devastating fires. Failure of the fire protection systems to extinguish a fire is most often the result of improper maintenance and repair of these systems. Each facility must have a program in place to properly maintain such systems.

Economic factors that may impact a facility may include the following:

1. Criticality of product

2. Exclusiveness of product

3. Stockpiled or reserve material

For planning purposes, you must assume that most disasters will arrive with little warning, develop rapidly, and have the potential for substantial destruction. The likelihood is small that the kinds of disasters that we will discuss and that you will plan for will ever happen to your business. However, if you expect your business to survive following an emergency, you must have an effective emergency action plan prepared for your facility.

Hazard and Risk Management Assessment

A Hazard and Risk Management Assessment (HRMA) is a comprehensive assessment of a business's potential for, and its projected ability to handle, an emergency situation and remain in business. It is designed to provide decision makers, such as corporate executives, safety professionals, bankers, attorneys, and insurance agents, etc., a fundamental knowledge of the potential risks present at a facility and its survivability following an emergency. The HRMA is a tool for effective management of a business's operations. Most executives fail to consider the risks from a catastrophic emergency and the ability of the business to handle the emergency, but without an effective analysis of a business's ability to survive an emergency situation, one cannot effectively gauge its long-term survivability. Every business owner or manager should ask the following questions about his or her operation:

- What would happen to your business if you were to have a catastrophic incident that required you to shut down for 30 days or longer?

- What effects would the incident have on the long-term survivability of your business?

- Would you be able to stay in business or would you lose a number of your customers?

Most business owners feel that by purchasing insurance they have protected themselves. But insurance is only one piece of the puzzle. Unless you are in a business with no competition, you may be in a great deal of trouble.

Look at your business and answer the following questions:

- Does your facility have the ability to go into limited production?

- Are all of your eggs in one basket, so to speak, in that all of your sales, management, production, and distribution activities are within one facility?

- How long would you be able to maintain your employees after a catastrophic incident before you would have to begin layoffs?

- If you were unable to supply your customers, would they go to your competition?

- What percentage of your "loyal customers" would remain with your competition after you reopen?

If you don't know the answer to the above questions you may be very vulnerable to business failure following an emergency.

Benefits of a Hazard and Risk Management Assessment

Put very simply, a properly conducted hazard and risk management assessment (HRMA) will provide management with an idea of the relative degree of risk that a facility may be vulnerable to, the facility's level of preparedness to handle an emergency, and its ability to survive the emergency situation and remain in business. Let's take a look at the areas of the HRMA that should be addressed.

Step 1   Determine the Potential Hazards
That Threaten the Facility

Risk Potential Analysis

The risk potential analysis is designed to determine the types of hazards that a facility might be vulnerable to. The following should be considered when conducting the risk analysis:

- **Type of business**
  Certain businesses will have a higher probability of incidents because of the type of activity that they are involved in. A metal-plating business that uses corrosives and other hazardous materials has a higher probability of fire, chemical spills, and employee injuries than a business involved in the development of computer software.

- **Materials involved in production**
  A business using highly reactive chemicals has a higher degree of risk than a facility involved in glass cutting.

- **Degree of fire protection**

  A facility with a moderate degree of risk from fire that has a well-designed fire sprinkler system and fire alarm system may present less of a risk than a facility with no special hazards that has no fire protection system in place.

- **Degree of safety training and prevention activities**

  A facility that has a good training program instructing employees in emergency procedures and a good safety inspection program will generally have less risk than a facility with no program in place.

Types of Hazards

Types of hazards that may threaten a business include the following:

1. **Fire and explosion**

   Every business is vulnerable to fires. Each year fires in the workplace cost in excess of $3 billion. Every business must be cognizant of the hazards from fire and take a proactive approach toward fire prevention. The American public is very lax when it comes to fire safety. We may be the most technologically advanced country in the world, but we lead all other countries in deaths, injuries, and dollar loss from fire. If your business relies fully on the fire inspection conducted by the local fire department to reduce your risk from fire, you may be a prime candidate for a fire. A fire inspection only looks at your potential for fire at the time of the inspection. Often the facility is given advanced warning that the fire inspection is to take place. Usually the fire inspector will call the facility manager to set up an appointment for a fire inspection. Most facility managers, when they receive word that a fire inspection is about to occur, will take extra time to straighten up the facility and make it look its best. Often this good housekeeping condition only lasts until the fire inspection has been completed.

   Unless your facility is located in an area with a large number of inspectors or unless you operate a high-hazard business that requires frequent inspections (six-month intervals), the most you will see a municipal fire inspector is once every one to two years. I have been to some facilities that have not had a fire inspection in over ten years. Do not rely solely on a fire inspection by the local fire department to identify fire hazards. Each facility must have a procedure in place to review safety practices and housekeeping on at least a monthly basis. Fire is the most common and most devastating form of destruction that threatens a facility. You must be prepared.

   It is important to keep in mind that your business's risk from fire is impacted by the community in which it is located. Your risk of destruction from a devastating fire is in part affected by the quality and preparedness level of the local fire department. Some facilities will be served by excellent well-trained and equipped fire department, while others will be served by something quite different. I have experienced incidents in which the response to a fire at a commercial facility consisted of as many as four engine companies, two ladder truck companies, one heavy rescue squad, and one chief officer, with a total response of 32 personnel. I have also experienced incidents in which the response to a similar facility consisted of only one engine and a total of two personnel. It should be obvious that the differing capabilities of these two communities to respond to emergencies will have profound impacts on the businesses that operate in their jurisdictions. With a fire station located close to your facility, fire personnel will be able to respond within a few minutes, but if you are located in a rural area served by volunteer fire department, it may take 15 to 20 minutes for the first fire department personnel to arrive. Do you know what the fire department response capability is in your locality? If not, you had better find out. Following an assessment of the local fire department's capabilities and response time, facility managers have had to drastically reevaluate their onsite fire training and capability to compensate for the inadequacy of local community response. Do not assume the level of capability; investigate and implement appropriate safeguards.

In addition, your neighbors could have a tremendous impact on your facility. Even if you have a very good fire protection and prevention program in place at your facility, if the business that you share the building with has no fire protection program in place and would be considered at a high risk from fire, then you share in your neighbor's risk. If a fire starts in your neighbor's business, it may very likely spread to yours. I have talked to many business owners who share a building with another business. It always amazes me that most of these owners have little idea what their neighbors do or have never been inside their neighbors' businesses to assess the degree of risk to their facilities.

2. Hazardous material releases

Your business may be vulnerable to the effects of a hazardous materials release whether or not your facility uses hazardous materials. Over the past few years, a tremendous amount of emphasis has been placed on the preparedness and response to hazardous materials releases. If you use hazardous materials, you must be prepared to react quickly to such incidents. Your personnel must be able to recognize the hazards presented by hazardous materials and must know exactly what procedures to follow to ensure safe handling of an incident.

Materials that can be hazardous when released are referred to by different terms. We call these materials *hazardous materials*, *hazardous substances*, *hazardous wastes*, *hazardous chemicals*, and *extremely hazardous substances*, to name just a few. For the purposes of this book, we will consider hazardous materials to be any material that can cause harm to people, the environment, or property when spilled or released. A hazardous material is not a problem until it leaves its intended containment system. We could have a cylinder of "methyl-ethyl-death" in our office and work day in and day out with no adverse effects occurring to us as long as the material does not leave its container. Hazardous materials do not generally present a hazard until they leave their containers.

3. **Severe weather and natural events**

All businesses are vulnerable to the effects of severe weather. The type and severity of weather will be greatly influenced by the location of your business. Severe weather is one of the least planned for emergency situations in most businesses. You can determine your vulnerability to the different types of severe weather by contacting your local emergency management office. This office should also be able to tell you specific hazards, such as flooding, that your facility may be subject to.

Over the past few years the United States has seen its share of natural disasters. In the past two decades there have been over 40 weather-related disasters that have each caused over $1 billion in damage. A few significant examples include:

- Hurricane Floyd in September 1999 caused an estimated $6 billion in damages and over 70 deaths. The majority of the deaths and damage came as a result of the flooding that followed the hurricane. Upwards of 2.6 million people were evacuated during Hurricane Floyd, making this the largest single evacuation effort in United States history.

- Drought and heat wave during the summer of 1998 caused an estimated $9 billion in damage from crop and related losses. Estimates of the number of heat-related deaths are as high as 5,000.

- The "Storm of the Century," in March 1993, hit the eastern seaboard with high winds, tornadoes, and snow, causing $6 billion in damages and 270 deaths.

- Hurricane Georges, in September 1998, caused an estimated $6 billion in damage and 16 deaths.

- Hurricane Fran, in September 1996, caused an estimated $5 billion in damage and 37 deaths. It was the most destructive hurricane ever to strike North Carolina.

- Hurricane Andrew, in September 1992, caused an estimated $30 billion in damage and 58 deaths. Hurricane Andrew destroyed or damaged 82,000 businesses and caused 86,000 people to lose their jobs. In addition, 90,000 homes were damaged or destroyed and 250,000 people were left homeless.

- Floods in the Midwest during the summer of 1993 claimed 48 lives and caused an estimated $20 billion in damage.

- The January 1994 Los Angeles earthquake claimed at least 60 lives, injured more than 9,000 and caused an estimated $30 billion in damages. Over 10,000 people filed quake-related requests for unemployment compensation in the first two weeks following the earthquake.

Types of severe weather that your facility may be subjected to include the following:

- Hurricanes

- Tornadoes

- Winter storms

- Floods

- Earthquakes

- Volcanic eruptions

Chapter 3 will go into some specifics concerning severe weather conditions.

4. Transportation incidents

All businesses are subject to hazards from transportation incidents. Trucks making deliveries to your facility may bring onto your property hazardous materials that are to be delivered to another facility. Many people are unaware of the hazards that are brought onto their property by common carriers. If there should be an incident involving a delivery truck while on your property, you will have to resolve the problem. A truck carrying hazardous materials may be involved in an incident as it passes by your facility, endangering the employees at your facility and requiring that you shut down or modify your operations.

You can find out what roads in your area are used extensively for hazardous materials transportation by contacting your county office of emergency management or the Local Emergency Planning Committee (LEPC). They may have information on transportation flow studies that may assist you in your risk analysis planning.

5. **Public demonstrations and civil disturbances**

Public demonstrations and civil disturbances have become commonplace throughout the country over the last 30 years. Your business may be the target of a specific public demonstration, or you may be impacted by a demonstration or disturbance at a nearby facility.

Police will generally be responsible for handling any violence or vandalism associated with such episodes, but you, as the employer, must also share in the responsibility for protecting your employees. I think that we can all see the impact that the April 1992 Los Angeles riots had on thousands of businesses and individuals. The Los Angeles County Economic Development Corporation estimated that 20,000 employees lost their jobs immediately following the riots. Of these, as many as 5,000 may have been permanent. Another report indicated that Los Angeles County may lose as much as $1.1 billion in visitor spending and 31,000 full-time jobs as a result of tourists being scared off by the riots.

I am certain that businesses in the Los Angeles area will consider early action should a similar situation arise in the future. Every business can learn from the problems that occurred during the Los Angeles riots.

It is important to note that civil disturbances are not experienced only by large cities such as Los Angeles. In 1996, St. Petersburg, Florida, experienced what may be the most significant episode of civil disturbances since the 1992 Los Angeles riots. In October 1996, the shooting of a black motorist by a white police officer sparked two nights of rioting and arson. In November 1996, further disturbances occurred following the release of the Grand Jury report that cleared the police officer involved in the incident. Over 100 businesses and homes were damaged or destroyed and over $6 million in damage was experienced.

6. **Terrorism**

In this day and time, almost every business and person has the potential to be touched by terrorism. Much of the recent focus on terrorism has involved incidents where explosive devices were used. However, terrorism also includes attacks with chemical and biological weapons, hijackings, kidnappings, maimings, assassinations, and assaults on facilities. Over the past 30 years, terrorism has been increasing at an alarming rate. During the 1970s there occurred a total of 8,114 reported acts of terrorism worldwide. A total of 4,978 people were killed and 6,902 were injured. The 1980s marked a substantial increase in worldwide terrorism. During the 1980s, there were 31,426 reported acts of terrorism, with 70,859 killed and 47,849 injured. During this 20-year period, the primary targets for terrorists have been businesses. What is not reported in any of the studies that I am aware of, is the cost of these acts of terrorism to the business community in terms of lost jobs, lost income, and the number of businesses that have failed following the incident.

Look at the impact from the bombing at the World Trade Center in New York City in February of 1993, when 6 persons were killed and over 1,000 were injured. This act of violence impacted 450 businesses and over 50,000 employees. A report by UPI in 1993 indicated that lost business and recovery work as a result of the World Trade Center bombing would exceed a half billion dollars. In addition, over 1,600 workers were laid off following the incident.

The most horrific terrorist event in United States history was certainly the bombing of the Alfred P. Murrah Federal Office Building in Oklahoma City on April 19, 1995. This act of terrorism killed 167 persons and caused the nation to come to the realization that we are vulnerable to terrorist attacks.

Acts of terrorism are increasing at an alarming rate. One of the greatest threats today is the use of weapons of mass destruction (WMD) as part of terrorist activities. Weapons of mass destruction include chemical, biological, nuclear, and radiological weapons or materials, and explosive or incendiary devices that can cause mass casualties among innocent civilians or government forces. The use of chemical and biological weapons is possibly of most concern to government and emergency preparedness officials in that a very small amount of certain materials can cause significant impact. The recent incident involving the release of sarin gas in a Tokyo subway on March 20, 1995, caused 12 deaths and over 5,000 injuries.

The concern over terrorism has caused the federal government and state and local agencies to take a hard look at their level of preparedness for such incidents. Consider that, in 1999 alone, spending by the U.S. government for terrorism prevention and preparedness activities is estimated at $7.7 billion dollars.

7. Sabotage

Sabotage is another problem that today's business executive cannot ignore. The threat from sabotage is very real, and you may be more vulnerable than you think. Very few businesses have adequate procedures in place to minimize the threat from sabotage. There are many similarities between sabotage and terrorism. At times it is hard to distinguish between the two. They are similar in that both of these types of action are carried out by individuals or groups in order to make a point.

Sabotage might be carried out by disgruntled present employees, former employees in retaliation for being fired, political groups that may disagree with your business activities, or by others for any number of reasons. Certain occurrences may make you more prone to sabotage, such as facility layoffs and labor disputes. Facilities must be aware that sabotage is a real threat in today's business environment and must be planned for.

In October 1998, the Vail Ski Resort in Vail Colorado suffered a series of arson attacks that caused an estimated $12 million in property damage. A group called the Earth Liberation Front claimed responsibility for the arsons in retaliation for the resort's plan to expand its ski areas.

Most people will remember the tragedy surrounding the 1984 release of the chemical methyl isocyanate (MIC) from the Union Carbide pesticide plant in Bhopal, India, which killed more than 3,800 people. What is not known by most is that this is probably the most horrific act of employee sabotage that has ever occurred. Although it was not known at the time of the incident, the toxic gas was formed when a disgruntled plant employee, apparently wanting to spoil a batch of methyl isocyanate, added water to a storage tank. The water caused a reaction that built up heat and pressure in the tank, quickly transforming the chemical compound into a lethal gas that escaped from the plant.

8. Workplace violence

Workplace violence has been increasing at an alarming rate over the past 10 years. Murder has become the number-one cause of death for women in the workplace; for men it is the third most frequent cause, after machine-related mishaps and auto accidents. More than 1,000 Americans are murdered on the job every year, which is about 20 every week. A 1993 survey by Northwestern National Life Insurance suggests that each year more than 2 million employees suffer physical attacks on the job and more than 6 million are threatened in some way. Many of these incidents are the results of robberies of retail store employees, delivery drivers and others who are vulnerable to such attacks. However, an increasing number of these incidents are the results of altercations among employees and conflicts with former employees or with customers.

Workplace violence is an issue that must be considered by facilities when they develop their emergency plans, and precautions must be taken to minimize the threat from such occurrences.

9. Strikes and work stoppages

Dealing with employee strikes and job actions must be a significant part of your emergency planning. When a strike occurs, it can have a severe impact—other than just financial—on your business. Facilities that have the potential for work stoppages or strikes should have a plan in place to provide for the safety of workers who will remain on the job and for the preservation and protection of facility assets. It is important that facilities develop an alternate emergency plan for dealing with emergency situations that arise during a strike. You must keep in mind that your emergency plan was developed based on the availability of your facility's normal workforce. Many of your personnel who are trained to respond to and handle emergency situations (such as emergency response team members and fire brigade members) will be on the other side of the fence and not part of your response. You may find that in some situations you do not have any qualified and trained personnel available to respond to and handle an emergency. It is important that management develop specific emergency procedures to be implemented during a strike or work stoppage. I would recommend that these procedures be kept separate from your emergency plan as a separate document maintained by top facility management.

Step 2 Determine the Prevention and Preparedness Level of the Facility

Step 2 examines those activities, procedures, and plans that are currently in place to prevent and react to an emergency situation at the facility. Consider each of the risks that you identified in Step 1, and determine your capabilities and those of your community to respond to any possible emergency.

What emergency planning documents do you have in place? Do they address these areas:

- **Prevention Activities**
  Prevention activities include safety inspections, employee training, and early warning detection systems.

- **Response Capability**
  What is the capability of the facility to respond to an emergency situation to protect its employees and company assets? You should also consider the capability of the local community's emergency response services (fire, police, and medical) to handle an emergency situation at the facility.

Step 3 Determine the Ability of the Facility to Protect Company Assets

Protection of company assets is one of the major factors in determining whether or not a facility will be able to stay in business following a major emergency situation. The most important part of this assessment is the protection of vital records, since you should have adequate insurance to cover equipment and machinery. You must determine how your vital records are being protected and whether that level of protection is adequate in view of the perceived hazards at your facility. Vital records include financial, corporate, customer, and manufacturing information—to name just a very few. Chapter 6 goes into detail on record protection strategies.

Step 4 Assess the Capabilities of Your Personnel

The actions that your employees will take in an emergency will have a profound impact on how well your facility fares. One of the techniques that I use when I conduct facility assessments is to randomly interview employees. I ask them what their actions would be during an emergency situation. You may be very surprised at the answers your employees will give. Often the action that an employee plans to take during an emergency would actually increase the vulnerability of the facility and the employee for greater damage or injury.

Step 5 Putting It All Together

If you take the information that you obtained from the first four steps, you should have a good idea of the types of hazards that your business is vulnerable to and your capability to handle emergencies. This information will be used to develop a site-specific emergency action plan.

Planning Considerations

This chapter will examine in greater detail some of the types of emergency situations that were introduced in Chapter 2. Suggestions for emergency preparedness planning will be provided for each of the examined hazards.

Hurricanes

The National Weather Service is responsible for issuing warnings when hurricanes appear to be a threat to the United States mainland, Puerto Rico, the Virgin Islands, Hawaii, and the Pacific Territories. As soon as conditions intensify to the tropical storm level—even though the storm is a thousand miles or more from the mainland—the storm is given a name and the National Weather Service begins issuing advisories. The advisories are issued every six hours when a hurricane is more than 24 hours away from land and every three hours or less when it is closer. These advisories tell where the storm is located, the intensity of its winds, and the speed and direction of movement.

If a hurricane moves toward the mainland, hurricane watch notices are given. A *hurricane watch* indicates that (1) the hurricane is a threat to coastal areas, and that (2) everyone in the area covered by the watch should listen for further advisories and be ready to take precautionary actions, including evacuation, if directed.

As soon as the forecaster determines that a particular section of the coast will feel the full effects of a hurricane within 24 hours, a hurricane warning is issued. *Hurricane warnings* specify coastal areas where winds of 74 mph or higher or a combination of dangerously high water and very rough seas are expected. *Tropical storm warnings* are also issued for those areas that are expected to receive gale force winds (greater than 40 mph).

At the beginning of the hurricane season, your facility should take early action to prepare for a hurricane. Check all drainage pumps, battery-powered equipment, and backup power sources. Ensure that sewers and drains for flood water removal are in working order. Brace storage tanks and all outer structures that may be vulnerable to high winds. Keep company vehicles fueled. When the warning is issued, immediately take all precautions against the full force of the wind. Board up windows or protect them with tape. Secure all outdoor equipment. Store drinking water for post-hurricane operations. Listen for local emergency weather advisories or special instructions from local government before, during, and after the storm. Prepare to evacuate if the order comes. Be alert for tornado warnings, as hurricanes often spawn tornadoes. Since some industries may require one to three days to prepare (petrochemical manufacturers, offshore oil drill rigs, etc.), carefully planned procedures must be implemented as soon as advisories indicate a hurricane may affect such facilities.

The local office of the National Weather Service will provide all severe storm data following a general storm warning, including tornadoes and hurricanes. The Latest Forecast lines for the local weather office will be listed under the Department of Commerce in the U.S. Government listings in the local telephone book. These lines are frequently answered 24 hours a day. There will be a regularly updated taped forecast, or in some cases, an individual will answer questions. Weather alert radios are also a very good means to keep updated on hurricane information. Every facility should have at least one weather radio. Do not overlook the Internet as a means of keeping advised of breaking weather conditions.

Stay indoors during the hurricane. After the storm, turn off all damaged utilities at central control points and report problems to the appropriate utility services. Check for gas leaks or hazardous materials release. Take special precautions to prevent fires because lowered water pressure makes firefighting difficult. Avoid possibly contaminated drinking water. If you must venture outdoors, stay away from loose or dangling wires.

Tornadoes

Tornadoes are violent local storms with whirling winds that can reach velocities of 200 to 400 mph. The individual tornado appears as a rotating, funnel-shaped cloud which extends toward the ground from the base of a thundercloud. It varies from gray to black in color. The tornado spins like a top and may sound like the roaring of an airplane or locomotive. These small, short-lived storms are the most violent of all atmospheric phenomena and, over a small area, are the most destructive.

The width of a tornado path ranges generally from 200 yards to 1 mile. They travel 5 to 50 miles along the ground at speeds of 30 to 75 mph. Tornadoes sometimes double back or move in circles, and some have remained motionless for a while before moving on. They have struck in every state, but areas of frequent occurrence are the middle plains and southeastern states. Because tornadoes are highly localized and recurring in some areas, companies in tornado-prone areas should participate in a tornado watch system built around a local emergency management agency.

The National Weather Service issues severe weather warnings, using the following terms:

- *Severe thunderstorm* indicates the possibility of frequent lightning and/or damaging winds with wind velocity greater than 50 mph, hail ¾ inch or more in diameter, and heavy rain.

- *Severe thunderstorm watch* indicates the possibility of tornadoes, thunderstorms, frequent lightning, hail, and wind velocity of greater than 75 mph.

- *Tornado watch* means that tornadoes could develop in the designated area.

- *Tornado warning* means that a tornado has actually been sighted in the area or is indicated by radar.

Since tornadoes occur with little or no warning, very little planning can be done before the event. However, permanent mitigation measures can be taken to upgrade existing buildings and can be included in new building designs. Management should assign specific areas in the facility to shelter employees. The best protection is an underground area. In buildings without basements, managers should designate interior hallways on the lowest floor as tornado shelter areas. Shelter high-rise building occupants in small interior rooms or hallways. Continuously monitor news broadcasts following a tornado watch announcement. When a tornado warning is issued, direct employees to take shelter immediately and to crouch down and cover their heads with their arms. Close all doors to outside rooms. Conduct training and periodic drills to ensure that employees know where and how to best protect themselves. Those employees who work outside should be advised to lie flat in the nearest ditch, ravine, or culvert with their hands shielding their heads if there is not time to reach indoor shelter. In the aftermath of the tornado, check all damaged facilities for injured personnel. Avoid downed powerlines, check for gas leaks, and extinguish or contain small fires.

Winter Storms

Winter storms vary in size and intensity. A storm may affect only part of a state or many states and may be a minor ice storm or a full-blown blizzard. Freezing rain or sleet, ice, heavy snow, or blizzards can be serious hazards. A facility can lessen the impact of hazardous winter storms if management observes storm warnings and makes adequate preparations to protect its employees and operations.

The forecast terms for hazardous weather conditions which should alert a facility to take precautionary measures include the following:

- *Winter storm watch* indicates severe winter weather conditions may affect the area. Freezing rain, sleet, or heavy snow may occur either separately or in combination of the three forms of precipitation.

- *Winter storm warning* indicates that severe winter weather conditions are imminent.

- *High wind watch* indicates that sustained winds of at least 40 mph, or gusts of 50 mph or greater, are expected to last at least one hour. In some areas this means strong gusty winds occurring in shorter time periods.

- *Heavy snow warning* indicates snowfalls of at least 4 inches in 12 hours or 6 inches in 24 hours are expected.

- *Blizzard warnings* are issued when sustained wind speeds of at least 35 mph are accompanied by considerable falling and/or blowing snow. Visibility is dangerously restricted.

- *Travelers' advisories* are issued to indicate that falling, blowing, or drifting snow, freezing rain or drizzle, sleet, or strong winds may make driving difficult.

Take all preseason preparedness measures appropriate to your geographical area before the first snowfall. Assure that employees are aware of cold weather safety rules and understand company policy for operations and closing under adverse weather conditions.

Floods

Except in the case of flash flooding from thunderstorms, coastal storms, or dam failure, the onset of most floods is a relatively slow process with adequate time for warning the public. The buildup usually takes several days. A *flash flood warning* is the most urgent type of flood warning issued. These warnings are transmitted to the public over radio and television. They may also be transmitted through local warning systems by sirens, horns, or whistles; through telephone alerts; or by police cars using loudspeakers.

If your community has a history of recurring floods, the community's minimum precautionary requirement is to establish continuing communications with the National Weather Service. For example, flood forecasts and warnings should be telephoned to the local police headquarters or some other centralized facility at agreed-upon periods. The location of your facility with respect to potential flooding is critical, and planning must be done accordingly. Therefore, you should contact your local and/or state emergency management agency to determine vulnerability of your facility's location and to obtain information and maps, where appropriate, and other details pertaining to flood plains and other flood prone areas.

Water damage can be prevented or lessened by floodproofing buildings, constructing levees, and sandbagging, by relocating equipment and records, and by installing pumps and emergency power supplies. Some methods to assist in minimizing water damage include the following:

- **Maintain an adequate supply of sandbags**

  Sandbags are not watertight, but they are usually adequate as short-term emergency flood barriers for shallow flooding conditions. Sandbags may be fabric or plastic sacks which are usually filled with sand or soil at the site where they are to be used. Sandbags are commercially available throughout the country. The local emergency management office can usually provide information on suppliers in the area. You should stockpile a reasonable number of sacks for any anticipated flooding. The cost is small, the storage space is minimal, and when the flood occurs sandbags may not be available in adequate supply.

- **Move critical records and equipment**

  Placing items up off the ground onto shelves and tables may provide enough clearance to prevent damage from minor flooding. In multistory buildings, items can be moved to an upper level. Relocation to another facility may be required if the expected flood water elevation will be more than 2 or 3 feet above the facility's floor level. In new construction, key pieces of equipment, such as emergency generators, can be positioned above an expected flood water elevation by using steel support legs, by bolting to wall supports, or by placement in upper stories or on roofs. Quick-disconnect electrical plugs can be installed to permit rapid removal and reinstallation of larger machinery.

- **Provide pumps and emergency power sources**

  Pumps can be used to dewater localized areas (e.g., basements or areas protected by berms or sandbags). Care must be exercised in selecting pumps with adequate capacity to pump the water out faster than it enters. Also, there must be adequate power supply to drive the pumps. It should not be assumed that normal electric power will be available. Gasoline powered pumps or emergency generators may be required.

Earthquakes

Although many earth scientists are searching for means of predicting impending earthquakes, accurate predictions of the exact time and place of earthquakes are not yet possible. However, it can be assumed that earthquakes will continue to occur in areas where they have been relatively common in the past. They may range in intensity from slight tremors to great shocks and may last from a few seconds to as long as 5 minutes. They could come in a series over a period of several days. The actual movement of the ground in an earthquake is seldom the direct cause of injury or death. Most casualties result from falling materials and building collapse. Severe quakes usually destroy power and telephone lines and gas, sewer, or water mains. They may also trigger landslides, rupture dams, and generate seismic waves.

Employees should be warned that during an earthquake they should (1) stay indoors if already there; (2) take cover under sturdy furniture (such as work tables), brace themselves in a doorway, or move into a corner and protect the head and neck in any way possible; (3) stay near the center of the building; (4) stay away from glass windows, skylights, and doors; and (5) not run through or near buildings where there is danger of falling debris. If employees are outside, they should stay in the open, away from buildings and utility wires.

After the earthquake, employees should exit the building by the stairs, never the elevators. They should stay out of damaged buildings as the aftershock can cause the building to collapse. Facility officials should check utilities. If water pipes are damaged or electrical wires are shorting, turn them off at the primary control point. If gas leakage is detected, evacuate the building and keep the building cleared until utility officials say it is safe to return. At some facilities, shutdown of high voltage and fuel systems is necessary immediately following earthquake damage and before evacuation so personnel will not be endangered by lines that might be ruptured. In other plants, evacuation might not be jeopardized, but recovery operations might, unless shutdown was completed beforehand.

An important fact to keep in mind is that virtually all areas of the United States have the potential to experience an earthquake. We all recognize that California has a high incidence of earthquakes, but how many of you realize that Missouri is considered as being the next most likely area to experience a devastating earthquake? In all, 41 states are considered to have a moderate to high potential to experience an earthquake. The Federal Emergency Management Agency (FEMA) has identified a number of heavily populated areas of the United States that are particularly susceptible to high-intensity earthquakes. These areas include Honolulu, HI; San Diego, Los Angeles, and San Francisco, CA; Puget Sound, WA; Anchorage, AK; Salt Lake City, UT; the seven-state area of the central United States (MO, KY, TN, MS, AR, IN, IL); Charleston, SC; Boston, MA; New York; Puerto Rico; and the Virgin Islands.

Facility Fires

Because prompt and well-directed action can be decisive in escaping a major fire loss, it is important to have in place an organization to prepare for and conduct emergency functions. The size, style, and makeup of your facility's emergency organization will depend on many factors such as plant size, the hazard present, the type and condition of available fire equipment, and the nearness and reliability of the local fire department. Local ordinances, and state or federal regulations may require your facility to choose among several response options for fire control and to define your response in written procedures. These procedures would be inspected periodically and reevaluated for merit. The following options are representative of the choices industry has for responding to facility fires under OSHA 1910.156 Fire Protection:

- *Option One* calls for immediate evacuation on alarm. The employer is not required to train employees in firefighting but must take steps to ensure safe egress.

- *Option Two* requires every employee to be trained in the use of fire extinguishers. Employees in the vicinity of the fire make the initial attempt at control. If the fire is beyond self-help control, the alarm is sounded and all employees evacuate.

- *Option Three* assigns designated employees only to self-help firefighting. The other employees in the affected area, who have not been assigned emergency duties, evacuate.

- *Option Four* establishes a fire brigade to fight only incipient fires that can be controlled without resorting to breathing apparatus or protective clothing. Beyond this level, the brigade must break off and evacuate.

- *Option Five* establishes a structural fire brigade. Employees so assigned must be trained and equipped to fight fires beyond the incipient stage using breathing apparatus and protective clothing.

The most important aspect of planning to cope with major facility fires is the development of mutual assistance agreements with local governments, other plants, and nearby federal installations. Smaller businesses usually cannot afford to maintain the standing forces required to meet a major fire situation, so they rely on local government services and mutual aid. To be effective in cases of large fires, industrial explosions, and forest fires, mutual aid requires good communications, accessibility to the fire scene, prearrangements for use of apparatus and personnel, and centralized command.

The most important factor in fire control is not personnel and equipment. Most often it is the ability to respond quickly and to confine the fire to manageable limits before it reaches the disaster stage. This calls for a plan of action for mutual aid response by existing local fire organizations. Where such plans exist at the time of a large fire, the emergency usually is manageable, with life and property loss held to a minimum. For the safety of employees, install smoke detectors and a fire alarm system with automatic notification to the local fire department; adequately mark fire escapes and ensure that they are accessible at all times; post evacuation plans in prominent areas throughout the building; conduct periodic fire drills; and install a fire suppression (water sprinkler) system where practical.

Hazardous Materials

Several thousand chemicals and other hazardous materials in daily use can cause an emergency which would affect a substantial number of employees and others in the area of the facility. These effects could include injury to the eyes, respiratory system, and skin; contamination of a community; explosions; and fires. Facility officials should ensure that extreme care is taken in the use of hazardous materials in all processes, production stages, storage, and shipment. Management should also be aware of the presence and use of hazardous materials in neighboring facilities.

Post a plot plan throughout the plant indicating the location, hazardous properties, and characteristics of individual chemicals and their potential hazardous reaction to each other. Your plot plan will organize most of the basic information needed to make response decisions for onsite hazards and will be valuable for both planning and operations when an incident occurs. Provide a copy of this plot plan, including location of storm drains, shutoffs, hydrants, etc., to the local fire department along with a facility contact list containing names and contact information for persons to notify in case of an emergency at the facility.

The major planning requirements for employee protection include an audible warning system and evacuation plans. Once basic personnel safety has been addressed, the next management decision point is how to contain, control, and conclude onsite incidents. Management may rely on outside agencies to handle the situation or may maintain an onsite emergency response team (ERT) for this task. The choice will probably depend on facility size and how much property damage is acceptable as the result of a delayed response.

If your facility decides to leave the response to onsite hazardous material incidents to the community emergency services, you should inform emergency service providers of the decision and supply them with detailed information about facility hazards. Determine exactly how emergency service providers want an incident reported to them, and develop an acceptable backup incident reporting system.

If management decides to maintain an onsite ERT for hazardous material incidents, then, in addition to the above, you need to determine the potential impact from these incidents and the limits of onsite team response, develop response procedures to deal with the incidents, and initiate a program of preventive countermeasures.[5] The bulk of these additional planning needs can be determined from the inventory of hazardous materials, their quantities, locations, the manufacturers' material safety data sheets, the range of the threat from each material, and what is at risk. The preventive and response countermeasures that address the specific circumstances of hazardous materials should take into account complications from possible concurrent incidents such as fire. Also, remember that your onsite problem could become a neighbor's offsite hazard, so give adequate warning of the danger to the surrounding community.

---

[5] OSHA 1910.120(q) Hazardous Waste Operations and Emergency Response.

On October 17, 1986, Public Law 99-499, the Superfund Amendments and Reauthorization Act of 1986 (SARA) was passed. SARA specifies requirements for state and local government and the private sector related to hazardous chemicals. Title III of SARA, known as the Emergency Planning and Community Right-to-Know Act of 1986, specifically requires the governor of each state to establish a State Emergency Response Commission (SERC). SERCs, in turn, designate emergency planning districts within the state and appoint a Local Emergency Planning Committee (LEPC) for each district. SERCs and LEPCs are responsible for implementing various emergency planning provisions of Title III as well as serving as points of contact for the community right-to-know reporting requirements. The Title III provisions which apply to the private sector are included in the following sections of the law.

- **Section 302 Substances and Facilities Covered and Notification**

    Requires facilities producing, storing, or using certain extremely hazardous substances in excess of threshold planning quantities to notify the SERC if these substances are present at the facility. The presence of these chemicals triggers certain local emergency planning requirements under Title III.

- **Section 303 Comprehensive Emergency Response Plans**

    Requires covered facilities to provide the LEPC with the name of a facility representative who will participate in the emergency planning process as a facility representative. Facilities are also required to provide to the LEPC information necessary for developing and implementing an emergency plan.

- **Section 304 Emergency Notification**

    Requires covered facilities to notify appropriate authorities upon the release of certain hazardous chemicals.

- **Section 311 Material Safety Data Sheets**

    Requires each facility that must prepare or have available material safety data sheets (MSDSs) under Occupational Safety and Health Administration regulations to submit either copies of MSDSs or a list of MSDS chemicals to the SERC, LEPC, and local fire department with jurisdiction over the facility.

- **Section 312 Emergency and Hazardous Chemical Inventory Forms**

    Requires each facility having MSDSs to submit an inventory form annually to the SERC, LEPC, and local fire department including information aggregated by categories on estimated amounts and locations of chemicals in the facility. The facility may also be requested to provide this information on a chemical-by-chemical basis.

- **Section 313 Toxic Chemical Release Forms**

    Requires facilities to complete an annual inventory of toxic chemical emissions for specific chemicals.

Transportation Incidents

Almost every facility is exposed daily to the possibility of air, highway, railroad, or shipping accidents in or near its boundaries. Facility officials should be prepared to handle the type of problems they will have to face if their facility is involved in transportation incidents.

The U. S. Department of Transportation (DOT) regulates the movement of hazardous materials. When hazardous materials that would pose a significant hazard to the public if released from their packings are transported interstate, they must be labeled with appropriate hazard warnings. Shipping papers identifying the hazardous material being transported are required to be in the cab of the motor vehicle, to be in the possession of train crew members, to be kept in a holder on the bridge of a vessel, or to be in the possession of an aircraft pilot.

Since not all facilities have the same degree of vulnerability or the same resources to handle such emergencies, each facility should develop its own plan of action, including agreements for giving and receiving mutual aid. These plans should include listings of the type of equipment or services needed, the source and location of the equipment or services, the person or point of contact to give or obtain immediate response to an emergency request, and the means and method of compensating (if appropriate) for the use of the equipment or services in an emergency.

Major transportation accidents often cause chemical spills, fires, explosions, and other problems, which call for special operations such as rescue and evacuation. Usually, transportation accidents affect only relatively small areas and involve only a small number of people.

An airplane crash may create the need for firefighting and other operations in the area of impact. An automobile crash with a bus or a carrier of hazardous cargo can involve substantial rescue, firefighting, and evacuation operations. A railroad accident can produce hazardous situations when it occurs in or near plant facilities, particularly if the cargo is flammable or explosive. This can also involve substantial rescue, firefighting, and evacuation operations.

Regardless of the type of transportation accident, the first consideration should be to save lives. This can be accomplished through quick response and coordination of the facility's emergency services and local police, fire, and medical services. Again, effective warning devices and evacuation procedures are essential.

Public Demonstrations/Civil Disturbances

In recent years protest demonstrations for different purposes have occurred in many locations throughout the country. Some demonstrations develop slowly, allowing the authorities to assess the problem, to conduct negotiations with the organizers, and to arrange for control measures. On other occasions, violence may flare up with little advanced notice. However, these incidents are usually preceded by earlier indications of a buildup of tensions and pressures.

In a situation which is developing slowly and deliberately, facility officials may operate out of their regular offices during the preliminary or negotiating phase, calling in staff directors as required, and routinely circulating information to departments concerned.

In a situation where there is a sudden eruption of violence, accompanied perhaps by attempted arson and assault, facility security personnel usually will be involved initially and will serve as the source for information regarding the characteristics and extent of the disturbance. The facility security personnel should cooperate completely with local law enforcement agencies, which will provide the information needed to make appropriate decisions. Consider early release of employees or a request that employees stay home. An effective employee notification/recall system is a must.

Terrorism

Compared with other facility emergencies, the covert and criminal nature of terrorism, including bombing incidents, bomb threats, and the taking of hostages, is a highly complex problem for management and emergency service personnel. Consequently, planning to meet the threat must include prompt contact with the local law enforcement agency, particularly if it has a bomb disposal unit, and the local office of the Federal Bureau of Investigation.

Experience shows that over 95 percent of all written or telephoned bomb threats are hoaxes. However, there is always a chance that a threat may be authentic. In 1996, the Bureau of Alcohol, Tobacco and Firearms reported that there were over 2,500 bombings in the United States. These incidents caused over $50 million in damage and 23 fatalities. Appropriate action should be taken in each case to provide for the safety of employees, the public, and property and to locate the suspected explosive or incendiary device so it can be neutralized.

The first line of response to a bomb threat is threat analysis. In order to do this effectively, it is necessary to get all the information possible on the person or group making the threat and the size and location of the bomb. Industries concerned about such threats will want receptionists who can remain calm and have had training in what questions to ask. A prepared questionnaire placed near the phone can be very useful in such an emergency situation. (See Appendix Documents for a sample of such a questionnaire.)

The information gathered on this questionnaire may be sufficient to discount the threat or may indicate that actions other than evacuation be taken. And it is not as unlikely as you may think that the caller will give his/her address. According to the FBI many of these callers are really looking for someone to talk to, and a simple ruse such as saying, "We'll have the manager get back to you on that. Could I have your name and address so he/she can do so?" may be all it takes to get such information. Therefore, this question-naire may be the most important resource in dealing with bomb threats.

While the responsibility for action rests primarily with the law enforcement agency, the course of action will be affected to some degree by the other persons involved. For example, the facility manager must be prepared to warn employees and must decide whether or not to evacuate the building after a bomb threat and where to send the people who are evacuated. Also, individuals who know what does or does not belong in or near the building should be available to assist law enforcement officials in conducting the search for a suspected bomb.

If a suspicious object is located and thought to be a bomb and the local law enforce-ment personnel cannot dispose of it, the services of a bomb disposal unit previously ar-ranged for should be requested. Contact the state police or a military explosive ordinance disposal team, if there is a military installation located nearby, for assistance and training.

Sabotage

No facility is immune to sabotage. However, the types of targets for sabotage usually can be predicted with reasonable accuracy. The saboteur will generally look for a target that is critical, vulnerable, accessible, and at least partially conducive to self-destruction. Sabo-teurs in general are enemy agents, disgruntled employees who commit sabotage for re-venge, or individuals who are mentally ill or have been duped by enemy propaganda. Sabotage may be linked to or be another form of terrorism.

The methods of sabotage may be classified as follows:

- **Chemical** - the addition or insertion of destructive or polluting chemicals

- **Electric or electronic** - interrupting or interfering with electrical or electronic pro-cesses or power and jamming communications

- **Explosive** - explosive materials used to destroy or damage a facility and its assets

- **Incendiary** - fires ignited by chemicals, electrical, electronic, or mechanical means or by any ordinary means of arson

- **Mechanical** - breaking or omitting parts, using improper or inferior parts, or failing to lubricate or properly maintain

- **Psychological** - inciting strikes, boycotts, unrest, personal animosities, or causing slowdowns or work stoppage by excessive spoilage or inferior work

Sabotage may be prevented by reducing target accessibility and vulnerability. Allow only authorized access to the potential target; screen and place employees in accordance with security requirements; design, construct, and modify equipment with built-in protection against sabotage; conduct continuing education for employees on prevention of sabotage; and have a plan with procedures for handling potential or actual sabotage.

Secondary Disasters

A range of secondary disasters may strike facilities at any time, with or without warning. The probability of secondary disasters should be anticipated. For example: an earthquake could cause a structural fire which may, in turn, burn out circuits resulting in a power failure. Severe winds might damage a chemical plant, or spilled chemicals could start a fire that releases toxic smoke. Intense rains can cause flooding which may set off landslides.

The multihazard situation creates an environment in which resource availability and priorities may be radically different from the norm. In large-scale events, services and options would likely be severely curtailed and/or adversely affected. Your facility would still be responsible for doing what can be done to protect lives and property. A change in priorities as a result of a multihazard disaster might influence critical decisions, especially when the event is in your control, such as during an onsite toxic smoke release, and when it affects people both onsite and off. Your planners should take into account the extra demands secondary disasters would place on facility resources and emergency response capabilities. Assessing these ramifications will involve considerations that are site and operations specific and should be made by someone familiar with the site and the operations, someone who has given thought to what kinds of events might be expected onsite from the primary hazards that pose threats to the facility.

Whether the emergency preparedness program developed for multihazard situations is comprehensive or austere, there are certain minimum legal obligations (Occupational Safety and Health Act of 1970) to life and safety, as well as the moral obligations. Your employees are among your most important resources, and the most fundamental functional responses are to protect lives and prevent injuries. In addition to life and safety considerations, additional preparedness measures will be profitable to consider from an operational standpoint to ensure continuity of operations, protect property, and reduce potential product and market loss.

Chapter 4

Survival after an Emergency

Will you be in business following an emergency at your facility? Don't just assume that you will. In Chapter 1, I discussed why insurance was not enough to ensure the survivability of your business following an emergency. Just as you must have an effective emergency response plan to manage an emergency situation at your facility and to protect your employees from harm, you must have a plan in place for business recovery. If you want to maintain your market share and stay in business, you must develop an effective plan for the recovery of your business in advance of an emergency. Estimates following Hurricane Andrew indicated that only 11 percent of the businesses damaged by the storm had any business recovery plans or programs in place. However, business is apparently not learning from past experience. In 1999, estimates are that upwards of 70 percent of businesses do not have a business recovery plan in place.

This chapter will examine a number of areas that you should assess as part of your business recovery plan. A well written plan will be valuable whether you experience either a minor or a catastrophic incident at your facility.

Following an emergency there are literally dozens of things that need to be accomplished. Fortunately, not all of them have the same degree of importance, but you will still need to address them. This is especially true when you have to deal with many of the federal, state, and local governmental agencies, insurance adjusters, the news media, union officials, and a host of others that may appear at your doorstep. If you do not assign certain members of your staff to business recovery functions, they will get tied up with other activities associated with the emergency. Business recovery must begin the moment that the emergency phase of the incident is over. If you wait even a few days to initiate your business recovery plan and concentrate only on dealing with the events related to the emergency incident, it may be too late to salvage your business. The bottom line is that the majority of businesses that do not have formal business recovery plans in place will fail in the five years following the disaster.

Organizations with Post-Emergency Responsibilities

The following is a list of some of the organizations and personalities that you may need to deal with following an emergency situation. The number of government officials and organizations appearing at your facility tends to grow at an exponential rate based on the size and magnitude of the incident.

Local Officials

- **Fire department**
  Involved in conducting investigation of the incident.

- **Police department**
  May be involved in investigation if arson or other criminal acts were involved in the incident.

- **Building officials**
  Depending on the degree of damage to the facility, local building officials may be called to assess the degree of building stability and whether you may access your facility.

- **Elected officials**
  Elected officials like to get involved and will likely visit your facility if the event is newsworthy and they can get their names and pictures on television.

County Officials

- **Environmental affairs**
  An incident involving hazardous materials has potential impact on air and water.

- **Emergency management**
  Depending on the severity of the situation, emergency management officials will be at the scene of the emergency.

- **Elected officials**
  They like to get in the paper, too.

State Agencies

- **Department of Environmental Protection**
  Assessment of site for ground, water, and air pollution.

- **Department of Labor**
  Investigation into employee injuries/deaths and compliance with state safety and health regulations.

- **State Department of Transportation**
  Involvement when incident involves transportation issues.

- **State fire marshal**
  Often involved in the investigation of large-loss fire incidents and explosions.

Federal Agencies

- **Occupational Safety and Health Administration (OSHA)**
  Investigation of incident, which may include a review of your emergency procedures, safety practices, training programs and record documentation.

- **Environmental Protection Agency (EPA)**
  Investigation of incident when hazardous wastes or hazardous materials were involved that present a threat to the environment; often provides assistance to the state environmental officials.

- **Department of Transportation (DOT)**
  Involvement if transportation related; generally assist state transportation officials.

- **Department of Energy**
  May get involved if the incident involved radioactive materials or processes utilizing radioactive materials.

- **Chemical Safety and Hazard Investigation Board**
  Relatively new federal agency given the responsibility for investigating significant chemical emergencies; functions in a manner similar to the National Transportation Safety Board (NTSB) in that it issues reports of findings and issues recommendations to help prevent a reoccurrence.

Other Organizations and Agencies

- **Labor Union Officials**
  Concerned with many of the side issues related to the incident, including worker protection, potential for company layoffs, and nonunion workers involved in cleanup and recovery operations at the facility.
  Many unions have initiated investigation teams that get involved with serious injuries or deaths to union members. If your facility is covered by a union contract then you should be aware of whether they have a program in place to investigate such incidents. If so, then it is very important that you develop procedures to deal with this issue. Many facilities have learned of the existence of such investigating teams only after an incident when the union investigators showed up at the facility.

- **Insurance carrier**
  One or more individuals on scene investigating the incident as part of your claim.

- **News media**
  Amount of news media present at the incident site and in the days following the incident generally dependent on how significant the incident was (major fire and chemical released which forced the evacuation of thousands of people) and its impact to the community (layoffs as a result of the incident).

- **Attorneys**
  Your facility attorneys and also attorneys representing employees and/or their families and area businesses impacted by the incident.
  They want to be compensated for business they lost while evacuated from their facilities during your incident.

Other Issues of Concern

- **Hazardous waste cleanup/removal**
  Very complicated and costly effort depending on the degree of contamination and types of hazardous material that were involved in the incident.
  Often the cost of hazardous waste cleanup and removal will far exceed the damage to the facility. This process could take hours, days, weeks, months, or even years, complicating your recovery procedures.

- **Customers**
  Want to know the status of your facility and if and when you will be delivering your product or service to them.

- **Public demonstrations**
  Depending on the impact to the community, your facility may be viewed as having little concern for the public or environment.
  One incident that I am familiar with had local citizen groups picketing the facility following an incident because of the impact the incident had on the community.

A cardinal concept to remember is this:

Your clients and customers are only concerned about your ability to supply them with the products and services that they need, not with the devastation you have experienced. If you cannot supply them with what they need they will go elsewhere.

Political Issues

The types of agencies and organizations involved in the hours and days following an emergency incident can become a tremendous drain on your management personnel. Not all of these agencies or organizations have the same degree of importance, at least in your mind, but they are there and you will have to deal with them. It is important to keep in mind that the majority of the governmental agencies listed have a legal right to be at your facility and have responsibilities designated to them by local, state, and/or federal laws and regulations. It is important that you deal with these agencies in a fair and considerate manner. You must understand that they have a job to do and if you make their job difficult by not providing requested information or not actively participating, they can, and in many cases will, make your life miserable.

Five Steps to Business Recovery

This section will outline a five-step process that I feel is necessary for you to accomplish in order to develop an effective business recovery program.

Step 1   Assign Responsibility for Business Recovery

Any effective business executive will tell you that it is critical to properly deploy personnel to key activities in order for a business to prosper and survive. Handling an emergency at your facility is no different. You must determine which members of your staff will be assigned to work with agencies and organizations pertaining to the emergency phase of the situation and which members of your staff will be concerned with business recovery activities. I recommend that you develop an organizational chart to help clarify duties and responsibilities. Keep in mind that, as time passes, many of the people assigned to the disaster end of the situation will be relieved of their tasks and can be assigned to recovery activities. It is also important to note that, depending on your business, your income will be drastically curtailed and you may have very limited cash flow. How many of these key personnel will you have to lay off? I have talked with a number of business executives who have told me they would have to start layoffs within seven days of the emergency. You must consider what impact a minimal number of personnel will have on the implementation of your recovery plan.

When developing your recovery plan and assigning activities to personnel, you must anticipate the number of personnel that you will be able to maintain on your payroll. It would have a crippling effect on your recovery efforts if your plan is developed under the assumption that you will have thirty employees to accomplish recovery activities when in reality you will only have five.

Step 2   Make Plans to Establish Temporary Facilities

Where are you going to conduct daily operations? If your facility was extensively damaged and you have no other offices in the area, you will need to establish temporary offices to deal with emergency activities and business recovery activities. Depending on your needs, there are a number of options that you can look at. You may be able to temporarily operate out of a home or make arrangements with another area business that you can share offices or warehouse space with. You must have arrangements for temporary facilities in place prior to an emergency occurring. Keep in mind that, during a community-wide disaster such as earthquake or hurricane, your primary arrangements for alternate facility locations may also be damaged. Many of the other businesses in your area will also be trying to obtain temporary facility locations. It is of critical importance to have arrangements for alternate temporary facilities located outside of your local area should a community-wide disaster strike you.

Step 3   Prepare to Contact Your Customers

You must make immediate contact with your customers. Let them know that you are still alive and kicking and to what extent you will be able to serve them while you are rebuilding. Set up an emergency client contact system (ECCS). An ECCS is a set procedures that you have in place to communicate with your clients following an emergency. It is intended to provide them with information on how to contact you and how and when you will be able to service their needs.

The following is a sample message that a company could send to its customers following a major emergency situation using an ECCS.

SPORT & PATCHES DISTRIBUTION
200 Industrial Drive
Jennifersville, AL 34587
999-888-5555

Dear valued customer:

I wanted you to be among the first to know that today Turbo Sport Widgets suffered a fire at our facility. I am happy to report that there was no loss of life associated with the fire. In spite of the fire, we will still be able to honor your orders and provide service to you while we rebuild our facility. Your sales representative will personally contact you within the next few days to insure that we have not lost any of your orders during the fire. Please note that we may be reached at 999-888-5555. Please feel free to contact us if you have any questions.

We look forward to serving you.

Sincerely,

Sidney Norman
President

Using current technology such as email and automated faxing, I could have this message sent to 50 or 50,000 of my customers in a matter of a few hours. A number of companies can provide you such a service. Some will even allow you to preload the names and fax numbers or email addresses of your customers into the system so that your message can be delivered immediately. The cost of this service is surprisingly low when compared to the cost of losing your customers. If you do not communicate with you customers, your competition will. Were I an aggressive salesperson also selling Widgets for another company, after hearing about the fire at Turbo Sport Widgets, I would immediately get on the phone to grab as many of Turbo's customers as I could.

Here is the conversation of an aggressive salesperson:

YC = Your Customer   C = Competition

YC: Hello.

 C: Mr. Jones, my name is Jennifer Nicole and I represent Aggressive Widgets. I wanted to let you know that Aggressive Widgets can supply all of your widget needs.

YC: Well, thank you, Jennifer, but we've had a long-standing relationship with Turbo Widgets and have always been pleased with their service and delivery.

 C: I guess you didn't hear that the Turbo Widgets facility was destroyed by a fire yesterday.

YC: No, I didn't.

 C: Unfortunately yes, but I just wanted to let you know that we can provide the same quality widget that Turbo always has, and we will match or beat their price.

YC: Well, I certainty appreciate you contacting me with this information.

 C: Did you have any widgets on order with Turbo at the time of the fire?

YC: Well, no, but we just received word that we have obtained a major contract for one of our products and will need to produce an additional 100,000 Zip Wipes next month to meet the order.

 C: We would be happy to give you a price on the widgets that you need, and we can have them delivered in time for your increased production.

TC: (*YC has now become TC—Their Customer—since you just lost an order.*)
     Yes, I would like you to talk with Don English who is my purchasing manager and can arrange all the details.

PM: (*The purchasing manager, being the sharp individual that he is, knows that the salesperson might be trying to pull a fast one. He puts Jennifer on hold and dials the number for Turbo Widget. Unfortunately, Don gets the following recorded message when he dials Turbo Widgets' number: "The number you have dialed is temporarily out of service." Apparently Turbo Widgets did not have a procedure in place to deal with telephone system disruptions.)*

Is it true that Turbo Sport Widgets could not deliver the order as placed? Maybe not. Turbo may have been able to handle their customers' orders, but did their customers know that? You must communicate with your customers as soon as possible. If not, your competition will. Do you have a specific plan in place to contact at least your best clients within 24 hours of an emergency? Do you have records that would not have been destroyed in the fire of telephone numbers, fax numbers, email addresses, and mailing addresses for your customers?

Step 4   Establish Joint Alliances

"Business is war." "Let's kill the competition." How many times have we heard these statements? Well, I am here to tell you that if you take that attitude when it comes to business recovery, you will have lost the war and your competition will become king of the mountain. There are some exceptions to the concept that I am going to propose to you, but I feel that it will work for the majority of businesses, especially those that are regional in nature.

Most businesses do not have totally proprietary products. There are probably a number of businesses that manufacturer an identical product or provide the same service that you do. Let's take Sidney's and Sport's Plastics as an example.

Sidney's and Sport's Plastics had attended one of my seminars on disaster planning and learned the value of having a business recovery plan and forming joint alliances. Following a fire at their facility, Sidney's and Sport's Plastics immediately sent faxes to all of their customers indicating how to contact them and that they would continue to be able to supply customers' needs. Even though all of Sidney's and Sport's Plastics inventory was damaged or destroyed in the fire, they had formed a joint alliance with Bradley's Plastics which is located about 400 miles away. Both companies provide their services to customers within their respective geographic regions and were therefore not competing with one another. They had made an agreement that if either facility suffered a major loss, the other would provide inventory and supply as available to assist the damaged business in meeting the demands of its customers. Through this arrangement, Sidney's and Sport's Plastics was able to supply all of their customers and did not suffer a loss of market share during their rebuilding process.

Perhaps many of you are thinking that this would never work, that there is no way that my competition would ever work with me. Why should they? If I have an emergency they would benefit by my going out of business. But it can work if you want it to. This is a win-win situation for both of you. You might need to form such an alliance with two of more businesses so that all of you will have adequate supply to serve your customers. The businesses that will survive in the future will be those that are innovative. Unbelievable ideas have made a lot of people a lot of money over the years. Remember that Federal Express was thought by many people to be an idea that would fail. Who would ever spend ten dollars to get a letter sent overnight? Now millions of letters and packages are sent every day by overnight mail services.

I cannot tell you what joint alliances you should or could form. The suggestions presented here may help save your business. One of the key concepts to remember is that you must remove yourself from your traditional thinking and be proactive to prevention and preparedness activities.

Step 5   Establish Agreements With Your Vendors

Another option to increase your ability to service your customers is to establish agreements with many of your vendors. An example of this is to make arrangements with some of your vendors to drop-ship to your clients while your shipping and receiving facilities are nonfunctional. This will probably increase your unit cost but it might be a way to continue to supply your customers. The key to survivability following a disaster and while your facilities are not fully functional is to supply your clientele and not necessarily to make a profit. If your goal is to continue making a profit during recovery operations, you will probably fail. Likewise, cutting costs will probably not be possible at this time. Your chief goal during the recovery phase of the emergency should be to hold on to your market share. Remember that if you lose your customers, you may not get them back following the incident.

One business executive told me that there was no way his primary vendor would drop-ship product because it was very clearly written in their catalog that they would only ship in case lots of 144 units, and the majority of this executive's clients only purchased 4 to 12 units at a time. However, he admitted that he had never asked the vendor whether such a service could be provided for a short time during an emergency. When asked if this was a proprietary product or whether there were a number of suppliers he could purchase from, he said it was a very competitive market and there were a number of vendors. The solution: inform the vendor that if they would not agree to such an arrangement he would go to another vendor who would. You hold a lot more power and leverage than you might think. Use it to your advantage.

Specific Situations and Solutions

Let's look at some specific situations that should be included as part of your recovery plan. Most businesses will never experience a catastrophic emergency, but most will experience at least one of the disruptions in routine business described below. Your recovery plan should cover a magnitude of topics, but you will only need to implement those portions that are applicable to the event. Let's take a look at a few.

Telephone Disruption

The telephone is the lifeblood of many businesses. What happens if your telephone system fails? How much money would you lose for every day, hour, or minute that your telephone system is out of service? Do you have a specific policy for handling telephone system failures? Let's look at some specific telephone systems and strategies to deal with interruptions.

The easiest thing to do is to call-forward your phone line to another location. Call-forwarding is a service available in most areas of the country for a very nominal fee and should be placed on all critical phone numbers going into a facility. Following a problem with your phone system, you should be able to contact your telephone company and have them call-forward your line from their end. A number of options are available. You can forward your calls to your home, to a cellular phone, or to another one of your facilities. One of my clients who does a tremendous amount of telephone sales has taken the precaution that, in the event of telephone system failure, all of the company's 1-800 order lines are transferred to one of the company's five other facilities located across the country. The customers never know that their calls have been answered in California instead of Texas.

I would recommend that every business spend some time discussing with its local and long distance carriers the business's telephone needs and options during emergency situations, as well as the availability of enhanced telephone services.

Central Telephone Systems

Most businesses with 20 or more phones will have a central phone system. A central phone system has many advantages, such as a single incoming phone number for all individuals within the facility, but it also places all of your eggs in one basket.

Most central phone systems will fail if power is lost to the building. If power is lost, your phone system is dead in the water. Do not automatically assume that your system has a backup power supply. You must investigate and determine how your system works. A battery backup system is the most commonly used. If your phone system uses a battery backup, it must be checked on a regular basis. I have seen systems where the batteries were dead when inspected. The business owner never knew that the phone system had a battery backup or that it needed to be checked on a regular basis. Your system should be checked according to the manufacturer's instructions. If there are no guidelines available, check the system monthly.

Here is a situation that could happen at any business. How would you handle it?

During a storm you lose all power to your building and your phone system goes dead. At the same time, you discover that one of your employees has experienced a heart attack. How will you call for an ambulance?

Don't know? You'd better. Today, almost every business has one or more fax machines. Many fax machines are not tied into the central telephone system. Often, a fax machine will have a separate line outside of the central system. Many businesses, especially manufacturing facilities, will have one or more pay telephones in reception areas or employee break rooms. These will be on a separate system and may still work when the regular phone system goes down.

Insurance Policies

Having the proper insurance is critical to the long-term survivability of a business following an emergency. Although I am no expert on insurance, you are probably not either. I would recommend that you obtain the services of a good insurance agent or insurance consultant. A qualified individual who understands your business and your needs can be very valuable in helping you obtain the insurance that you need. Find out exactly what is and is not covered by each policy. In addition, find out exactly what documentation your insurance carrier requires when filing a claim. Documentation pertaining to inventory, machinery and equipment, daily net sales, and many other areas may be required to obtain the full value of your insurance. This information must be maintained in a safe location away from your facility, such as in your safe deposit box.

Inventory Records

Do you have current and up-to-date inventory records? Is this information stored in a safe offsite location? If not, you may not be able to claim the actual value of your equipment and inventory on your insurance. Dun & Bradstreet claims that 80 percent of all business failures are due to poor records. The University of Pittsburgh found that 40 percent of those businesses that they surveyed did not keep proper records. If businesses in general do not keep proper business records, how many do you think would have up-to-date inventory records?

Recently I asked a client if the company had a current inventory of its equipment and merchandise. The client indicated that they did indeed and a few minutes later produced a document that was dated two years earlier. I asked the client if the company had purchased any new equipment or increased the dollar value of its inventory in the past two years. The company had indeed done these things, but for some reason they had never gotten around to updating their inventory sheets. The company president, appearing somewhat annoyed that his staff had not maintained accurate documentation, called one of his vice presidents into the conference room and instructed him to drop everything and have an up-to-date inventory on his desk before going home. The next day I was provided a copy of the updated inventory. The difference was approximately $270,000. How would this difference have affected the survivability of this company if they suddenly experienced a major loss and were required to file their claim based on two-year-old information?

Lease Agreements

I am certain that many of you lease your business property. A number of business executives with whom I have talked have had long-term leases on their business property. What would happen if the facility you were leasing had a major fire which devastated the property? The property owner tells you that he will rebuild, but it could take 6 to 8 months. Knowing that you cannot wait 6 to 8 months to reestablish your operations, you go out and find a suitable property to move your operations to. Since the lessor was unable to fulfill their contract in providing you a suitable facility, you move to the new facility, breaking the contract. Do you really have the right to break this lease? What will happen if the lessor demands that you adhere to the contract by either moving back into the newly rebuilt facility or buying your way out of the lease? Well, if there was nothing in your lease agreement to cover such an occurrence, it becomes a matter for your attorney to handle. I am certain that if you have a good attorney you will get out of the contract, but what will it cost you to have your attorney represent you and write a few letters? Would it not have been easier to have an additional clause written into your lease agreement that would cover such an occurrence?

Receivables

How important are your receivables to the long-term survivability of your business? For me, collecting on my receivables is of critical importance. What would happen if you lost a few invoices? What would happen if you lost a week's or even a day's worth of invoices? If you do not have a system in place to back up this data and keep it well protected, a fire or other major disaster could eliminate your business. If you had a fire and lost all records of who owed you money, what would it cost you? You would probably receive most of the due amount, but what about those people who say, "Hey, they had a fire. Probably lost their records. I'll wait until they send me a late notice before I pay."

Computer Data

Most companies I have dealt with have a written policy concerning the backup of computer data. This is good, but most employees do not follow the company policy. The type and frequency of data backup will depend on the type of information stored, its degree of importance to your operations, and how frequently you change the information in the database. A business entering hundreds or thousands of orders per day and shipping thousands of products per day might need to back up its data on an hourly basis. A business making minimal entries, however, may only need to back up once a day.

The best way to ensure that your data is backed up in a timely manner is to use an automated system, thus relieving your personnel of the need to perform backups. Numerous software packages are available that will automatically back up your data at the times you specify. Now computer companies offer backup services by satellite or telephone line transmission.

Once you have a good procedure in place for the backup of your computer data, you must look at the proper storage of your data. Keep a minimum of three sets of data, all in different locations. Chapter 6 has specific guidelines for the storage and rotation of computer media.

Also, you should store one set of backups in a fire-rated computer media cabinet. Please note that the typical fire-resistant safe or filing cabinet will not provide adequate protection for your computer media. Fire-resistant safes and filing cabinets are designed to protect paper materials, such as files and records, from damage. Computer tape and disks will melt at temperatures well below those at which paper is destroyed. There are several manufacturers who make fire-resistant safes and storage devices that are designed specifically for the special needs of computer media.

Another problem is that you should have a contingency plan for accessing your data following an emergency. Let's say you have a fire that destroys your computer system. Your data might be safe because you maintained a copy off site. The problem is how to access the data. If you are using a simple PC, there is probably no problem in that this is a readily available system. But let's say you use a mainframe system that uses very specialized software. What hoops will you have to jump through to get your data up and running again?

Record Protection

Chapter 6 provides specific guidelines on the proper storage of vital business records. In the following section, you will learn that business records can be damaged, destroyed, or lost because of storage methods used by most businesses.

Every business should have a minimum of one fire-resistant filing cabinet for storage of important business records and files. Fire-resistant filing cabinets cost more than the typical filing cabinet used in offices, but what is your real savings if you have to spend hundreds of hours reconstructing a filing cabinet full of documents damaged or destroyed in an incident?

Record Protection for Field Personnel

How well protected are the records of your field personnel and salespersons? If your field personnel store their files in the manner of many that I have encountered, these records are probably very vulnerable to loss or damage. It is critical for your field sales staff to maintain their records as you would at your offices. The information that your salespersons have may be needed following a major incident to help reconstruct customer records and sales information. A few questions that you might want to address include the following:

- Can the records, files, invoices, and orders of field personnel be easily damaged by an accident or theft?

- If field personnel use portable computers, how frequently do they back up their data?

- Do the field personnel keep their backup data in a safe places?

Chapter 5

Generic Emergency Action Plan

From your own deliberations and readings, it should be apparent that the development of an emergency action plan involves a variety of activities that cannot be completely defined in any textbook or manual. Certain planning considerations (direction and control; alert and warning; and the protection of employees, company equipment, and facilities) will require attention, whatever the emergency. These planning considerations tend to be interwoven with variations that depend somewhat on the particular combinations of hazards that threaten the facility. For planning to be truly comprehensive, it must be based on the hazards you are vulnerable to, with additional attention given to unique characteristics of pertinent hazards.

The emergency action plan establishes the framework for an effective emergency response capability. The introductory (basic) portion of the plan describes the situation and assumptions for the execution of the plan, explains the overall concept of operations, and specifies the organization and responsibility for emergency operations.

The operational section of the plan provides specific information and direction. It defines and describes policies, procedures, responsibilities, tasks, and operational actions as they pertain to each response function before, during, and after any emergency situation. To ensure adequate planning for all applicable hazards, the content of your plan must be responsive to the results of the vulnerability analysis.

One of the more important things you should do early in the planning process is to select the functions to be included in your plan. These choices will be influenced by such factors as the size and organizational structure of your company, the company's emergency response capabilities and resources (firefighting, security, medical, etc.), and the established policy or intentions regarding the company's concept of operations for response to emergencies. Accordingly, it may be more suitable for a small company to develop an emergency action checklist rather than a formal emergency operations plan. Review the discussion in this chapter to determine what form of written procedures best meets your organization's requirements to protect employees, facilities, equipment, and inventory.

Successful emergency and disaster preparedness is the business of dealing with whole sequences of undesirable events. While in some instances all you may be able to do is warn personnel to hasten evacuation and attempt to get more outside help, it is valuable to recognize as many of the potential complications that might arise as possible. This will facilitate making quick decisions when these situations do occur. For example, what would happen if your automatic warning system stopped functioning as a result of the incident? In the end, the objective is to develop the capability to activate a functional response and to exercise or rehearse that response with the people familiar with the plan.

No single listing of planning considerations can be prescribed for all business and industry. The primary concern is that all important activities be properly covered in your plan. At a minimum, you should include direction and control, alerting and warning, facility shutdown, evacuation, and shelter.

The following functions represent the recommended core that should be included if you write a plan. These functions should be adapted, as appropriate, if you use the checklist format. Inclusion of additional functions or the combination of related functions such as alerting, warning, and communications may be preferable for your company. The provisions listed below each function are suggested for your consideration in developing your plan and should be used prior to developing your plan to review and evaluate your company's preparedness status and to determine planning voids and weaknesses.

This chapter will outline the topics that you might want to include in your emergency action plan (EAP). The topics included in this generic plan would be appropriate for the majority of facilities with an average degree of risk. It is intended to cover the typical hazards present at nearly all facilities. The information concerning each topic has been purposely kept brief so as not to overwhelm the reader. At the same time, there is enough information provided to get you pointed in the right direction.

I am strongly opposed to boilerplate emergency action plans. There are numerous sources from which to obtain a boilerplate emergency action plan and simply fill in the blanks. These plans have statements such as:

It is the policy of _____ to protect its employees and the surrounding community from all types of hazards that may present themselves.

If you are looking for such an easy way out, don't be surprised that, when you have an actual emergency, things do not happen as you expect them to. I firmly believe that each and every emergency action plan must be tailored to the individual facility. The information that you have been provided with in this book will give you the tools you need to develop an effective emergency action plan for your facility.

I have included in Chapter 7 a sample emergency plan that was developed for a small manufacturing facility. It is provided as a model to guide you in developing your own facility emergency plan.

Generic Emergency Action Plan

I. Introduction

A. Purpose of the Emergency Action Plan

What is the emergency action plan designed to accomplish? Most EAPs are designed to provide for the safety and welfare of facility personnel, the community, the environment, and property.

Are the following covered as appropriate:

❏   *Does the EAP specify the specific purpose of the plan?*

❏   *Does the plan account for the safety of facility personnel, the community, environment, and facility property?*

B. Legal Authority

This section typically indicates what specific regulations the plan is designed to meet. The specific regulation and title should be listed, such as OSHA 1910.38(a) Employee Emergency Plans and Fire Prevention Plans.

Is the following covered as appropriate:

❏   *Are all regulations that the plan is to address properly referenced?*

C. Assumptions and Situations

Detail out any assumptions that may have been made in the content of the EAP. Common assumptions are that the local fire and police department will respond and assist the facility for emergency situations at the facility. Situations would define the specific provisions that the plan is designed for, such as fires, hazardous material spills, bomb threats, hurricanes, etc.

Is the following covered as appropriate:

❏   *Are the assumptions clearly stated?*

D. Facility Health and Safety Policy

This should provide an overview of the facility's health and safety policy as it relates to the identification, response, and handling of an emergency at the facility.

Is the following covered as appropriate:

❑ *Is the plan consistent with the facility health and safety policy?*

E. Organization and Personnel Responsibilities

This section should outline the organization of the facility as it relates to emergency operations and the primary and alternate personnel who will be utilized to handle the emergency situation. Key positions include the facility emergency coordinator, plant manager, human resource director, safety director, and response team members.

Are the following covered as appropriate:

❑ *Does the plan indicate who is in charge of each emergency situation, and does it cite the location of the emergency operations center (EOC) or the on-scene command post from which direction and control will emanate?*

❑ *Does the plan identify an alternate EOC site to serve as a backup if the primary EOC is not able to operate?*

❑ *Is there an adequate number of primary and alternate personnel assigned to the EOC and command and control functions so that personnel will always be available, even during peak vacation and holiday periods?*

F. Plan Update Procedures and Revisions

Specific procedures should be followed to update the EAP. The EAP should be considered a controlled document. This means that all copies of the EAP should be numbered and assigned to specific individuals or offices. Each copy of the EAP should have one person who is responsible for ensuring that the plan is updated. There should be a check sheet in each copy of the EAP recording the date and the name of person updating the plan. I have found that when you do not control the distribution of the EAP and the responsibility for updating, it will not get done. The individual who is in charge of EAP activities for the facility should periodically inspect each plan to ensure that all revisions and updates have been made.

Are the following covered as appropriate:

❑ *Have one or more individuals been given the specific responsibility for revising and updating the EAP?*

❑ *Is there a specific timetable given for plan revisions and updates?*

G. Plan Distribution

This section deals with the specific list of individuals and offices within the facility that are to receive a copy and any updates of the EAP. This should include both internal and external distribution of the plan. External distribution includes the local fire department, police department, and local emergency planning committee.

Are the following covered as appropriate:

❑ *Is there a list of all personnel and facility offices that are to receive a copy of the EAP?*

❑ *Is there a list of all external organizations that are to receive a copy of the EAP?*

❑ *Is the plan distributed as a controlled and numbered document to maintain accountability?*

II. Facility Hazard and Risk Analysis

A. Overview of Facility

This section provides a basic overview of the facility, its activities, processes, and materials used in production.

Are the following covered as appropriate:

❑ *Is there an overview of the facility provided that gives a clear indication as to the use of the facility?*

❑ *Are all hazardous processes and materials identified?*

B. Facility Risk Evaluation

This section should provide information on the assumptions that you have made regarding the types of hazards the facility is vulnerable to and the degree of risk and impact anticipated from these hazards.

Are the following covered as appropriate:

❑ *Have all risks been appropriately analyzed and addressed?*

❑ *Have all hazardous materials been identified and their degree of risk evaluated?*

❑ *In addressing the potential risk to the facility, have you considered past incidents and incidents at similar types of facilities?*

❑ *Are procedures in place to allow for assessment of new hazards or vulnerability as facility processes and operations change?*

C. Offsite Risk Evaluation

This section looks at the types of offsite risk that may impact the facility and its operations. Offsite risks are those posed from other local facilities or transportation routes. An example is a railroad yard located one block from the facility. A chemical spill or fire at this location could cause evacuation and shut down of your facility.

Are the following covered as appropriate:

❑ *Have offsite hazards that may impact the facility been addressed?*

❑ *Does the EAP address procedures for the identification and warning of offsite incidents to facility management?*

III. Prevention

A. General Prevention Policy

This looks at the basic facility policy which addresses how incidents will be minimized through inspections, engineering controls, employee training, and independent consultations.

Are the following covered as appropriate:

❑ *Does the EAP address the responsibility for the prevention of incidents?*

❑ *Does the plan incorporate prevention procedures into all new facility equipment and processes?*

❑ *Does the plan reduce risk to the facility by minimizing hazardous materials and processes?*

B. Fire Prevention Policy

Specific procedures should minimize the occurrence of a fire at the facility. Include specific inspection guidelines and inspection frequency.

Are the following covered as appropriate:

❑ *Does the fire prevention policy clearly address the facility's commitment to the prevention of fires?*

❑ *Do the components of the fire prevention policy cover all of the requirements as addressed in OSHA 1910.156 for fire protection?*

❑ *Are major workplace fire hazards identified, including the proper handling and storage procedures that are to be followed by personnel?*

❑ *Does the plan specify the frequency for the inspection of fire protection, detection, and response equipment?*

C.   Facility Safety Inspections and Audits

This section should look at the specific inspection procedures that you have developed to identify safety hazards and housekeeping violations. There should be a specific timetable for inspections and responsibility for conducting the inspections. Audits should also be conducted to verify compliance with the facility inspection program. In addition, you should develop specific checklists to emphasize the key areas to be inspected. The completed checklist will also serve as the documentation for your compliance audits and for OSHA facility inspections.

Are the following covered as appropriate:

❑   *Are there procedures in place to address the auditing of the plan for compliance?*

❑   *Have inspection checklists been developed for all critical areas and processes?*

❑   *Has responsibility been assigned for conducting safety inspections and audits?*

❑   *Have training and knowledge requirements of inspection personnel been addressed within the EAP?*

D.   Facility Health and Safety Committee

Each facility should establish a health and safety committee. The health and safety committee should be composed of personnel from management and labor and should be designed to assist the facility in providing a safe workplace. The safety committee should be given specific responsibilities as it applies to the emergency action plan. You may want to give the safety committee members special training and have them conduct safety inspections or audits.

Are the following covered as appropriate:

❑   *Has a facility health and safety committee been established with clear-cut responsibilities as they relate to the EAP?*

❑   *Has training in activities related to the EAP been provided to members of the health and safety committee?*

IV. Preparedness

This section will examine the efforts that have been made and the plans that are in place to prepare the facility and its employees for an emergency situation.

A.   Training

Identify the specific types of training for employees by job classification and/or responsibility. Specific training outlines and topic material should be referenced in this section.

Are the following covered as appropriate:

❑ *Are personnel provided with adequate training to cover their responsibilities and duties as required by the EAP?*

❑ *Are the frequency of training and the topics to be covered referenced in the EAP?*

❑ *Is the person(s) responsible for ensuring that training activities are completed identified in the EAP?*

❑ *Are training records maintained for all personnel instructed in EAP responsibilities or actions?*

B. Drills and Exercises

Drills and exercises of the EAP should be carried out at least annually. I recommend that each facility exercise its EAP every six months. Specific guidelines pertaining to drills and exercises should be addressed in this section.

Are the following covered as appropriate:

❑ *Are the methods to be used in exercising the EAP identified?*

❑ *Is the frequency of drills and exercises specified in the plan?*

❑ *Are tabletop and full-scale exercises identified, as well as their frequency?*

❑ *Are procedures in place that will involve in the exercises outside organizations and agencies that may be affected by an emergency at the facility?*

❑ *Are procedures in place to revise the plan based on results of drills and exercises?*

❑ *Are all levels of the facility, from entry level to top level management, included in the EAP exercises?*

C. Facilities, Supplies, and Equipment

Provide specific information on the location of equipment and supplies that will be used in the handling of an emergency situation. Included should be specific inspection guidelines for response equipment. Under OSHA regulations, equipment to be used in an emergency must be inspected at least monthly. Checklists should be created to identify equipment that requires inspection and specific items to check during the inspection.

Are the following covered as appropriate:

❑ *Are all equipment and supplies to be used for emergency clearly identified?*

❑ *Are there specific guidelines for the inspection and maintenance of all emergency equipment?*

❑ *Are records of equipment inspection, deficiencies, and repairs properly maintained?*

❑ *Is emergency equipment clearly marked and accessible by employees?*

D. Facility Security

Are procedures in place for the security of the facility and its assets during and after an emergency situation? For facilities that do not have their own onsite security personnel, arrangements will need to be made with a security guard service.

Are the following covered as appropriate:

❑ *Are provisions in place to ensure the security of the facility during an incident?*

❑ *If onsite security personnel are not available or adequate for the potential situation, are there procedures in place for obtaining security personnel from private contractors or from the local police department?*

❑ *If security personnel are assigned to response activities, is security for the facility addressed?*

E. Media Relations Policy

Every business should have a specific media release policy. Very simply, it should designate who is allowed to talk with the media during and following an emergency situation. One of the worst things that can happen is allowing your employees to talk with the media. The message that your employees have may not be the same message that you want to convey to the public. Your employees may not have all of the facts concerning the incident. Remember—what is reported will have a profound impact on your business.

In one incident that I am very familiar with, the facility management had prohibited entry onto the facility property by all news media. The news media finally found an employee who was offsite and who would talk to them. Jokingly, he told the media that it was the worst thing that he had ever seen. Keep in mind that this employee had been nowhere near the incident and did not see the injured workers. This became the lead story on the television and in the papers: "Serious chemical explosion. Employee says that it was the worst thing he had ever seen." This report was a complete distortion of reality, but this was the only perspective that the public had about the incident.

You must talk with the media, because if you don't, they will continue to dig until they get a story. If you talk with the media you have a greater chance of controlling the message about the incident so that it will best represent the truth about the situation at your facility. Accordingly, you must be honest with the media. If you lie about an incident, it will probably come back to haunt you.

Are the following covered as appropriate:

❑   *Does the facility have a specific media release policy that addresses responsibilities for press releases concerning the incident?*

❑   *Have personnel been given specific training to deal with the media?*

V. Detection, Alarm, and Notification Procedures

The EAP must include procedures to detect the occurrence of an emergency, make the initial notifications to alert employees, and begin the evacuation of employees.

A. Incident Discovery

What procedures are in place to discover the occurrence of an incident that either has impacted or may impact the facility? Numerous methods can be used, such as employee observations, alarm and detection systems, and severe weather alert radios, to name a few.

Are the following covered as appropriate:

❑   *Are procedures addressed that will provide for the discovery of incidents both onsite and offsite that may impact the facility?*

❑   *Does the EAP identify the types of detection and alarm systems that will be utilized?*

❑   *Are procedures in place for the monitoring of detection equipment, such as smoke alarms and process control alarms?*

❑   *Is training provided to personnel to allow them to properly interpret the meaning and response actions required by an alarm system?*

❑   *Are there specific inspection and maintenance guidelines and checklists for detection and alarm equipment?*

B. Initial Notification

Initial notification procedures identify persons to be contacted first and provide all contact information. Typical notifications include facility emergency response teams, company management, and local emergency response organizations, such as the fire and police departments.

Is the following covered as appropriate:

❑   *Are critical personnel, internal response teams, and outside organizations identified, as well as the primary and secondary methods to contact them?*

C.   Emergency Alerting Procedures

Specify procedures that will be used to alert employees and others of an emergency situation at the facility.

Are the following covered as appropriate:

❑   *Are procedures in place for alerting all personnel of an emergency situation?*

❑   *Are primary and backup methods to notify personnel of an emergency situation identified?*

❑   *Are critical personnel accessible 24 hours a day by pager, cellular phone, or other method?*

❑   *Are periodic tests conducted to ensure that the notification systems work as intended?*

❑   *Does the alerting system meet the requirements as outlined in OSHA 1910.165?*

❑   *Are alarm systems adequate to be heard or noticed in high-noise areas of the facility?*

D.   Evacuation and Personnel Accountability

Specify procedures for evacuating personnel from the facility during an emergency. These procedures must provide a means to account for all personnel to ensure that everyone has been safely removed from a hazard area.

Are the following covered as appropriate:

❑   *Does the plan provide for the evacuation of all personnel from the facility?*

❑   *Are procedures in place to account for all facility personnel and visitors?*

❑   *Does the plan specify persons who are responsible for determining that all employees and visitors were safely evacuated?*

❑   *Does the plan specify how to determine the need to evacuate the facility or site and when to issue evacuation orders?*

❑   *Does the plan identify the individuals responsible for issuing evacuation orders and how evacuation orders will be announced?*

❑   *Does the plan specify arrangements to assist employees who may need special assistance during evacuation?*

E.   Emergency Notifications

1.   Internal Facility

Specify procedures for notifying key personnel within the facility during an emergency.

Is the following covered as appropriate:

❑ *Does the plan identify the procedures to be followed to notify key facility personnel and does it provide necessary contact information, such as office, cellular, and pager numbers?*

2. External Facility

Specify procedures for notifying personnel and organizations that may be needed to assist in an emergency at the facility.

Is the following covered as appropriate:

❑ *Does the plan identify procedures to be followed to notify external personnel and organizations that may be needed to assist in the emergency?*

F. Regulatory Notifications

1. Regulatory Reporting of Incidents

Specify procedures for notifying regulatory agencies. In addition, the person(s) within the facility responsible for making these notifications must be identified.

Are the following covered as appropriate:

❑ *Does the plan identify the procedures for notifying regulatory agencies?*

❑ *Is the individual responsible for making the regulatory notifications identified in the EAP?*

2. Regulatory Requirements

Facilities should develop a spill and emergency reporting matrix that can be referenced during an emergency. This matrix would identify agencies that must be notified and those situations that require notification.

Is the following covered as appropriate:

❑ *Does the EAP contain a spill and emergency reporting matrix?*

3. Notification Telephone Numbers

Provide a list of telephone numbers to aid in making regulatory notifications.

Are the following covered as appropriate:

❑ *Are all telephone numbers of organizations, services, personnel, and regulatory agencies identified in the EAP?*

❑ *Is there a procedure in place for the verification of the contact numbers?*

❑ *Is responsibility assigned for verification of the contact numbers?*

VI. Incident Handling Procedures

Some facilities like to classify incidents by their severity. Typically, incidents are classified into three or four levels. Generally, incident classification will be used at larger facilities and will indicate, depending on the severity of the incident, the internal and external resources required to handle the emergency.

A.   Fires and Explosions

Specify procedures for the handling of fires and explosions.

B.   Hazardous Material Releases

Specify procedures for the handling of hazardous materials releases and spills.

C.   Medical Emergency

Specify procedures for handling a medical emergency or injury.

D.   Severe Weather Incidents

Specify procedures for the handling of severe weather conditions that may impact the facility.

E.   Bomb Threats

Specify procedures for handling reports of bomb threats at the facility.

F.   Transportation Accidents

Specify procedures for the handling of a transportation accident at the facility.

G.   Public Demonstrations/Civil Disturbances

Specify procedures for dealing with public demonstrations and civil disturbances that may impact the facility.

H.   Terrorism

Specify procedures for handling acts of terrorism that may impact the facility.

I.   Sabotage

Specify procedures to be used for the detection of possible acts of sabotage.

J.   Workplace Violence

Specify procedures for dealing with workplace violence and providing for the safety of facility personnel and visitors during such incidents.

K.   Strikes and Work Stoppages

Specify procedures for dealing with emergency situations and for ensuring recovery of operations during a strike or work stoppage. This section should generally be kept as a separate appendix item maintained by facility management.

Are the following covered as appropriate for the above Sections A to K:

❑   *Have specific procedures for all potential emergency situations that the facility is vulnerable to been provided?*

❑   *Do the procedures clearly specify the responsibilities of each facility employee?*

❑   *Are safety concerns adequately addressed as part of the response procedures?*

❑   *Do the response procedures adhere to national, industry-specific, or regulatory requirements?*

VII.   Facility Shutdown Guidelines

If the facility has critical equipment that must be shut down during an emergency situation, this equipment should be identified here.

A.   Emergency Shutdown Procedures

Specify emergency shutdown procedures of critical operations and equipment and identity of persons responsible for this.

Are the following covered as appropriate:

❑   *Does the EAP address requirements for the emergency shutdown of critical equipment and systems?*

❑   *Have checklists of procedures required for shutdown been developed?*

❑   *Have personnel received proper training in shutdown procedures?*

❑   *If personnel are required to stay behind after evacuation to operate or shutdown critical equipment, how is their safety provided for?*

VIII. Terminating the Emergency

This section deals with the specific activities that a facility will need to undertake following an emergency situation.

A. Recovery of Operations

Specify procedures for the recovery of the facility and the reestablishment of facility operations, as well as the assignment of responsibility for carrying out these tasks. This section is just as critical as the handling of the incident if you want to minimize losses and not be part of the 50 percent of businesses that fail within the two years following an incident.

Is the following covered as appropriate:

❑   *Does the plan specifically address critical procedures and activities that will be required for recovery activities?*

B. Documentation

All emergencies that occur at a facility must be documented. Documentation is needed for insurance claims and regulatory reporting. In addition, you should gather documentation just as if you were preparing to go to court over the incident, because you might be.

Are the following covered as appropriate:

❑   *Are the required types of documentation for insurance, regulatory, and legal purposes identified?*

❑   *Is the responsibility for collecting and recording documentation addressed?*

C. Incident Investigation

Specify procedures and responsibility for the investigation of incidents that occur at the facility. Incident investigation is important in that it can provide critical documentation about the incident and can identify problems that management will be able resolve to prevent a reoccurrence in the future.

Are the following covered as appropriate:

❑   *Are procedures in place for the investigation of incidents at the facility?*

❑   *Has specific responsibility been assigned to personnel responsible for conducting the investigation?*

D. Damage Assessment

Specify procedures and responsibility for assessing damage and cost impact to the facility as a result of the incident.

Are the following covered as appropriate:

❑ *Are procedures in place for assessing the damage to facility equipment and resources?*

❑ *Have personnel who will be responsible for damage assessment been designated?*

❑ *Have designated personnel received training in damage assessment techniques?*

F. Post-Emergency Activities

The following post-emergency activities will generally take place within 72 hours of the incident, depending on need.

1. Incident Debriefing

The purpose of debriefing is to inform personnel about the hazards, such as chemicals, that were involved in the incident and to identify damaged equipment and unsafe conditions that require immediate attention. Some employees may be profoundly impacted by the incident in a traumatic manner. In some cases, it may be necessary to arrange for a mental health professional to intervene and help employees deal with the situation. This is especially true when there are serious injuries or deaths as a result of the incident.

2. Critique

A critique is a discussion among those people involved in the handling of the emergency situation. It is designed to allow personnel to talk about what went right and what went wrong. It is not designed to be a shouting match or a session to place blame. It should allow for the flow of ideas and recommendations to improve the emergency action plan and facility policies and procedures.

IX. Appendix Materials

The basic emergency operations plan or action checklist should be supported by appropriate appendices providing samples of documents that may be needed during an emergency.

A. Maps

Building floor plans, plot plan (site plan map of building and grounds), street maps, and other appropriate maps that can be tacked to sheets of wallboard in the EOC should be provided. The EOC staff can use pins, stick-ons, grease pencils, and erasable marking pens on clear plastic overlays to depict emergency situations and show the locations of available manpower and equipment. This method of illustrating what is happening will help direction and control staff decide what emergency actions should be taken.

B. Procedure Charts

Simple organizational charts with the names, titles, addresses, and telephone numbers of key emergency personnel should be provided. These charts will be useful before and during emergency operations. The charts should also show which members of the direction and control staff are responsible for certain actions, such as dealing with the local governments, other industries, or contractors who have emergency equipment or supplies on hand.

C. Callup Lists

Callup lists of key personnel responsible for activating the basic plan should be included. These lists should include names, addresses, telephone numbers, and organizational responsibilities for emergency operations. Alternates should be listed in case primary personnel are not available. Company officials should carry pocket cards containing the names, telephone numbers, and locations of local government and company emergency services staff and facilities.

D. Emergency Contact Numbers

Every emergency plan should have a detailed listing of telephone numbers for contacting government and other agencies and organizations.

1. **Local and county government**
2. **State government**
3. **Federal government**
4. **Other numbers**

Each plan should contain a list of essential services that the facility will need to reestablish operations following an emergency.

E. List of Local Resources

Prepare a resource list of major sources of additional workforce, equipment, and supplies. The data should list by company and location the kind and number of skilled workers, equipment, and supplies available in the community. The resource list should be updated at least annually.

F.   Mutual Aid Agreements

The EAP appendices should include agreements among companies and government agencies to assist one another, within defined limits, during major emergencies. The direction, control, and emergency service staffs should be aware of the provisions of these agreements.

G.   Glossary of Terms

To be effective, the plan should use terms that mean the same thing to everyone concerned. To accomplish this, include a glossary of terms.

Additional Plan Observations

The following questions are some general considerations that should be kept in mind as you formulate your emergency action plan. They include items that are common to most facility emergency plans.

- ❑   *Is the EAP similar in format to other facility policies and procedures?*

- ❑   *Has the plan been given the full support of company management?*

- ❑   *Do all personnel know of their roles and responsibilities during a facility emergency?*

- ❑   *Is the safety of visitors to the facility properly addressed?*

- ❑   *Is the plan easily understood by all employees?*

- ❑   *If the facility has bilingual employees, have the special communication problems of these employees been addressed?*

- ❑   *Is a table of contents included in the EAP?*

- ❑   *Is there a sheet for recording all changes and updates to the plan?*

Chapter 6

Preservation of Records

Preservation and protection of vital records in an emergency is essential for rapid return to normal operations. Destruction, disruption, or loss of records, even if only temporary, can significantly delay recovery operations. To ensure that those records deemed essential for the continuity of business are properly safeguarded, take the following steps:

- Identify, in advance, priority categories of essential records.

- Label all records within the priority categories with identifiable markings. Priority of evacuation should be noted on record containers.

- Assess the vulnerability of stored records to direct and secondary damage from various disaster threats; i.e., fire, water damage, chemical damage, aftershock, vandalism, etc.

- Evaluate alternate record storage locations in light of hazard analysis.

- Make arrangements for transportation to relocate records to alternate locations if the need arises.

- Identify and retain copies of the records that will be needed by management or the emergency response teams during the emergency operations.

Vital Records

Vital records that are necessary to ensure the survival of a business constitute a small part of a company's records, usually no more than two percent. Therefore, it is important that vital records be given maximum protection from every disaster. Indeed, for some businesses, the information contained in their records is their most valuable asset. The loss of processing and trade secrets, drawings, and formulas could easily end a prospering business.

What Records Are Vital?

What records must a company have in order to function? This varies depending upon the type of business; i.e., manufacturing, financial, institutional, etc.. But there are certain fundamental records vital to any corporate organization; for example, the incorporation certificate, the bylaws, the stock record books, ownership and leasing documents, insurance policies, and certain financial records.

In addition, a manufacturing organization requires engineering drawings and specifications, parts lists, work processes and procedures, lists of employee skills required, and similar information. Without these it is impossible to produce a product. A banking institution requires current information about the status of depositors' accounts, accounts with other banks, loan accounts, and related banking services. The task of re-creating all of this information would be virtually impossible.

Selecting Records to Be Protected

The vital records protection program is an administrative device for safeguarding vital information, not for preserving existing records. Management begins to protect vital records by systematically determining what information is vital and which records contain this information. If a record contains vital information, it should be protected against all possible peril. If a particular record does not contain vital information, it has no place in the company's vital records protection program.

Record Analysis Procedure

The following procedure is suggested for analyzing a company's vital records. A management project team analyzes a company's vital records information needs in four steps. The logical team leader is the company records manager.

Step 1

The project team classifies company operations into broad functional categories. These functions will be different in each company, but in general they should include at least the following categories:

- **Finance**: bill payment, account collection, and cost accounting
- **Production**: research, engineering, purchasing, and related activities
- **Sales**: inventory control and shipping activities
- **General Administration**: personnel, legal, tax, public relations, and similar staff activities

Step 2

The project team determines the role of each function in an emergency. Not every current company function and activity will be essential for prompt post-disaster recovery. Some activities must be suspended during the recovery period; some can be eliminated completely in spite of possible inconvenience. If elimination or curtailment of an activity after a disaster will restrict the company's ability to restore some essential aspect of its operations, then that activity is vital. Also, the information needed to maintain it is vital and should be protected.

Step 3

The project team identifies the essential information that must be readily accessible during a post-disaster emergency to ensure that vital functions are performed properly. For instance, to stabilize customer account collections, it may be necessary to have the most recent account statement showing the outstanding balance at the time of the disaster as well as a record of subsequent purchases and payments. Or, to clarify field parts inventory conditions, it may be necessary to have access to a copy of the most recent sales agents' reports. This step may disclose that some of the records needed in an emergency are not created in the routine of daily business. In such a case, a system should be developed to ensure that these records are available for possible post-disaster use.

Step 4

Finally, the team identifies the particular records that contain this vital information and the departments in which they are, or should be, maintained.

In today's society, the majority of vital information is processed by computers and captured on the distinctive media associated with electronic data processing. In some businesses, however, certain vital information must be maintained as paper records. The same planning considerations should be given to protecting both kinds of vital records.

Protecting Vital Records

Vital records may be protected by dispersal of duplicated copies or may be secured in protected onsite or offsite storage. The dispersal of duplicate vital records lends greater assurance that the information needed to reconstitute the business after a disaster would be available in a location unaffected by the incident. While onsite storage in fire resistant files, vaults, or safes may be acceptable for temporary storage of vital documents and records, a significant disaster could damage or destroy even these special containers. Offsite storage in a vital records facility located outside the risk area offers the advantages of quick retrieval from a single location, security, air and humidity control, and trained staff.

Prior to determining the best method for protecting vital records, consider the hazards to which your site, buildings, and computer equipment are vulnerable and the consequences an emergency resulting from these hazards would impose.

The following recommendations are the result of experience gained from Hurricane Andrew and other recent disaster situations.

- One set of critical business records should be kept at a safe and secure site 100 miles or more from the facility. During Hurricane Andrew there were a number of instances in which the facility was damaged and so was the location chosen to maintain the backup sets of business and computer records.

- Do not wait until the last minute to move critical business records or equipment from the area. During Hurricane Andrew many facilities waited too long to move records and then were unable to get flights out of the area, or found that the interstate highways were clogged with several hundred thousand people trying to leave the area.

Safeguarding Vital Computer Information and Records

Effective protection of vital computer information is more complicated than safeguarding paper vital records for the following reasons:

- Information that was formerly dispersed is usually consolidated in electronic form, which intensifies its exposure to possible destruction or compromise. Paradoxically, this consolidated information becomes, through remote data transmission equipment, more accessible to more people. Greater accessibility to this information means greater chances for compromise and the introduction of error.

- The data processing medium is extremely vulnerable to a wide variety of perils: fire, water, dirt, static electricity, transients (surges) over electrical and telephone lines, and hazardous chemical gases, to name a few. Even a sharp blow through careless handling can rearrange and render worthless the magnetic data impulses that it records.

- Information transmitted over a distance for remote computer processing or handled by a computer service bureau is out of the company's direct control and custody for an extended period of time.

- The computer and the physical area in which it is located must be protected along with the vital information which is so closely linked to it.

- The adequacy and validity of the programs used to process this information and related computer operations documentation must be safeguarded to ensure the usefulness, currency, and accuracy of the basic information.

Much of what already has been said about selecting and protecting vital records applies to records processed by a computer. Many of the general measures taken to protect vital data processing operations and records are measures that ordinarily should be taken to ensure the general efficiency of the computer and its use by the company. However, procedures used to protect vital data processing records must be compatible with the information system design policies and the computer programming concepts used by the company.

In protecting vital records on paper or microfilm, it is necessary to safeguard only the record itself. In contrast, in protecting vital data processing records there are three distinctive elements: (a) the computer facility, (b) the physical data processing media, and (c) the inherent integrity of the information itself.

Controlling the Central Computer Facility

Prior to computer installation, it is preferable to build many protective features into the area in which it is to be operated. However, where these features have been omitted or function inadequately, it is possible to remedy some defects even when the computer has been operating for some time. The following recommendations for improving computer facility security are not meant to cover every aspect of computer area design and layout.

- Make the central computer facility as inconspicuous as possible. Remove door and direction signs that identify the computer's location. It may be preferable to leave the computer facility entrances unmarked. Block off, or otherwise eliminate, display windows originally installed to permit exhibiting computer operations to visitors or those passing the building on the outside.

- Strengthen controls over access to the computer facility. Provide 24-hour security guard surveillance of the area. In some companies, this may be supplemented by installation of closed circuit video equipment to permit monitoring of computer facility approaches by the security center duty officer. Install security hardware on all computer facility entrance doors. Maintain a record of all visitors, both outsiders and nonassigned company employees, and require that they wear distinctive badges while they are in the computer facility. Encourage assigned employees to question visitors about their right to be in the facility, even when they are wearing visitor badges. Prohibit delivery by vendors of forms and other supplies directly to the computer facility. Do not permit vendor representatives to stack these materials in halls or corridors.

- Review possible computer facility exposure to water and fire damage. Determine whether the walls, ceiling, and air-conditioning system are sufficiently watertight to prevent possible damage in an emergency. Be sure that drainage under the facility's raised floor is adequate to avoid water accumulation wherever flooding might occur or water might be used to extinguish a fire. Install a dedicated heating and cooling system. Computer room fires are rare, but smoke damage from someone else's fire is common according to insurance company reports. Reduce exposure to arson attempts by moving air-conditioning and ventilation air intake ducts from the ground floor to well up on the building side, possibly even under the eaves. Make prompt removal of paper accumulation and similar waste a part of computer facility work routines. To further reduce fire hazards, prohibit smoking and eating within the computer facility.

• Provide sufficient emergency power generation capacity to compensate for voltage surges or extended voltage reductions, and otherwise maintain uninterrupted power input to the computer. A battery pack with converter, possibly integrated into a motorized generator, will be required. Most mainframe and minicomputers have optional batteries.

The minimum power failure reserve needed is from 15 to 18 minutes, sufficient to reach the nearest restart point and to shut operations down in an orderly manner. Attach an audible warning device to the emergency power source to ensure that the computer operator and others are notified promptly of the shift to reserve power.

• Alternate computer facilities to be used in an emergency must be truly compatible with the company's computer and the work performed on it. The alternate facility should have sufficient reserve processing capacity and mainframe schedule time to permit it to handle the company's work and its own during the emergency. Be sure that the two computers are comparable in memory size, hardware options available, resident operating or executive system, and peripheral equipment. Determine the impact of any differences on the programs themselves and the data preparation routines used in the material to be processed on this alternate computer. Alternate computer facilities may be a duplicate company facility, either in-house or at a separate headquarters, or various levels of facility backup available from commercial firms.

Ensuring Information Integrity

The integrity of computer processed vital records is maintained by limiting data access to authorized users and then by careful control over data input and user file access, program content revisions, and computer facility operating practices. In each of these areas, some protection will be provided by normal data processing management practices. However, special attention should be given to their impact on computer processed vital records.

- **Input and file access**

  Input data editing routines can be designed to detect and automatically reject spurious information. Vital records processing programs also can be designed to selectively limit user access to key file segments and to restrict user ability to modify certain types of information in the file. In addition, the resident supervisor or operating system programmer should maintain a log inaccessible to assigned computer operators. This log should routinely record programs processed, files used, computer operator assigned, and travel use rate and elapsed time. Where the computer facility services a data transmission network, this log also should record user terminal identification and the type of inquiry made. Computer facility supervisors and company security officers should review the log jointly at least once weekly and investigate questionable inquiries and apparent irregularities.

- **Program content revisions**

  Computer programs used to process vital information should be fully documented. A current copy of this documentation should be stored off site with the dispersed file copy tapes. Programs purchased or leased from another company should receive protection equal to that given to company-developed programs. Programs from outside sources may have been adapted in some way to the company's specific data processing needs. Documentation incorporating all the necessary features for such an adapted program may be difficult or impossible to obtain from the supplier on short notice. Computer facility operating policies will determine full documentation file content, but the program segment of it should encompass at least the following: A plain English narrative description of what the program does; definition of transaction content; block or program logic diagrams; decision tables; source coding; assembly listing; a register of checkpoints, error messages, and interruptions, together with restart and recovery instructions; and a description of input, output, and transaction processing controls.

As company operating policies and procedures evolve, the programs used to process computer vital records must be altered to reflect these changes. Program changes should be fully documented, programmers involved in these changes must be clearly identified in the program documentation, and both the user department and computer facility supervisor must review and approve these changes before they are implemented. Programmers must not be permitted on their own initiative to make even minor changes in the production programs they are running.

Personal Computers

Personal computers (PCs) and small business computers are more susceptible to data security breaches than large centralized or distributed systems. They are often located in open areas and are operated by nontechnical users who use widely distributed applications software. While these systems are often the first place data is entered in a large corporation before transmission to mainframe data storage, they might be the only computers a small business has. The information generated on this type of equipment is as valuable as that generated on any other type of equipment.

The problems in protecting data on PCs are complex. These problems include a lack of software reliability, data integrity, backup/recovery procedures, and physical protection. Also lacking is protection for data resident on hard disk or in system memory. Further, there is no differentiation between public and private data sectors in small multi-user systems in which all files are currently available to all users.

A growing number of tools, both software and hardware, to combat these problems are entering the market. These include physical locks to prevent unauthorized individuals from turning the equipment on, as well as software locks, which require passwords to gain access to various applications. Special security measures similar to those for mainframe computers are becoming available for personal computers. Extra care must be taken to back up and store data disks in remote locations from the site of the personal computer.

Testing the Vital Records Program

The vital records protection program is designed to protect and provide the information needed by the company for survival in a disaster or emergency. But will it? Management must know whether the planned safeguards will work in an emergency. Periodic vital records protection program tests will provide the answer.

Chapter 7

Sample
Emergency Action Plan

Emergency Action Plan

AirCraft Parts Service
200 Industrial Drive
Jennifersville, Alabama

Employee and Management Procedures

January 200_
Version 1.0

Contents

Section V   Terminating the Emergency

Appendix Documents

Section I   Administration

I.1   Policy Statement

The purpose of this Emergency Action Plan is to assist employees and management in making quality decisions during times of crisis. This plan is simply a resource tool providing guidance in determining the appropriate actions to take to prevent injury and property loss from the occurrence of emergency incidents.

The plan will also assist facility management in ensuring the survivability of the various business activities provided by AirCraft Parts Service in the event of an incident impacting upon the facility.

The plan will meet the applicable requirements of federal regulations, including 29 CFR 1910.38(a), as well as state and local regulations regarding emergency action planning.

When an emergency situation occurs at the facility, the safety of employees and visitors will be coordinated by the Facility Emergency Coordinator.

I.2   Scope of Plan

It is AirCraft Parts Service's intent to prevent all foreseeable emergency situations that might impact the safety of employees and visitors through the implementation of a facility safety and health program and the regular training of personnel in emergency procedures. However, it is recognized that emergency situations are not totally preventable. Therefore this plan has been developed to achieve the following objective:

Provide employees with procedures to follow for effective and safe actions during an emergency situation, including evacuation.

This plan will serve as the emergency action guide for employees and visitors in the event of an emergency. The plan is divided into six separate action guides based on the nature of the emergency. The six areas of concern are these: 1) Emergency Medical Situations, 2) Fires, 3) Severe Weather, 4) Bomb Threats, 5) Chemical Releases and 6) Power Failures. The contents pages will enable the user to quickly find the appropriate section during an emergency incident.

While no plan can take into consideration all possible emergency situations, the guidelines included in this plan should assist you in making proper decisions.

I.3   Legal Compliance

This plan will comply with the following federal regulation:

29 CFR 1910.38(a) Employee Emergency Plans and Fire Prevention Plans

As regulations are revised, the plan should reflect these changes as necessary. Plan updates will be completed as described in Section I.6, Plan Updating Procedures.

I.4   Authority Statement

The management of AirCraft Parts Service recognizes that during emergency situations special procedures must be followed to control and mitigate an emergency. Therefore management, by the acceptance of this Emergency Action Plan, grants authority to those responsible individuals and/or positions named or unnamed in these procedures to implement and carry out the Plan to the termination of the emergency situation.

Management also recognizes that those individuals authorized to respond to emergency situations shall be properly trained in those procedures and emergency techniques, such as evacuation, first aid, use of fire extinguishers, and other areas as determined by their duties and responsibilities.

I.5   Plan Distribution

The Emergency Action Plan will be distributed to all departments with a master copy being maintained by the Facility Emergency Coordinator. The plan will be available for review by all employees.

I.5.1   Location and Plan Identification Numbers

All copies of the plan will be identified with a copy number on the binder spine. The following is a list of the plan copies by number and their locations in each department.

Plan Number	Department	Location
EAP-1	Administration	President's Office
EAP-2	Operations	Vice President of Operations
EAP-3	Safety	Safety Director
EAP-4	Manufacturing	Foreman's office
EAP-5	Transportation	Foreman's office
EAP-6	Shipping/receiving	Foreman's office

I.5.2 Plan Information and Contact Person

Information concerning the plan can be obtained from department supervisors, the Facility Emergency Coordinator, or the Safety Director.

I.6 Plan Updating Procedures

The Emergency Action Plan will be reviewed at least annually by the facility safety committee with recommendations for changes and/or modifications. These recommendations will be forwarded in writing to the Facility Emergency Coordinator who, in conjunction with the Safety Director, will implement changes to the plan as necessary. The Facility Emergency Coordinator will keep the Safety Director advised of any changes that may be necessary based on changes to federal, state, and/or local regulations and requirements.

I.6.1 Revision Notation

a) When revisions are made to the plan, the page(s) affected by the revision will be provided with a date of issue and version number.

b) Each person/department identified in I.5.1 will receive a copy of the changes. Along with the changes, a Notification of Change form will be provided which must be signed by each responsible party indicating that the party has received a copy of the changes and that the copy of the plan assigned to that party has been updated. This form is to then be submitted to the Facility Emergency Coordinator.

I.7 Plan Training

To ensure that the plan is properly followed during facility emergencies a training program shall be provided to employees. The objectives of the training program shall be as follows:

a) To ensure that personnel are knowledgeable of their roles and responsibilities concerning the plan.

b) To ensure that personnel are knowledgeable of the plan's procedures to effect a safe response to facility emergency situations.

c) To ensure that personnel are knowledgeable of the evacuation procedures to effect a safe and expedient evacuation of the appropriate areas of the facility impacted by an emergency situation.

I.7.1 Training Program

Facility personnel will receive training in the plan appropriate to the level of their expected involvement. The specific lesson plans and training topics are to be maintained by the Facility Emergency Coordinator. The following is the general training program for each of the identified groups:

I.7.1.1 Employees

- **Training frequency**

  Employees will receive training during initial employment orientation and refresher training at least quarterly during safety meetings.

  When employees change areas or departments in which they work, they will receive from their department supervisor appropriate training in their responsibilities and actions as required by the plan for their new area. All employees will be trained whenever the plan is changed.

- **Training level**

  Employees will receive training in the general plan procedures and specific departmental procedures related to the plan.

  Training should cover evacuation procedures, incident discovery, notifications, fire extinguishers, and first aid.

- **Supervisor training**

  All supervisors will receive additional training, beyond that received by employees, dealing with actions that are necessary to provide for the safety of personnel and visitors, and the protection of facility assets.

- **Facility Emergency Coordinator training**

  All Facility Emergency Coordinators will receive additional training on the specific duties, actions, and responsibilities of their position during an emergency situation as identified in the emergency action plan.

- **Emergency response team member training**

  All emergency response team members shall receive specialized training for the response to and handling of emergency situations that could occur at the facility.

I.8 Plan Drills and Exercises

To ensure that the plan will meet current conditions and that all involved individuals will respond properly, the plan will be tested on a regular basis.

I.8.1 Frequency of Drills/Exercise

The plan will be exercised at least monthly on varied work shifts. Specific areas to be evaluated during the monthly exercise will include the following:

a) Evacuation and accountability of personnel

b) Proper functioning of alarm system

c) Special procedures for evacuation of personnel with special disabilities or impairments

d) Response time of emergency response personnel to emergency situation

e) Adherence to plan procedures

I.8.2 Exercise Documentation

All drills and exercises of the plan will be documented, indicating the results of the exercise and any problems that were encountered, along with recommendations for plan modifications. The Facility Emergency Coordinator will complete an Emergency Action Plan Exercise Evaluation Form and maintain copies for review by the Safety Committee. The Facility Emergency Coordinator shall submit a report to the Safety Director indicating results of an exercise and changes necessitated by the exercise.

Section II   General Information

II.1 Description of Facility and Operations

The facility is involved in the manufacture and distribution of specialty components used in the manufacture of aircraft. The facility is protected by a modern fire protection system, including automatic sprinklers in all areas of the two facility buildings, and a fire alarm system. Hazardous materials, such as solvents and corrosives, are used in the manufacturing process. There are no special or highly hazardous processes taking place at the facility.

II.2 Emergency Recognition and Prevention

Through the use of regularly scheduled safety meetings, employee orientations, safety procedures, training programs, and operational procedures, facility employees will be trained in identifying conditions that might lead to a facility emergency condition. Employees are instructed, as part of their training and orientation, in the steps to take to prevent and report facility emergency situations when these conditions are found to exist.

Regular safety training, covering actions of employees, will be provided as identified in I.7.1 of this plan.

II.2.1 Fire Prevention

Listed below are specific procedures that shall be addressed by the facility to minimize the occurrence of and impact from a fire emergency. There are no unusual fire hazards present at this facility. Special emphasis is placed on housekeeping and storage practices in the maintenance and manufacturing areas because flammable and combustible materials are used and stored here.

a) The facility is committed to preventing the occurrence of fires and situations that may promote a fire at the facility.

b) Fire prevention is the responsibility of all facility personnel. Employees should follow safe practices to minimize fire hazards, and supervisors must ensure that safe practices are followed on a daily basis. Supervisors shall check their work areas daily for fire prevention problems and report these problems promptly to the Facility Emergency Coordinator for corrective action.

c) All fire protection equipment will be inspected monthly by the Facility Emergency Coordinator or designee. Results of inspection will be recorded on the Fire and Safety Equipment Monthly Inspection Form, and the results will be reviewed by the Safety Committee. Results of these inspections will be provided to the Safety Director.

   1) Equipment to be inspected will include the following:
      • Fire extinguishers
      • Smoke detectors
      • Fire alarm system
      • Fire sprinkler system
      • Emergency lighting
      • Emergency generators

2) All areas in the facility will be inspected to check for the following unsafe conditions:

- Blocked or locked fire exits
- Poor housekeeping procedures
- Smoking in nondesignated areas
- Flammable/combustible materials not stored properly
- Obstructed access to electrical rooms and panels

II.3 Organization and Personnel Responsibilities

During an emergency situation, the Facility Emergency Coordinator will have the responsibility for ensuring that proper actions are taken to ensure the safety of employees and visitors to the facility. Management grants the Facility Emergency Coordinator the authority to carry out those tasks and functions identified in the plan that provide for the safety of personnel. In the event that the primary Facility Emergency Coordinator is not available, the next alternate in the order listed will assume the responsibilities of Facility Emergency Coordinator.

Facility Emergency Coordinator

Sidney Hampton

321-5000	Office
621-4534	Home
324-1221	Pager

Alternate Emergency Coordinators (In Order)

The Senior Onsite Facility Foreman will serve as the alternate Facility Emergency Coordinator.

In the event that the Senior Onsite Facility Foreman is unavailable or unable to function as the Facility Emergency Coordinator, the first on-scene emergency response team member will function as the Facility Emergency Coordinator.

The alternate Facility Emergency Coordinator will notify the primary Facility Emergency Coordinator, as needed, based on the severity of the situation. Upon arrival, the primary Facility Emergency Coordinator will assume the duties and responsibility of the Facility Emergency Coordinator, as needed.

Emergency Response Team

The facility maintains an Emergency Response Team that has received specialized training to respond to emergency situations at the facility. The Emergency Response Team will be under the direction of the Facility Emergency Coordinator.

II.3.1 Key Facility Personnel and Phone Numbers

The following is a list of individuals and groups that may be needed during a facility emergency. The list is separated into two parts: facility or onsite personnel and offsite or community organizations and services.

- **Facility personnel**
  This would include facility employees who may be needed during an emergency situation.

- **Organizations**
  This would include local, state, and federal organizations that may be needed to assist in providing services to the facility during an emergency situation.

The list provides phone numbers (facility and home) and pager numbers when available. This list is to be verified every six months and updated whenever an employee or organization advises that a change has occurred.

II.3.2 Onsite Personnel

Key facility personnel who may need to be contacted in the event of an emergency include:

Jennifer Jetson, President
321-5001	Office
621-3333	Home
324-1111	Pager

Laurie Kay Johnson, Vice President of Operations
321-5005	Office
654-2287	Home
324-1321	Pager

Sidney Hampton, Facility Emergency Coordinator
321-5000	Office
621-4534	Home
324-1221	Pager

A list of all onsite employees is contained in the Appendix.

II.3.3 Local and State Organizations and Services

Organization	Emergency Number	Administrative Number
Jennifersville Fire Department	911	373-7556
English County Sheriffs Office	911	373-3327
English County EMS	911	373-7565
Power Company	800-555-5555	800-555-3434
Southern Bell Telephone	800-222-8240	800-222-8240
American Natural Gas	378-1111	378-1213
Jennifersville Water Department	373-2344	373-2344
Jennifersville Sewer Department	373-2344	373-2344
English County Emergency Management	373-2278	373-2278

II.3.4 Miscellaneous Services

Organization	Number
Truck Rental	
Storage Facility	
Mechanical	
Telephone - System	
Portable Rest Rooms	
Bottled Water	
Fire Alarm Service	
Cellular Phone	
Water Removal	
Equipment Rental	
Waste Removal	

II.4 Media Relations Policy

AirCraft Parts Service recognizes that it is essential to present accurate information to the news media concerning an emergency situation involving our facility. In the event of an emergency involving AirCraft Parts Service, the President or his/her designee are the only authorized individuals who may speak with the media.

Any requests for information concerning the facility, employees, or visitors will be referred to the President or designee for handling.

II.5 Emergency Alerting Procedures

In order to provide for the safety of employees and visitors, it is essential that early warning of emergency situations be made so that evacuation procedures can be implemented and emergency response organizations notified of the situation.

The facility uses a state-of-the-art incident reporting and notification system. When an incident is reported by means of a fire alarm pull station or activation of the fire protection system, the location of the alarm is transmitted by means of a computer printout at the security station and a verbal report is transmitted over the facility hand-held portable radios.

Emergency alerting procedures shall be tested as part of the monthly drills as identified in I.8 of this plan and as part of the monthly emergency equipment inspection as identified in II.2 of this plan.

II.5.1 Notification for Small Area-Specific Incidents

Incidents such as individual medical emergencies will generally not require the notification of the entire facility.

- **Preferred means of notification**
  The telephone will be the preferred means of reporting such emergencies. Reports of emergency situations will be reported to the security office. When available, the hand-held portable radios may be used to make notification of an emergency situation.

- **Secondary means of notification**
  A runner will be sent to the Security Office for a verbal notification of the situation.

II.5.2 Notification of Serious or Facilitywide Emergency Situation

Facilitywide emergency situations include incidents, such as a fire or explosion, which require that all or the majority of the facility be notified.

- **Preferred means of notification**

  The preferred means of notification is the activation of the fire alarm pull station.

- **Secondary means of notification**

  The secondary means of notification is by telephone from an area not involved in the emergency situation or by hand-held portable radio if available.

II.6 Evacuation and Personnel Accountability

Evacuation of employees and visitors from the facility is of the utmost importance. Most emergency situations will require the evacuation of all or part of the facility. In order to achieve a safe and timely evacuation, it is critical that an early warning of the emergency situation be communicated to personnel and action implemented to remove personnel from the hazard area.

The following procedures will be applicable for all evacuations called for under the specific emergency situations of the plan outlined in Section IV.

II.6.1 Management Responsibility

The management of AirCraft Parts Service has the responsibility to ensure a safe workplace for its personnel and visitors to its facility. As part of this responsibility, each supervisor and employee has a responsibility to ensure that all personnel are evacuated in a timely and safe manner from the facility and that all personnel are accounted for following evacuation. The following will outline the responsibility of each level of facility management during an evacuation:

II.6.1.1 Facility Emergency Coordinator

a) Ensures that facility personnel are trained in proper evacuation methods through facility safety training and evacuation drills.

b) Ensures that alarms are sounded in a timely manner when an emergency situation is encountered.

c) Determines that all personnel onsite have been accounted for following an evacuation.

d) Reports status of evacuation to the fire department upon its arrival.

II.6.1.2 Supervisors

a) Will be familiar with the requirements of the plan and their responsibilities during an evacuation of their assigned area(s).

b) Ensure that personnel assigned to their area(s) are trained in the requirements of the plan as it relates to them and procedures to following during an evacuation.

c) Determine any special evacuation needs or assistance that personnel within their assigned area(s) might have.

d) Account for all personnel assigned to their areas following an evacuation and report this information to the Facility Emergency Coordinator.

II.6.1.3 Employees

a) Will be familiar with their responsibilities during an evacuation of their assigned work area(s).

b) Assist their department supervisor as needed in the evacuation of other employees and visitors to a safe area.

II.6.2 Evacuation Points

Each area of the facility has designated primary and secondary evacuation points. In the event of an emergency requiring the evacuation of the facility, all employees are to immediately leave the facility by the designated route and report to their assigned evacuation point. Should the primary evacuation point be in a hazardous area, employees will then proceed to the designated secondary evacuation point for their assigned work area.

On arrival at your designated evacuation point, report to your supervisor. Supervisors will notify the Facility Emergency Coordinator as to the status of personnel assigned to them.

- All accounted for, or
- Names of missing personnel and location last seen

II.6.2.1 Primary Evacuation Points

Administration Building personnel	North employee parking lot
Distribution Warehouse personnel	North employee parking lot
Manufacturing Area 1	Field adjacent to Highway 710

II.6.2.2 Secondary Evacuation Points

Administration Building personnel	Parking lot of ABC Distribution
Distribution Warehouse personnel	Parking lot of ABC Distribution
Manufacturing Area 1	Jennifersville Elementary School parking lot

Section III   Maps and Diagrams of the Facility

The following maps and diagrams are included with this plan to assist those who have a need to use this document, but who may not be familiar with the layout of the AirCraft Parts Service facility. More detailed versions of the facility layout and control points are available from the Facility Emergency Coordinator.

III.1 Map of Facility and Designated Evacuation Meeting Points

Section IV   Emergency Procedures

The following are instructions for facility personnel about proper actions to be taken for personal safety and the procedures that are to be implemented to help guide management efforts during an emergency situation.

IV.1 Emergency Medical Situations

IV.1.1 Employee Procedures for Medical Emergency

a)   Dial 444 for Security Dispatcher.

b)   Inform dispatcher of the nature of problem.

c)   Inform dispatcher of your exact location.

d)   Inform dispatcher of the severity of the problem.

e)   Render first aid if you have been trained to do so.

f)   If enough personnel are present, send another employee or bystander to the building entrance to direct the emergency response team members.

IV.1.2 Security Officer Procedures for Medical Emergency

a)   Obtain from the caller:
    1)   Exact location of the emergency.
    2)   Nature of problem.
    3)   Severity of problem.

b)   Notify 911.

c)   Notify facility Emergency Response Team members.

d)   Send one person to main entrance to meet fire department ambulance.

IV.1.3 Emergency Response Team Procedures for Medical Emergency

a)   Upon receipt of call immediately respond to the location.

b)   Security will provide updated information if available.

c)   The first arriving Emergency Response Team member will report by radio that the team is on scene and give an initial assessment of the situation.

d)   Advise security of any additional resources required.

e)   Render first aid as appropriate.

IV.2 Fires

IV.2.1 Employee Procedures for Fires

a) **Fire discovered by employee**

1) Clear the area of all other personnel and visitors. Instruct all personnel to evacuate the facility.

2) Confine the fire by closing the door to the area.

3) Activate the fire alarm pull station.

4) Use portable fire extinguisher to contain the fire if it can be done safely.

5) Send one employee, if available, to meet the Emergency Response Team and lead the team to the fire.

6) Advise the Emergency Response Team on its arrival if all personnel are accounted for. If an employee or visitor is missing, advise response team as to the last known location of the individual.

7) Provide assistance to the Emergency Response Team as requested.

b) **Fire alarm activation - employee procedures**

1) On hearing the fire alarm, employees will evacuate the building using the closest exit route. Once emloyees have left the building, they may not go back in until instructed to do so by their supervisors.

2) Employees will assist visitors with evacuation as they exit the facility.

3) Employees will report to their supervisors in the designated evacuation areas for their buildings.

IV.2.2 Emergency Response Team Procedures for Fires

a) Upon receipt of a call, immediately respond to the location.

b) Security will provide updated information if available.

c) The first arriving ERT member will report by radio that they are on scene and give an initial assessment of the situation.

d) Assist in evacuation of employees and visitors.

e) If fire is still in incipient stage, attempt to extinguish it.

f)   One ERT member shall go to the fire department sprinkler connections and ensure that there is free access to them and that the post indicator valve is in an open position.

g)   Assist fire department officials as requested.

IV.2.3 Security Officer Procedures for Fires

a)   Obtain from the caller:
1)   The exact location of the fire
2)   Nature of problem

b)   Notify fire department at 911.

c)   Notify ERT members.

d)   Send one person to front entrance to meet fire department.

IV.2.4 Facility Emergency Coordinator Procedures for Fires

a)   Respond to all reported fires and direct the actions of the emergency response team and facility employees.

b)   Ensure that necessary actions, such as evacuation, accountability of personnel, fire suppression of incipient fires, etc., are initiated.

c)   Advise the fire officer in charge as to present conditions in the building (location of fire, missing personnel, chemicals involved, etc.).

d)   Advise the fire officer in charge of the available assistance AirCraft Parts Service personnel can provide (utility shut down, floor plan layout, contents of facility, hazardous materials storage, etc.) via the Emergency Action Plan.

e)   Relocate employees and visitors to an area of safe refuge, if necessary.

f)   Establish a telephone communication capability to allow employees and visitors to notify relatives/friends of their whereabouts and status.

g)   Establish a telephone response line for incoming questions from employee and visitor relatives concerning site activities. Security will be assigned this task.

h)   Assess damage impact and determine which areas of building cannot be reoccupied.

i)   Once the fire department returns control of the building to AirCraft Parts Service management, the Facility Emergency Coordinator shall assess whether temporary repair work can feasibly be performed by employees to minimize further damage. Such work might include covering ventilation openings made by the firefighters, securing doors that were forced open during rescue operations, and shutting down any unnecessary utilities to prevent further incident.

IV.3   Severe Weather/Natural Disasters

Severe weather can take many forms, including tornado, hurricane, earthquake, flood, or winter storm. All of these situations can impact the facility. Most severe weather situations provide some degree of warning or buildup which will allow for necessary preparations to be implemented. Of the types of severe weather listed above, a tornado is the most likely to impact the AirCraft Parts Service facility with little or no warning. The National Weather Service classifies tornadoes in the following manner:

- **Tornado Watch**

  A tornado watch means that tornadoes may occur in or near the area.

- **Tornado Warning**

  A tornado warning is issued when a tornado has been sighted or has been located by weather radar and may strike in the immediate area.

IV.3.1 Employee Procedures for Severe Weather

a) Tornado Watch

  1) Keep outdoor activities to a minimum. If outdoors, be observant for revolving, funnel-shaped clouds.

  2) Listen to the facility radio for weather updates.

  3) If a tornado is sighted, immediately take shelter and notify security.

b) Tornado Warning

  1) Immediately take shelter.
    (*a*) Your best protection is a reinforced concrete or steel-framed structure.
    (*b*) An interior hallway on the lowest level of the structure will be the safest.

  2) Take action to protect yourself from being blown away or struck by falling or flying objects.

  3) Stay away from windows to avoid flying debris.

4) If a tornado is rapidly approaching and you cannot reach a safe shelter, lie flat in the nearest depression or ditch and cover your head with your arms.

IV.3.2 Emergency Response Team Procedures for Severe Weather

Emergency Response Team members will respond as needed for severe weather conditions. The response to severe weather incidents by the Emergency Response Team will generally be an after-the-fact response and their primary responsibilities will be the evacuation of personnel and accounting for all employees and visitors.

IV.3.3 Security Officer Procedures for Severe Weather

Monitor Weather Alert Radio and report severe weather alerts from the National Weather Service as follows:

a) On receipt of a severe weather advisory, notify the Facility Emergency Coordinator.

b) Monitor the weather radio and provide any updates to the Facility Emergency Coordinator as received.

c) Implement any actions as requested by the Facility Emergency Coordinator.

d) If a tornado is sighted or reported to be approaching the facility, make an announcement over the radio system. Instruct all personnel to seek cover. Call 911 and report the situation.

IV.3.4 Facility Emergency Coordinator Procedures for Severe Weather

a) Respond to and direct the actions of the Emergency Response Team and facility employees in securing the facility in preparation for severe weather conditions and in response to such occurrences.

b) Ensure that necessary actions such as evacuation, accountability of personnel, and securing of facility property are initiated.

c) Relocate employees and visitors to an area of safe refuge, if necessary.

d) Establish a telephone communication capability to allow employees and visitors to notify their relatives/friends of their whereabouts and status.

e) Establish a telephone response line for incoming questions from employee and visitor relatives concerning site activities. Security will be assigned this task.

f)   Assess damage impact, areas of building that cannot be re-occupied.

g)   Assess whether temporary repair work by employees to minimize further damage is feasible.

IV.4   Chemical Releases

Chemical releases can be classified into two distinct categories: *incidental releases* and *emergency releases.*

- **Incidental Releases**

  Incidental releases are small isolated releases of chemicals, such as cleaning solvents, that do not present or have the potential to cause injuries or require evacuation other than from the immediate release area. Incidental spills can be cleaned up by personnel who have received proper training under the OSHA Hazard Communication Standard 29 CFR 1910.1200 and have the proper safety equipment. This type of incident would not require the response of the facility Emergency Response Team or local fire department.

- **Emergency Releases**

  Emergency releases are those incidents that involve large quantities of chemicals and/or have the potential to cause injuries. A release that requires the response of the Emergency Response Team and/or local fire department would be considered an emergency release.

  For the purpose of this Emergency Action Plan, only emergency releases will be addressed. Incidental releases of chemicals are covered in the AirCraft Parts Service Hazard Communication Program.

IV.4.1 Employee Procedures for Chemical Releases

a)   Clear the area of all personnel and visitors. Instruct personnel to evacuate the facility.

b)   Confine the release by closing the door to the area.

c)   Dial 444 for Security Dispatcher.
   1)   Inform dispatcher of the nature of the problem.
   2)   Inform dispatcher of the exact location of the chemical release.

d)   If the situation appears to be a serious release, activate the fire alarm pull station and begin evacuation of the involved building.

e)   If possible, send one employee to meet the Emergency Response Team and lead them to the incident area.

f) Advise the Emergency Response Team on their arrival whether all personnel are accounted for. If an employee or visitor is missing, inform response team of the last known location of the individual.

g) Provide assistance to the emergency response team as requested.

IV.4.2 Emergency Response Team Procedures for Chemical Releases

a) Upon receipt of call, immediately respond to the location. The actions of the Emergency Response Team during an emergency chemical release will generally be limited to securing the area and evacuation.

b) Security will provide updated information if available.

c) The first arriving ERT member will report by radio that the team is on scene and make an initial assessment of the situation.

d) Assist in evacuation of visitors and employees.

e) Assist fire department officials as requested.

IV.4.3 Security Officer Procedures for Chemical Releases

a) Obtain all pertinent information from the caller:
    1) Their exact location
    2) Nature of problem

b) Notify fire department at 911.

c) Notify ERT members.

d) Send one person to main entrance to meet fire department.

IV.4.4 Facility Emergency Coordinator Procedures for ChemicalReleases

a) Respond to all reported chemical releases and direct the actions of the emergency response team and facility employees.

b) Ensure that necessary actions such as evacuation, locating and accounting for personnel, and restricting access to hazards area are initiated.

c) Advise the fire officer in charge as to present conditions in the building (location of chemical release, missing personnel, chemicals involved, etc.).

d) Provide a copy of material safety data sheets for chemical(s) involved to the fire officer in charge.

e) Advise the fire officer in charge of any assistance that facility personnel can provide (utility shutdown, floor plan layout, contents of facility, hazardous materials storage, etc.) via the Emergency Action Plan.

f)   Relocate employees and visitors to an area of safe refuge, if necessary.

g)   Establish a telephone communication capability to allow employees and visitors to notify their relatives/friends of their whereabouts and status.

h)   Establish a telephone response line for incoming questions concerning site activities from employee and visitor relatives. Security will be assigned this task.

i)   Provide for the proper cleanup and removal of chemical materials.

j)   Assess damage impact and determine areas of building that cannot be reoccupied.

k)   Once the fire department returns control of the building to AirCraft Parts Service management, the Emergency Coordinator will assess whether temporary repair work to minimize further damage can feasibly be performed by employees.

IV.5   Bomb Threats

IV.5.1 Employee Procedures for Bomb Threats

a)   If you receive a telephone call from an individual reporting a bomb threat, try to transfer them to Security at 444. If this is not possible, ask the following questions:

   • When is the bomb going to explode?

   • Where is the bomb?

   • What does it look like?

   • What kind of bomb is it?

   • What will cause it to explode?

   • Did you place the bomb?

   • Where are you calling from?

   • What is your name?

b)   Immediately following the completion of the call, notify security. Dial 444 for Security Dispatcher. DO NOT USE YOUR RADIO TO REPORT THE PROBLEM. Radio transmissions can detonate an explosive device.

c)   If you discover an explosive device do not touch it or move it in any way. Immediately notify Security and your supervisor.

IV.5.2 Emergency Response Team Procedures for Bomb Threats

The ERT will not respond to the scene of a bomb threat unless requested to assist Security and the Facility Emergency Coordinator.

IV.5.3 Security Officer Procedures for Bomb Threats

a) Obtain as much information as possible concerning the bomb threat. Use the bomb threat checklist for documentation purposes.

b) Notify the Facility Emergency Coordinator and inform the FEC of the situation.

c) Security will notify English County Sheriff's Department at 911.

d) Assist Sheriff's Department as requested.

IV.5.4 Facility Emergency Coordinator Procedures for Bomb Threats

a) Coordinate activities of facility personnel to control the situation as necessitated by the emergency.

b) Ensure that all personnel and visitors have been evacuated from the involved area(s).

c) Provide assistance to Sheriff's Department as necessary.

IV.6 Power Outages

IV.6.1 Employee Procedures for Power Outages

a) Unless there is another related problem, such as a fire, remain in your designated work area until directed to do differently by a supervisor.

b) Assist visitors as necessary.

c) Use flashlights where available.

d) DO NOT use candles or other types of flame- or heat-producing devices for illumination.

e) Assigned personnel should place emergency generator on line to provide essential power to critical areas of the facility.

IV.6.2 Emergency Response Team Procedures for Power Outages

The ERT will generally not respond to the scene of a power outage unless requested by the Facility Emergency Coordinator.

IV.6.3 Security Officer Procedures for Power Outages

a) If power outage affects entire facility, notify power company at 1-800-555-5555.

b) Provide assistance as requested by Facility Emergency Coordinator.

IV.6.4 Facility Emergency Coordinator Procedures for Power Outages

a) Attempt to determine the cause and extent of problem.
   1) Problem is restricted to facility.
   2) Problem is area-wide.

b) Verify that facility emergency generator(s) are operating.

c) Provide portable lighting as needed.

IV.7 Temporary Sheltering Procedures

The following procedures are to be used by AirCraft Parts Service management personnel for the temporary sheltering of employees and visitors in the event of an emergency situation impacting the facility. The following procedures will be implemented following evacuation procedures for any of the emergency situations described in this plan.

IV.7.1 Localized Incident Impacting Only Part of Facility

This would involve a situation such as damage caused to one or more buildings from a fire or weather-related emergency.

a) Ensure the safety of all personnel and visitors. Provide shelter as necessary from inclement weather.

b) Move to an area that will not be impacted by operations being conducted to restore or resolve the emergency situation.

IV.7.2 Localized Incident Impacting Entire Facility

This would involve a situation such as a tornado or flood.

a) Ensure the safety of all personnel and visitors. Provide shelter as necessary from inclement weather.

b) Move to an area that will not be impacted by operations being conducted to restore or resolve the emergency situation.

   1) If the incident is affecting other parts of the community, English County Emergency Management may have opened shelters. Check

with English County officials at 555-5555 for information and disaster assistance.

2) The following hotels and motels can be used as needed to provide for lodging of residents and employees.

- **Crack of Dawn Hotel**
  204 Central Drive
  Jennifersville, AL
  910-555-5555

- **Jennifersville Airport Inn**
  Jennifersville International Airport
  Jennifersville, AL
  910-444-4444

Section V   Terminating the Emergency

This section of the Emergency Action Plan will deal with those activities necessary to support employees during and following an emergency situation and those activities necessary to restore operations at the AirCraft Parts Service facility.

V.1   Recovery of Operations

The recovery of facility operations and services will depend on the extent of damage suffered by the facility. The Facility Emergency Coordinator will need to prioritize activities that can be accomplished with available staff and resources. Immediately following the emergency phase of the incident, the Facility Emergency Coordinator and facility management will begin the implementation of the facility business recovery plan.

V.2   Documentation

Documentation of emergency activities is of critical importance following the emergency situation. All records and forms used during the incident to document activities must be retained for future reference.

V.2.1 Responsibility for Incident Documentation

a) Following an emergency situation, the Facility Emergency Coordinator will have the responsibility for collecting all records and forms used during the incident. These will be used for several purposes, such as incident investigation, insurance claims, and potential legal actions.

b) The Facility Emergency Coordinator must prepare a report documenting activities that took place during the emergency situation.

c) The report of the Facility Emergency Coordinator and all related documentation will be submitted to the President for review and necessary follow-up actions.

d) The Facility Emergency Coordinator shall report the findings and necessary corrective actions to the President of AirCraft Parts Service.

V.3 Incident Investigation

The emergency situation must be investigated as soon as possible following its occurrence. The investigation is designed to determine why the incident occurred and what precautions can be taken to prevent a recurrence. In general, the local governmental authorities will conduct investigations related to fires and explosions. The local fire and police department will generally solicit input and assistance from facility personnel during the investigation process. The Facility Emergency Coordinator will lead the investigation for AirCraft Parts Service, at least during the initial phases.

V.3.1 Investigation Responsibilities

The Facility Emergency Coordinator is responsible for ensuring that an incident investigation is conducted following all emergency situations that occur at the facility.

a) **Small Incidents**
For small incidents, the investigation will normally be conducted by the area supervisor. The Facility Emergency Coordinator will provide assistance as needed in conducting the investigation.

b) **Large Incidents**
For large incidents, especially those involving loss of life, local, state, and federal authorities will generally be involved in conducting the investigation. The Facility Emergency Coordinator and the Safety Director will assist the authorities as needed.

V.4 Damage Assessment

Following the incident, an assessment of damage that has occurred to facility properties and equipment must be conducted. The major goal of this assessment will be to determine the extent damage to facilities, safety hazards resulting from the incident, and repairs that must be initiated to minimize further damage and restore the facility for operational use.

V.4.1 Responsibility for Damage Assessment

The Facility Emergency Coordinator will have the primary responsibility for conducting the damage assessment following an incident. Assistance will be obtained as needed from facility personnel and outside organizations, such as structural engineering firms and local government.

V.5 Post-Emergency Activities

Post-emergency activities are those that tend to the welfare of facility personnel and provide for a review of facility actions during the incident

V.5.1 Incident Debriefing

The purpose of incident debriefing is to inform personnel about any hazards that may still remain on the facility property following the incident and to identify unsafe conditions that may still exist.

Some employees may be profoundly impacted by the events surrounding the incident, especially those involving injuries or loss of life. It may be necessary to provide critical-incident stress debriefing sessions following such incidents. The President shall make arrangements for counseling services as needed following an emergency situation.

V.5.2 Critique

The critique of the incident is a review of what actions took place during the incident, both good and bad. A critique is not designed to place blame, but rather to allow for the flow of ideas and recommendations to improve the emergency action plan and the facility policies and procedures.

Appendix Documents

Employee Emergency Roll Call

AirCraft Parts Service
200 Industrial Drive, Jennifersville, AL

(Check off each area as employees and visitors are accounted for.)

Office and Administration Areas—Building 1

❑ Administration   Accounted for   Y   N   Complete Missing Person Form

❑ Accounting   Accounted for   Y   N   Complete Missing Person Form

❑ Personnel   Accounted for   Y   N   Complete Missing Person Form

Manufacturing and Distribution—Building 2

❑ Shipping   Accounted for   Y   N   Complete Missing Person Form

❑ Maintenance   Accounted for   Y   N   Complete Missing Person Form

❑ Manu 1   Accounted for   Y   N   Complete Missing Person Form

❑ Manu 2   Accounted for   Y   N   Complete Missing Person Form

---

Missing Person Worksheet

Missing Person _____

   ❑ **Employee**   ❑ **Visitor**

Last Seen

Building or Location _____

Time _____ By Whom _____

Activities being taken to locate person _____

_____

_____

_____

_____

_____

_____

_____

_____

_____

_____

_____

Bomb Threat Checklist

Exact time of call _____

Exact words of caller _____

Questions to Ask

1. When is bomb going to explode? _____

2. Where is the bomb? _____

3. What does it look like? _____

4. What kind of bomb is it? _____

5. What will cause it to explode? _____

6. Did you place the bomb? _____

7. Why? _____

8. Where are you calling from? _____

9. What is your address? _____

10. What is your name? _____

Caller's Voice (Circle as many as appropriate)

Calm	Disguised	Nasal	Angry	Broken
Stutter	Slow	Sincere	Lisp	Rapid
Giggling	Deep	Crying	Squeaky	Excited
Stressed	Accent	Loud	Slurred	Normal

If voice is familiar, whom did it sound like? _____

Were there any background noises? _____

Remarks _____

_____

_____

Person receiving call _____

Telephone number call received at _____ Date _____

Emergency Action Plan
Exercise Evaluation Form

Facility _____

Date of Drill   ____ /____ /____

Time of Drill _____

Type of Drill Conducted

    ❑ Fire

    ❑ Severe Weather

    ❑ Medical Emergency

    ❑ Chemical Release

    ❑ Bomb Threat

    ❑ Power Failure

Length of time required to complete all exercise activities _____

List any problems encountered during the drill _____

_____

_____

_____

List any recommendations for improvement to the plan _____

_____

_____

_____

Signature of exercise evaluator _____

Send copy of completed form to Safety Committee and Facility Emergency Coordinator.

Internet Resources for Disaster Planning

For those of you who have access to the Internet and the information superhighway, there is a wealth of information available to assist you in the development of your facility emergency response and recovery plans. New sources of information that can be used for emergency planning are continuously being added. The following are some of the hundreds of websites on the Internet that address emergency planning and response. We have attempted to list those that would be of most value to facility personnel involved in emergency preparedness planning and response. We have intentionally omitted commercial sites, choosing to focus on those sites maintained by governmental agencies and organizations involved in emergency and safety. Every attempt has been made to ensure that the information is current and up-to-date; however, keep in mind that websites come and go and frequently change their URL addresses.

1906 San Francisco Earthquake—Museum of the City of San Francisco

http://www.sfmuseum.org/1906/06.html

Photographs and other historical information about the 1906 San Francisco earthquake.

Agency for Toxic Substances and Disease Registry—USA

http://www.atsdr.cdc.gov/atsdrhome.html

The goal of this agency is to prevent exposure and adverse human health effects and diminished quality of life associated with exposure to hazardous substances from waste sites, unplanned releases, and other sources of pollution present in the environment.

Air Force Reserve Command Fire

http://www.afres.af.mil/~fire/pages/firehome.htm

Contains information regarding fire department training. Also located at the site are fire safety materials, links, and other helpful information. If you're in the fire protection business, you'll want to visit this site.

Alaska and West Coast (U.S.A.) Tsunami Warning Center

http://wcatwc.gov/

The West Coast/Alaska Tsunami Warning Center (WC/ATWC), located in Palmer, Alaska, serves as the Tsunami Warning Center for Alaska, British Columbia, Washington, Oregon, and California.

Alaska Volcano Observatory

http://www.avo.alaska.edu/

Covers status of volcanoes in Alaska (80+ percent of active U.S. volcanoes), as well as volcanoes in the Northeast Asian area.

Alberta Safety Net

http://abirc.com/safetynet/mall.htm

The site is set up to be a virtual mall for safety-related information. You will find easy access to professional safety consultants, leading edge training, safety equipment suppliers, associations, newsletters, links, and much more.

Alert Net

http://www.alertnet.org

Reuters Foundation's AlertNet, a forum for the international emergency relief community with news from Reuters

American Meteorological Society

http://www.ametsoc.org/AMS/amshomepage.cfm

The American Meteorological Society currently promotes the development and dissemination of information and education on the atmospheric and related oceanic and hydrologic sciences.

American Psychological Association Disaster Response Network

http://www.apa.org/practice/drn.html

A pro bono service of the American Psychological Association and its members. The American Psychological Association developed its Disaster Response Network (DRN) in response to a perceived need. Over 1,500 psychologist volunteers provide free, onsite mental health services to disaster survivors and the relief workers who assist them.

American Radio Relay League (U.S.A.)—Emergency Services Backgrounder

http://www.arrl.org/pio/emergen1.html

Amateur Radio operators have informal and formal groups to coordinate communication during emergencies. At the local level, hams may participate in local emergency organizations, or organize local "traffic nets" using VHF and UHF frequencies. At the state level, hams are often involved with state emergency management operations. In addition, hams operate at the national level through the Radio Amateur Civil Emergency Service (RACES), which is coordinated through the Federal Emergency Management Agency, and through the Amateur Radio Emergency Service (ARES), which is coordinated through the American Radio Relay League. In addition, in areas that are prone to tornadoes, many hams are involved in Skywarn, which operates under the National Weather Service.

American Red Cross

http://www.redcross.org

Provides health and safety services to communities across the nation. Topics include first aid, swimming and water safety, and health and safety education. Also provides disaster services, blood and tissue donations, international services and armed forces emergency services.

Animal Disaster Planning Adivsory Committee (ADPAC)

http://www.fl-adpac.org/

ADPAC is an ad hoc group of organizations and individuals interested in promoting the effective development and implementation of disaster plans to protect animals. The group was organized after Hurricane Andrew killed, injured, and displaced tens of thousands of dogs, cats, horses, cattle, birds, exotic pets, and other animals.

Army Corps of Engineers

http://www.usace.army.mil/index.html

Information on resources inside and outside the corps, programs, emergency operations, and organizational elements

Association of State Floodplain Managers

http://www.floods.org

The Association of State Floodplain Managers is made up of professionals involved in floodplain management, flood hazard mitigation, the National Flood Insurance Program, and flood preparedness, warning, and recovery. The group is a respected voice in U.S. floodplain management practice and policy because it represents flood hazard specialists of local, state, and federal government, the research community, the insurance industry, and the fields of engineering, hydrologic forecasting, emergency response, water resources, and others.

Association of Traumatic Stress Specialists

http://www.atss-hq.com

Association of Traumatic Stress Specialists or ATSS is an international organization to provide professional education and certification to those actively involved in crisis intervention, trauma response, management, treatment, and the healing and recovery of those affected by traumatic stress.

Australia, Charles Stuart University Disasters Page

http://life.csu.edu.au/hazards/10General.html

Variety of disaster-related links and information papers.

Australian Red Cross—Australia

http://avoca.vicnet.net.au/~redcross/

Provides community services, emergency services, health and safety education, blood bank, Red Cross events, and services for youth.

Bureau of Alcohol, Tobacco and Firearms (ATF)

http://www.atf.treas.gov/

The Bureau of Alcohol, Tobacco and Firearms (ATF) is a federal law enforcement agency that is responsible for investigating arson and bombing incidents of a federal nature. ATF has four National Response Teams (NRTs) that respond to major arson and bombing incidents within 24 hours.

Business Emergency Preparedness Council (Shelby County, TN)

http://www.bepc.net/

The Business Emergency Preparedness Council (BEPC) is a coalition of business and government in Shelby County, Tennessee, dedicated to promoting business recovery planning and preparedness. BEPC's objectives are to educate the business community, provide preparedness and recovery resources, and serve as a liaison between business and government agencies to coordinate recovery and resumption activities.

CAMPUSAFE

http://www.disasterrecoverynet.net/

CAMPUSAFE is a consortium of emergency management professionals that addresses the emergency and disaster challenges of educational institutions around the world. The single focus is to aid administrators, safety officers, risk managers, and emergency management professionals who have the responsibility for maintaining operations of educational institutions.

Canadian Centre for Emergency Preparedness

http://www.ccep.ca/

The mandate of the Canadian Centre for Emergency Preparedness is to assist communities, governments, and private businesses to prepare for, prevent, respond to, and recover from manmade or natural disasters. The CCEP has emerged as one of the most recognized emergency response educational organizations in Canada. Through its affiliations and partnerships, it has gained recognition in the United States and throughout the world.

Canadian Coast Guard

http://www.ccgrser.org/

The Canadian Coast Guard is responsible for the safety and protection of national and international maritime transportation systems and conducts operations in Search and Rescue, Maritime/Boating Safety, and Environmental Response for the government of Canada.

Canadian Emergency News

http://www.pendragon.ab.ca/

Canadian Emergency News is a Canada-based magazine that deals with news and issues related to Canada's emergency response professionals.

Canadian Transport Emergency Centre

http://www.tc.gc.ca/canutec/

CANUTEC is the Canadian Transport Emergency Centre operated by Transport Canada to assist emergency response personnel in handling dangerous goods emergencies.

Caribbean Disaster Emergency Response Agency

http://www.cdera.org/

A comprehensive source of information on disaster management in the Caribbean.

Cascadia Region Earthquake Workgroup (CREW)

http://www.crew.org/

A public-private coalition working to reduce the risk of Cascadia region earthquake hazards.

Center for Excellence in Emergency Management

http://coe.tamc.amedd.army.mil/

Center for Excellence in Emergency Management and Humanitarian Assistance Program description as well as current activities.

Central Atlantic Storm Investigators

http://www.weatherwatchers.org/tropical/

This section contains extensive collections of links, up-to-date information, maps photos, video, live observations, and archives for the Atlantic tropical weather seasons.

Central U.S. Earthquake Consortium

http://www.cusec.org/

The Central U.S. Earthquake Consortium is a partnership of the federal government and seven states most likely to be affected by an earthquake in the New Madrid Seismic Zone—Arkansas, Illinois, Indiana, Kentucky, Mississippi, Missouri, and Tennessee.

Civil Air Patrol

http://www.cap.af.mil/

Program description, current activities, and membership information.

Civil Air Search and Rescue Association (CASARA-Canada):

http://www.casara.ca/

The Civil Air Search and Rescue Association, or CASARA, is a Canada-wide volunteer aviation association dedicated to the promotion of Aviation Safety, and to the provision of air search support services to the National Search and Rescue Program.

Community Preparedness Website

http://www.preparenow.org/

A Website designed to ensure that the needs and concerns of vulnerable populations are addressed in the area of emergency preparedness and response. This site has been developed through a cooperative agreement between the Federal Emergency Management

Agency (FEMA) and the California Office of Emergency Services (OES) and directly supported the OES Coastal Region.

Control The Nuclear Power Plant (Demonstration) by Linköping University, Linköping, Sweden

http://www.ida.liu.se/~her/npp/demo.html

This applet provides a (very rough) simulation of a nuclear power plant. This power plant consists of three major components: the reactor, turbine, and condenser. When components fail, the simulator calculates and displays the consequences for the powerplant system.

Current Weather, Climate, and Forecast Maps

http://grads.iges.org/pix/head.html

Contains information about the current weather conditions, forecasts, climate anomalies, and other National Oceanic Atmospheric Administration climate links.

Dartmouth Flood Observatory

http://www.dartmouth.edu/artsci/geog/floods/

This website is a research tool for mapping, measurement, and analysis of major flood events using remote sensing.

Department of Defense—Emergency Preparedness Policy

http://www.defenselink.mil/emerg/

The Directorate for Emergency Preparedness Policy (EPP) within the Office of the Under Secretary of Defense (Policy) has a wide variety of responsibilities relating to a broad spectrum of emergency situations worldwide.

Department of Defense—The National Guard

http://www.ngb.dtic.mil/

This home page provides on-demand information about the National Guard Bureau, the Army National Guard, the Air National Guard, and National Guard-sponsored organizations and events—including their vital support in disaster and emergency response operations.

Disaster Management Central Resource

http://206.39.77.2/DMCR/dmrhome.html

The intent of this project is to provide examples of medically relevant topics and examples of disaster related issues. Another goal is to make medical emergency management more understandable through use of examples provided by the Internet.

Disaster Mental Health

http://ourworld.compuserve.com/homepages/johndweaver/

This site contains a collection of detailed information designed to help mental health workers assist disaster/trauma victims and fellow relief workers/crisis counselors.

Disaster Preparedness and Emergency Response Association, International

http://www.disasters.org/deralink.html

The Disaster Preparedness and Emergency Response Association, International (DERA) was founded in 1962 to assist communities worldwide in disaster preparedness, response, and recovery, and to serve as a professional association linking professionals, volunteers, and organizations active in all phases of emergency preparedness and management.

Disaster Recovery Journal

http://www.drj.com/

This ten-year-old company has created a website devoted to the disaster response and emergency management industries. It contains various information, from dealing with the selection of alternative sites to utilizing proper disaster response procedures.

Disaster Research Center—University of Delaware

http://www.udel.edu/DRC/index2.html

The center conducts field and survey research on group, organizational, and community preparation for response to and recovery from natural and technological disasters and other communitywide crises.

Disaster Resources

http://www.ag.uiuc.edu/~disaster/disaster.html

Access to current events and conditions, disaster preparedness and recovery, agencies, organizations, networks, general disaster information, and important telephone numbers for Illinois residents.

DisasterRelief.Org

http://www.disasterrelief.org/

Worldwide disaster aid and information via the Internet.

DRI International

http://www.dr.org/

The purposes of the DRI are to create a base of common knowledge for disaster recovery/ business continuity planning filed through education, assistance, and the development of a resource base; to certify qualified individuals in the discipline; and to promote the credibility and professionalism of certified professionals.

Earthquake Activity Around the World

http://www.athena.ivv.nasa.gov/curric/land/todayqk.html

The site provides three sites with updated earthquake data in table format, plus map generators. The table shows the date, time, location, and magnitude of the most recent global earthquake activity

Earthquake Engineering Research Center, University of California at Berkeley

http://www.eerc.berkeley.edu/nisee/mission.html

Established in 1971 at the University of California, Berkeley, the National Information Service for Earthquake Engineering (NISEE) provides timely access to technical research and development information in earthquake engineering and related fields of structural dynamics, geotechnical engineering, engineering seismology, and earthquake hazard mitigation policy.

Earthquake Reporting Service

http://quake.wr.usgs.gov/

U.S. Geological Survey and UC Berkeley service for earthquake reporting.

EIIP Virtual Forum

http://www.emforum.org/

The Emergency Information Infrastructure Partnership (EIIP) Virtual Forum is designed to encourage emergency professionals to explore the use of current information technology to support emergency management and disaster response.

Emergency Animal Rescue Service

http://www.uan.org/programs/ears/articles.cfm

United Animal Nations has a program called Emergency Animal Rescue Service (EARS). This website provides specific information about how to prepare your animals for a disaster and how to keep them safe during a disaster.

United Animal Nations has a program called Emergency Animal Rescue Service (EARS). This website provides specific information about how to prepare your animals for a disaster and how to keep them safe during a disaster.

Emergency Management Australia (EMA)

http://www.ema.gov.au/

Their mission is to promote and support comprehensive, integrated, and effective emergency management in Australia and its region of interest.

Emergency Medical Services—USA

http://www.thirdstreet.com/ems/

EMS is a system for saving lives. Provides advice on what to do in a medical emergency and first aid tips.

Emergency Mgmt. Education Network

http://www.unex.ucr.edu/emen/emen.html

EMEN is a distance learning, resident, and workplace emergency management education, training, and consulting service provided by the Natural Sciences and Environmental Management Program, University of California, Riverside.

Emergency Preparedness Canada

http://www.epc-pcc.gc.ca/

A federal agency that is responsible for coordinating emergency planning for the government of Canada. Includes information materials, fact sheets, Federal Emergency Policy, selected videos, and EPC points of contact.

Emergency Response and Research Institute Emergency Net News Service

http://www.emergency.com/

EmergencyNet NEWS (ENN) is one of the nation's premier electronic news services that covers only fire, police, EMS, disaster, medical, and military topics.

Environment Canada

http://www.ec.gc.ca/ee-ue/

Environment Canada is an active player in confronting the environmental aspects of emergencies. The mission of the Environmental Emergencies program is to reduce the frequency, severity, and consequences of these events. The organization pursues this

·Environmental Protection Agency

http://www.epa.gov/

Access to EPA documents describing environmental information, as well as a number of links to Information Locators that can be obtained from the EPA and related organizations.

Environmental Refugees

http://pubpages.unh.edu/~leidermn/

The site is dedicated to 1) the plight of people fleeing communities and homelands because of a wide range of natural and manmade hazards and disasters, and 2) encouraging a sense of urgency for the ecological restoration of those areas.

EPA Chemical Emergency Preparedness and Prevention Office

http://www.epa.gov/swercepp/

This site includes press releases and advisories, periodic "alerts" which explain the specific dangers of hazardous substances that have become evident through accident investigations, fact sheets and technical assistance bulletins, general publications, frequently asked questions and answers, and technical guidance documents.

EPIX—Emergency Preparedness Information Exchange

http://hoshi.cic.sfu.ca/~anderson/index.html

The purpose of EPIX is to facilitate the exchange of ideas and information among Canadian and international public and private sector organizations about the prevention of, preparation for, recovery from and/or mitigation of risk associated with natural and socio-technological disasters.

Eye on the World—Violent Planet Page

http://www.iwaynet.net/~kwroejr/violent.html

Lots of links to lots of sites.

Fire Safety Institute

http://www.middlebury.net/firesafe/

The Fire Safety Institute is a not-for-profit information, research, and educational corporation that focuses on innovative approaches to fire safety science and engineering.

Firesafe—Fire and Safety—USA

http://www.firesafe.com/

FireSafe is a resource directory for safety information. The site contains general information about San Diego County fire agencies, California fire service agencies, federal fire service agencies, and fire safety education.

Firewise

http://www.firewise.org/

The Firewise home page was created for people who live, vacation, or own vacation homes in fire-prone areas of North America. The information contained here will help you to become a firewise individual and acquaint you with the challenges of living around interface/intermix wildfire.

HazardNet

http://hoshi.cic.sfu.ca/~hazard/

Contains operational background information and other information about hazard warnings, hazard impacts, monitoring programs, and emergency response and support organizations.

Home Office (United Kingdom) Emergency Planning Division

http://www.homeoffice.gov.uk/epd/

The Home Office is responsible for civil protection in England and Wales, and represents the U.K. in the European and international context. This responsibility involves planning for peacetime emergencies and civil defence.

Hurricane Hunters Home Page

http://www.hurricanehunters.com/

The 53rd Weather Reconnaissance Squadron, known as the Hurricane Hunters of the Air Force Reserve, is one-of-a-kind: the only Department of Defense organization flying into tropical storms and hurricanes on a routine basis.

Insurance Information Institute

http://www.iii.org/

For more than 30 years the I.I.I. has provided definitive, credible insurance information. Today the I.I.I. is recognized as a primary source of information, analysis and referral on property/casualty insurance. The site has information designed for both consumers and reporters.

International Association of Fire Chiefs

http://www.iafc.org/

Provides leadership to career and volunteer chiefs, chief fire officers and managers of emergency services organizations throughout the international community through vision, information, education, services, and representation to enhance their professionalism and capabilities.

International Critical Incident Stress Foundation, Inc.

http://www.icisf.org/

Provides the most current information available in the field of critical incident stress management.

Internet Sources for Earthquake Engineering and Natural Hazards Mitigation

http://mceer.buffalo.edu/default.asp

The Internet resources listed are not intended to be exhaustive. They represent sites which we have found useful in the past or which in some other way prove pertinent to the practice of earthquake engineering and earthquake hazards mitigation.

Kids Helping Kids Club, Kauai, Hawaii

http://www.hawaiian.net/~nbudd/kids/

In Hawaiian "mana'olana" means "floating thoughts." This page was created by kids on Kauai to give hope to other kids who have gone through natural disasters by sending them encouragement and advice.

Manitoba (Canada) Emergency Management Organization

http://www.gov.mb.ca/gs/memo/

Manitoba Emergency Management Organization (Manitoba EMO) has the responsibility of coordinating the overall provincial emergency planning, training, and response operations and the administration and delivery of the Disaster Financial Assistance Program, for the safety of the residents, protection of property, and the environment before, during, and after an emergency or disaster.

Michigan State Police, Emergency Management Division

http://www.msp.state.mi.us/division/emd/emdweb1.htm

This site provides information on the emergency management and preparedness activities for the State of Michigan.

NASA's Disaster Finder

http://ltpwww.gsfc.nasa.gov/ndrd/disaster/links/

This site provides a searchable index of disaster-related websites.

National Association for Search and Rescue

http://www.nasar.org/

National Association that provides a reference link for Search and Rescue Organizations in the U.S.

National Association of SARA Title III Program Officials

http://www.geocities.com/CapitolHill/6286/

An organization of state, local, tribal, and even some federal officials who are responsible for emergency planning, response, and training for hazardous materials emergencies.

National Earthquake Information Center

http://wwwneic.cr.usgs.gov/

The National Earthquake Information Center (NEIC), part of the National Ocean Survey of the Department of Commerce, is designed to provide accurate and timely information on the nature and size of all earthquakes that occur worldwide.

National Emergency Management Association

http://www.nemaweb.org/index.cfm

National Emergency Management Association (NEMA) is a unique partnership among State Directors of Emergency Management. NEMA is an affiliate of the Council of State Governments.

National Fire Protection Association

http://www.nfpa.org/

The mission of NFPA, which was organized in 1896, is to reduce the worldwide burden of fire and other hazards on the quality of life by providing and advocating scientifically based consensus codes and standards, research, training, and education.

National Institute for Urban Search and Rescue

http://www.niusr.org/

NIUSR provides a dynamic, stable platform for the exchange and advocacy of ideas. The NIUSR organization is enduring; the common theme is always the protection of lives, property, and institutions of the American people.

National Oceanic Atmospheric Administration

http://www.noaa.gov/

Describing, monitoring, and predicting changes in the earth's environment in order to ensure and enhance sustainable economic opportunities

National Response Center

http://www.nrc.uscg.mil/

The NRC is the sole federal point of contact for reporting oil and chemical spills. If you have a spill to report, contact them via their toll-free number or check out their website for additional information on reporting requirements and procedures.

National Response Team

http://www.nrt.org/

The National Response Team's membership consists of 16 federal agencies with interests and expertise in various aspects of emergency response to pollution incidents.

National SAFE KIDS Campaign

http://www.safekids.org/

The National SAFE KIDS Campaign is the first and only national organization dedicated solely to the prevention of unintentional childhood injury—the number one killer of children ages 14 and under.

National Weather Service

http://www.nws.noaa.gov/

The National Weather Service (NWS) provides weather, hydrologic, and climate forecasts and warnings for the United States, its territories, adjacent waters, and ocean areas, for the protection of life and property and the enhancement of the national economy. NWS data and products form a national information database and infrastructure which can be used by other governmental agencies, the private sector, the public, and the global community.

National Weather Service Disaster Survey Reports

http://www.nws.noaa.gov/om/omdis.html

National Weather Service teams document the impact of major weather systems. Reports include chronology of forecasting and storm tracking along with related events in the path of the storm.

Natural Hazards Center at the University of Colorado

http://www.colorado.edu/hazards/

The Natural Hazards Center, located at the University of Colorado, Boulder, Colorado, USA, is a national and international clearinghouse for information on natural hazards and human adjustments to hazards and disasters.

New England Floodplain and Stormwater Manager Association, Inc.

http://www.seacoast.com/~nefsma/

To promote public awareness of sound floodplain management practices and to develop the professional status of, and interaction between, individuals concerned with floodplain and stormwater management.

Northeast States Emergency Consortium

http://www.nesec.org/

NESEC is a not-for-profit natural hazard mitigation, education, and emergency management organization located in Wakefield, Massachusetts. It is the only multi-hazard consortium of its kind in the country and is supported and funded by the Federal Emergency Management Agency (FEMA). The consortium works in partnership with government and private organizations to reduce losses of life and property resulting from natural disasters.

Occupational Safety and Health Administration

http://www.osha.gov/

This is the home page for the U.S. Occupational Safety and Health Administration (OSHA).

Oklahoma State University—Fire Programs' Index—USA

http://www.fireprograms.okstate.edu/

Information about the three basic divisions of the Fire Programs Group: Fire Protection Publications, Oklahoma Fire Service Training, and International Fire Service Accreditation Congress.

Online Guide to Meteorology

http://covis1.atmos.uiuc.edu/guide/

The "Guide" is a collection of multimedia instructional modules that introduce and explain fundamental concepts in meteorology.

Pacific Disaster Center

http://www.pdc.org/

This website is sponsored by the State of Hawaii, State of Hawaii Civil Defense, and the Department of Defense.

Planned Response Exercises and Emergency Medical Preparedness Training (PREEMPT)

http://home.eznet.net/~kenberry/

PREEMPT, Medical Counter-Terrorism, Inc. is a not-for-profit corporate organization founded in 1997 by Kenneth M. Berry, M.D., for the express purpose of development and training of emergency medical personnel for responding to foreign or domestic terrorist attacks that use chemical, biological and/or nuclear weapons.

Provincial Emergency Program—British Columbia

http://www.pep.bc.ca/index.html

Maintains effective awareness, preparedness, response, and recovery programs to reduce the human and financial costs of emergencies and disasters.

Public Seismic Network

http://gandalf.ceri.memphis.edu/~rond/psn/

The Public Seismic Network, Memphis, is dedicated to the promotion of awareness and information about earthquakes in general, but particularly about earthquake activity in the New Madrid area.

RESCUE—Training Resource & Guide

http://www.techrescue.org/

Large training site on various forms of rescue including vehicle, cave, vertical or high angle, USAR, storm, flood, and water rescue. Contains various online tests and reference material. Created by a volunteer from the State Emergency Service, Victoria, Australia.

Rescue Coordination Centre NETwork

http://www.rcc-net.org/

A forum for the discussion and development of aeronautical and maritime search and rescue topics.

Royal Canadian Mounted Police

http://www.rcmp-grc.gc.ca/html/sar.htm

This page on the main Royal Canadian Mounted Police site outlines the force's role in search and rescue.

State of Alabama—Emergency Management Agency

http://www.aema.state.al.us/

The Alabama Emergency Management Agency coordinates emergency state assistance to local communities when they are affected by a disaster such as tornadoes, floods or hurricanes.

State of Alaska—Department of Military Affairs, Division of Emergency Services

http://www.ak-prepared.com/

The mission of the Division is to minimize the loss of life and property from disasters.

State of Arizona—Division of Emergency Management

http://www.state.az.us/es/

The Division of Emergency Management coordinates emergency services and the efforts of governmental agencies to reduce the impact of disasters on persons and property.

State of Arkansas—Office of Emergency Services

http://www.oes.state.ar.us/

The state Office of Emergency Services takes an integrated, all-hazards approach to emergency management. Local problems are often solved at the community level. However, when disaster is beyond local capabilities, the local CEO declares a state of emergency and state resources then become available.

State of California—Governors Office of Emergency Services

http://www.oes.ca.gov/

Includes legislative updates, Recovery Times Outline, fact sheets, images and links to the California Unified Information Coordination Center, the Emergency Information Infrastructure Project, and the Operational Area Satellite Information System.

State of Colorado—Office of Emergency Management

http://www.state.co.us/data2/oem/oemindex.htm

The Office of Emergency Management (OEM) is responsible for the state's comprehensive emergency services program that supports local and state agencies. Activities and services cover the four phases of emergency management: preparedness, response, recovery, and mitigation for disasters like flooding, tornadoes, wildfires, and hazardous materials incidents.

State of Florida—Division of Emergency Management, Department of Community Affairs

http://www.dca.state.fl.us/fdem/

The Division of Emergency Management is tasked by the state legislature to direct the state's programs to plan for and respond to natural or technological disasters.

State of Georgia—Emergency Management Agency

http://www2.state.ga.us/GEMA/

GEMA is Georgia's lead state agency for coordination of emergency and disaster response activities.

State of Idaho—Bureau of Disaster Services

http://www.state.id.us/bds/bds.html

The mission of BDS is to save lives and limit injury to people and reduce the damage to property, the environment, and the local economy by coordinating the state and federal response to emergencies and disasters in support of local jurisdictions.

State of Illinois—Emergency Management Agency

http://www.state.il.us/iema/

The Illinois Emergency Management Agency is the agency established within state government responsible for coordinating the efforts of the state and its political subdivisions to develop, plan, analyze, conduct, implement, and maintain programs for disaster mitigation, preparedness, response, and recovery together with private organizations, political subdivisions, and the federal government.

State of Indiana—Emergency Management Agency

http://www.ai.org/sema/index.html

The State Emergency Management Agency (SEMA), the Department of Fire and Building Services (DFBS), and the Public Safety Training Institute (PSTI) provide a wide range of public safety services to the citizens of Indiana. Those services include emergency management, emergency medical services, building safety, and fire protection, as well as professional training.

State of Iowa—Emergency Management Home Page

http://www.state.ia.us/government/dpd/emd/index.htm

This website helps support the State of Iowa Department of Emergency Management's mission. This mission is to establish, coordinate, and maintain state and local emergency management activities and intergovernmental, private, and volunteer partnerships to mitigate, prepare for, respond to, and recover from all disasters that might impact Iowa and its citizens.

State of Kansas—Division of Emergency Management

http://www.ink.org/public/kdem/

The mission of the Division of Emergency Management is to provide a 24-hour operation to reduce loss of life and property, protect Kansans from all hazards by providing and coordinating resources, expertise, leadership, and advocacy through a comprehensive, risk-based emergency management program of mitigation, preparedness, response, and recovery.

State of Louisiana—Office of Emergency Preparedness (LOEP)

http://199.188.3.91/

Site covers LOEP organization, operations, recovery services training, plans, and other public information.

State of Maine—Emergency Management Agency

http://www.state.me.us/mema/memahome.htm

Their mission is to lessen the effects of disaster on the lives and property of the people of Maine through leadership, coordination, and support in the four phases of emergency management: mitigation, preparedness, response, and recovery.

State of Maryland—Emergency Management Agency

http://www.mema.state.md.us/

The Maryland Emergency Management Agency (MEMA) is responsible for coordinating the state response to any major emergency or disaster.

State of Massachusetts—Emergency Management Agency

http://www.magnet.state.ma.us/mema/homepage.htm

MEMA is an executive branch of the government of the Commonwealth of Massachusetts with responsibility for coordinating federal, state, local, and private resources during disasters and emergencies.

State of Michigan—Emergency Management Division

http://www.msp.state.mi.us/division/emd/emdweb1.htm

This site provides information on emergency management programs and training in Michigan.

State of Minnesota—Dep't. of Public Safety, Div. of Emergency Management

http://www.dps.state.mn.us/emermgt/

This division's efforts encompass four areas: reducing the threat posed by hazards that can affect the state, planning ways to cope with disasters when they occur, coordinating the response of state and federal agencies in assisting local government when disasters occur, and coordinating the recovery efforts of state and federal agencies in conjunction with local governments when disaster strikes.

State of Mississippi—Emergency Management Agency

http://www.memaorg.com/index2.htm

The mission of the Mississippi Emergency Management Agency is to minimize the loss of life and property from disaster.

State of Missouri—Emergency Management Agency

http://www.sema.state.mo.us/semapage.htm

Assigned to protect the lives and property of all Missourians when major disasters threaten public safety in any city, county, or region of Missouri. SEMA responds to both natural and manmade disasters.

State of New Hampshire—Office of Emergency Management

http://www.nhoem.state.nh.us/

The New Hampshire Office of Emergency Management is a state agency charged with the preparation for the carrying out of all emergency functions, to prevent loss of life or property resulting from any natural or manmade cause, including, but not limited to, fire, flood, earthquake, windstorm, wave action, oil spill, or other water contamination requiring emergency action to avert danger or damage, epidemic, air contamination, blight, drought, infestation, explosion, or riot.

State of New Mexico—Department of Public Safety

http://www.dps.nm.org/emergency/em_index.htm

The mission of the Emergency Management Bureau (EMB) is to mitigate, plan for, respond to, and recover from natural and technological incidents, accidents, and disasters through a mandated statewide emergency management system.

State of New York—Emergency Management Office

http://www.nysemo.state.ny.us/

The New York State Emergency Management Office (SEMO) is a government entity that coordinates Emergency Management Services for the state by providing leadership, planning, education, and resources to protect lives, property, and the environment.

State of North Carolina—Division of Emergency Management

http://www.dem.dcc.state.nc.us/

The North Carolina Division of Emergency Management provides a variety of services to local governments and citizens of the state.

State of North Dakota—Department of Emergency Management (DEM)

http://www.state.nd.us/dem/

This site provides information about the DEM staff, local emergency situation reports for current incidents, and summaries of presidential disaster declarations in the state.

State of Ohio—Emergency Management Agency

http://www.state.oh.us/odps/division/ema/

The Ohio Emergency Management Agency is the central point of coordination within the state for response to and recovery from disasters.

State of Oklahoma—Department of Civil Emergency Management

http://www.onenet.net/~odcem/

The mission of the Oklahoma Department of Civil Emergency Management (ODCEM) is to minimize the effects of technological and natural disasters upon the people of Oklahoma by preparing, implementing, and exercising preparedness plans, assisting local government subdivisions with training for and mitigation of disasters, and by coordinating actual disaster response/recovery operations.

State of Oregon—Emergency Management Division

http://www.osp.state.or.us/oem/oem.htm

Meets the governor's responsibilities to maintain an Emergency Services System. Includes sections on technology, operations, plans, training, and financial services.

State of Pennsylvania—Emergency Management Agency (PEMA)

http://www.pema.state.pa.us/

The Pennsylvania Emergency Management Agency (PEMA) is charged with the management and coordination of the commonwealth's emergency management programs.

State of Rhode Island—Emergency Management Agency

http://www.state.ri.us/riema/

The Rhode Island Emergency Management Agency is responsible for the planning and implementation of all hazard preparedness programs at the state level and providing appropriate support to community hazard response activity.

State of South Carolina—Emergency Preparedness Division

http://www.state.sc.us/epd/

The mission of the division is to provide leadership and support to reduce the loss of life and property in South Carolina and protect the state's institutions from all types of hazards through a comprehensive, risk-based, multi-hazards emergency management program.

State of South Dakota—Division of Emergency Management

http://www.state.sd.us/state/executive/military/sddem.htm

The Division of Emergency Management provides planning and training assistance to city, county, and tribal governments, as well as the general public in preparing for, responding to, and recovering from the effects of an emergency or disaster situation.

State of Tennessee—Emergency Management Agency

http://www.state.tn.us/military/tema.html

The Tennessee Emergency Management Agency is responsible for ensuring the establishment and development of policies and programs for emergency management at the state and local levels.

State of Texas—Department of Public Safety

http://www.txdps.state.tx.us/dem/

The Division of Emergency Management (DEM) is tasked with administering a program of Comprehensive Emergency Management, designed to reduce the vulnerability of the citizens and communities of the state to damage, injury, or loss of life and property.

OSHA
Emergency Hotline

OSHA maintains a free telephone hotline for reporting life-threatening workplace hazards:

1-800-321-OSHA

The Occupational Safety and Health Administration (OSHA) provides this free hotline for reporting workplace safety or health emergencies. The service provides a 24-hour point of contact so that those who want to notify OSHA as soon as possible of imminent dangers on the job can do so. Two kinds of service will assist callers to the OSHA hotline. The type of service provided depends upon the time of the initiating call.

Daytime Calls

For telephone calls received during normal working hours—8 a.m. to 4:30 p.m. local time, Monday through Friday—the answering operator requests the caller's name (optional), a daytime telephone number (also optional), and a zip code (required). The caller is asked to hold while the representative determines the appropriate area office and then transfers the call to that office.

If the transfer is completed, the representative notes the call's disposition. If the transfer for a complaint is unsuccessful, a manual callback form will be completed and telefaxed to the area office. The caller is assured of a callback.

For an unsuccessful transfer of a call determined to be an emergency, alternate numbers and OSHA contact persons will be tried. The transfer will be repeated until successful.

After-Hours Calls

After normal working hours—4:30 p.m. to 8 a.m. local time, Monday through Friday, and all day Saturday, Sunday, and official government holidays—the same information is requested as with the daytime calls, with an additional request for the best time for a callback.

If the caller expressly states that the call is an emergency, an information form is completed and the caller is assured that the appropriate representative will be contacted immediately. The OSHA representative will also request information about the location of the emergency.

If the call is not an emergency, the nature of the complaint is noted by the operator and telefaxed to the appropriate area office. These call reports are telefaxed to the area office by 11 a.m., local time.

Facts about SBA Disaster Loan Programs

In the wake of hurricanes, floods, earthquakes, wildfires, tornadoes and other physical disasters, the U.S. Small Business Administration (SBA) plays a major role. SBA's disaster loans are the primary form of federal assistance for nonfarm, private sector disaster losses. For this reason, the disaster loan program is the only form of SBA assistance not limited to small businesses. Disaster loans from SBA help homeowners, renters, businesses of all sizes, and nonprofit organizations to fund rebuilding. SBA's disaster loans are a critical source of economic stimulation in disaster-ravaged communities, helping to spur employment and stabilize tax bases.

By providing disaster assistance in the form of loans which are repaid to the U.S. Treasury, the SBA disaster loan program helps reduce federal disaster costs compared to other forms of assistance, such as grants. When disaster victims need to borrow to repair uninsured damages, the low interest rates and long terms available from SBA make recovery affordable. Because SBA tailors the repayment of each disaster loan to each borrower's financial capability, unnecessary interest subsidies paid by the taxpayers are avoided. Moreover, providing disaster assistance in the form of loans rather than grants avoids the creation of an incentive for property owners to underinsure against risk. Disaster loans require borrowers to maintain appropriate hazard and flood insurance coverage, thereby reducing the need for future disaster assistance.

The need for SBA disaster loans is as unpredictable as the weather. In the aftermath of the Northridge earthquake, SBA approved more that 125,000 loans for more than $4.1 billion in 1994. In 1997, SBA approved 49,515 loans for $1.138 billion. Since the inception of the program in 1953, SBA has approved over 1,300,000 disaster loans for more than $25 billion.

The SBA is authorized by the Small Business Act to make two types of disaster loans:

- **Physical disaster loans** are a primary source of funding for the permanent rebuilding and replacement of uninsured disaster damages to privately owned real and/or personal property. SBA's physical disaster loans are available to homeowners, renters, nonfarm businesses of all sizes, and nonprofit organizations.

145

- **Economic injury disaster loans** help provide necessary working capital until the resumption of normal operations after a physical disaster. The law restricts economic injury disaster loans to small businesses only.

The disaster program is SBA's largest direct loan program, and it is the only SBA program assisting entities other than small businesses. By law, neither governmental units nor agricultural enterprises are eligible. Agricultural producers may seek disaster assistance from specialized programs run by the U. S. Department of Agriculture.

Disaster victims must repay SBA disaster loans. SBA can only approve loans to applicants with a reasonable ability to repay the loan and other obligations from earnings. The terms of each loan are established in accordance with each borrower's ability to repay. The law gives SBA several powerful tools to make disaster loans affordable: low interest rates (about 4 percent), long terms (up to 30 years), and refinancing of prior debts (in some cases). As required by law, the interest rate for each loan is based on SBA's determination about the ability of each applicant to obtain credit elsewhere (the ability to borrow or use their own resources to overcome the disaster). More than 90 percent of SBA's disaster loans are to borrowers without other available credit, and these loans carry an interest rate of about 4 percent.

SBA Disaster Area Offices

Niagara Falls, New York

360 Rainbow Boulevard South, 3rd Floor, 14303
(716) 282-4612

Serves: *Connecticut, District of Columbia, Delaware, Maine, Maryland, Massachusetts, New Hampshire, New Jersey, New York, Pennsylvania, Puerto Rico, Rhode Island, Vermont, Virgin Islands, Virginia, and West Virginia*

Atlanta, Georgia

One Baltimore Place, Suite 300, 30308
(404) 347-3771

Serves: *Alabama, Florida, Georgia, Illinois, Indiana, Kentucky, Michigan, Minnesota, Mississippi, North Carolina, Ohio, South Carolina, Tennessee, and Wisconsin*

Fort Worth, Texas

4400 Amon Carter Boulevard, Suite 102, 76155
(817) 885-7600

Serves: *Arkansas, Colorado, Iowa, Kansas, Louisiana, Missouri, Montana, Nebraska, New Mexico, North Dakota, Oklahoma, South Dakota, Texas, Utah and Wyoming*

Sacramento, California

P.O. Box 13795, 95853
(916) 566-7240

Serves: *Alaska, American Samoa, Arizona, California, Guam, Hawaii, Idaho, Nevada, Oregon and Washington*

Principal Threats
Facing Communities
and
Local Emergency Management Coodinators

Federal Emergency Management Agency, Office of Emergency Management

Contents

SUMMARY

As part of the review process for the Fiscal Year (FY) 1991 budget of the Federal Emergency Management Agency (FEMA), the Senate Appropriations Committee (hereinafter referred to as the "Committee") has directed FEMA to update annually the study on the principal threats facing communities and local emergency management coordinators. The specific task (originally assigned in FY 1990) was as follows:

> *The Committee directs FEMA to prepare a study on the principal threats facing communities and local emergency management coordinators. The Committee understands that certain natural and man-made disasters threaten communities with a varying degree of severity and frequency. The study should rank the principal threats to the population according to region and any other factors deemed appropriate.*

The Threats

Every day, the population of the United States is at risk from a broad spectrum of threats. The scope of these threats ranges from the impact of a house fire in an individual home to a hazardous materials incident, perhaps on an Interstate highway, to the devastating effect a catastrophic natural disaster such as a major earthquake would have on many thousands of square miles. It also includes the social threats posed by various forms of attack and civil disturbances.

These points were brought home vividly during 1992, which will probably rank as one of the most devastating in US history. Among the most notable incidents in 1992 was the Chicago Tunnel Flood, the series of earthquakes that occurred along California's San Andreas Fault and the Los Angeles riots. Perhaps the most significant aspect of 1992, though, was the series of hurricanes that battered states on both the Atlantic and Pacific. Hurricane Andrew, which tore across Florida and Louisiana resulted in 15 deaths and billion dollars in damage (an estimated $27 billion in Florida alone). Hurricane Andrew will probably rank as the most costly natural disaster in U.S. history. Hurricane Andrew was followed by Typhoons Omar and Brian hitting Guam, and Hurricane Iniki which caused over a billion dollars in damage. The events of the past year demonstrate the need to prepare for all potential hazards, some common, others newly recognized.

Types of Threats

For the purposes of this report, there are two basic categories of threats:

Natural threats, the largest single category of repetitive threats to communities and emergency management coordinators, come from weather-, geological-, seismic- or oceanic-related events. They pose a threat to any area of the country; their impact can be localized or widespread, predictable or unpredictable. The damage resulting from natural disasters can range from small to major (depending on whether they strike major or minor population centers). The impact of extremely severe natural disasters can have a long-term effect on the infrastructure of any given location. Natural threats include avalanche, dam failure, drought, earthquake, flood, hurricane/tropical storm, landslide, thunderstorm, tornado, tsunami/seiche, volcano, wildfire and winter storm.

Technological/man-made threats represent a category of events that has expanded dramatically throughout this century with the advancements in modern technology. Like natural threats, they can affect localized or widespread areas, are frequently unpredictable, can cause substantial loss of life (besides the potential for damage to property), and can pose a significant threat to the infrastructure of a given area. In this category are those social threats that primarily come from actions by external, hostile forces against the land, population or infrastructure of the United States, or from domestic civil disturbances. Technological/man-made threats include civil disorder, hazardous materials incidents at fixed facilities and in transport accidents, power failures, radiological incidents at fixed facilities or in-transit accidents, missile attack, nuclear attack, structural fires, telecommunications failures, terrorism, and transportation accidents.

Disaster Impact

What is the potential impact of these disasters on the population and the government of this country? The rapid technological growth in the United States during this century has resulted in an infrastructure, tightly interconnected by vast systems of sophisticated communications and transportation, integrating industry, government and even other nations. This infrastructure is continually exposed to disruption—or destruction in a catastrophic event—by the full range of disasters that threaten this country. The concurrent urbanization of the United States, particularly since World War II, has substantially increased the numbers of people exposed to a particular threat in a given area.

Our vulnerability to threats is complicated by the identification of newer threats, some of which were virtually unknown 20 or 30 years ago. Advancements in technology and the increased development and use of chemicals over the past decades have resulted in the rise of a new and wide range of threats. Estimates of the impact of some of these threats are often difficult because of a lack of experience with them or a thorough knowledge of the full range of their impact. For example, the potential for injury and loss from the failure of some of the technical systems we rely on each day has yet to be adequately measured.

The same is also increasing true for other types of threats. Preparing and attempting to mitigate the effects of landslides is becoming an increasing concern in the West, as urban development moves into more areas subject to ground failure. The wildfires that hit the hills of Oakland, California in October 1991 illustrate another hazard that will represent an increasing familiar threat to people and property in the future. The Chicago Tunnel Flood of April 1992, illustrate the vulnerability of our society to technological failures.

There are new changes to our environment that may affect the spectrum of hazards the nation faces. There is concern expressed by some on the potential atmospheric and other environmental changes caused by phenomena such as *acid rain* and the *greenhouse effect* on the United States. A growing consensus believes that weather trends on the African Continent, where most hurricanes that affect the continental United States form, could result in an increase in the frequency and severity of hurricanes hitting the United States mainland during the next decade. The severe hurricane season of 1992 seems to confirm this view.

Ranking of the Threats

In its direction to FEMA, the Committee stated that it:

"...understands that certain natural and manmade disasters threaten communities with a varying degree of severity and frequency..." and specifically requested that the study, "...rank the principal threats to the population according to region and any other factors deemed appropriate."

However, it is important to note that any ranking of the. threats to communities and emergency management coordinators is potentially misleading because of: (1) the wide variations that can occur with the application of different criteria to the same threat, (2) the significant differences that can occur from the impact of a particular threat on a region and the individual States within that region, (3) the fact that threats in one region are not necessarily applicable to another region, (4) variances in the types of data collected on each threat and (5) the lack of available data in some cases with which to develop a reasoned ranking.

Floods, hurricanes, tornadoes, winter storms, earthquakes, fires and hazardous material incidents represent the primary threats facing communities and emergency management coordinators. This by no means diminishes the magnitude of the many other threats discussed in this report. All hazards must be addressed in the effort to adequately protect the nation's people and property from the threats they face.

Agency Mission

FEMA is responsible for ensuring the establishment and development of policies and programs for emergency management at the Federal, State and local levels. This includes developing a national capability to mitigate against, prepare for, respond to and recover from the full range of emergencies .

In view of the broad range of threats the population and industry of the United States face, FEMA is also responsible for ensuring that plans are in place as part of an integrated, all-hazard emergency management program. While the nature of some emergencies (e.g., earthquakes, hurricanes, tornadoes, radiological emergencies) does require certain hazard-specific procedures and activities, the goal of the Agency is to ensure the establishment of an integrated, all-hazards emergency management capability.

The Agency has a wide range of programs available to provide financial and technical assistance to State and local governments. The purpose of these programs is to help State and local emergency managers coordinate their governments' mitigation, preparedness, response and recovery activities for protecting the population from the numerous hazards that threaten their communities.

The FEMA program of developing a Federal-State-Local infrastructure of emergency managers is essential to ensure that the nation is properly protected from the hazards they face. Regardless of whether the programs listed above are provided in the form of financial assistance, technical assistance or guidance, they provide the primary system within the Federal government to assist State and local governments in developing a readiness capability against threats. They cover the full range of emergency management activities—mitigation, preparedness, response and recovery—required against the full range of emergencies.

In 1992, FEMA used the Comprehensive Cooperative Agreement (CCA) process to distribute more than $129 million in direct assistance to State and local governments in 1992. These programs provided support to State and local governments across the full range of threats.

The importance of all elements of the FEMA program were never more apparent than in 1992. In Florida, an estimated 700,000 people were safely evacuated, and 80,000 sheltered, from areas endangered by Hurricane Andrew. This effort, possible only because of the emergency plans and personnel supported by FEMA, greatly reduced the potential death toll from the hurricane. In the disasters that occurred, the Federal Response Plan coordinated the immediate response to prevent suffering. During the year, over 7 million meals were served, over 18,000 people received medical treatment, and tons of ice, plastic sheeting and other supplies were provided to meet immediate needs. In recovery, over a quarter of a million families applied for FEMA assistance to get back on their feet.

The effort to protect the nation's people and property against disaster will gain in importance over the next few years. The recent trend has seen more and more disasters occurring. Increases in population and development, changes in our environment and the emergence of new threats means that the nation's emergency managers will have increasing challenges in the future.

INTRODUCTION

As part of the review process for the Fiscal Year (FY) 1991 budget of the Federal Emergency Management Agency (FEMA), the Senate Appropriations Committee (hereinafter referred to as the "Committee") has directed FEMA to update annually the study on the principal threats facing communities and local emergency management coordinators. The specific task (originally assigned in FY 1990) was as follows:

> *The Committee directs FEMA to prepare a study on the principal threats facing communities and local emergency management coordinators. The Committee understands that certain natural and man-made disasters threaten communities with a varying degree of severity and frequency. The study should rank the principal threats to the population according to region and any other factors deemed appropriate.*

Background

Every day, the population of the United States is at risk from a broad spectrum of threats. The scope of these threats ranges from the impact of a house fire in an individual home to a hazardous materials incident, perhaps on an Interstate highway, to the devastating effect a catastrophic natural disaster such as a major earthquake would have on many thousands of square miles. It also includes the social threats posed by various forms of attack and civil disturbances.

What is the potential impact of these disasters on the population and the government of this country? The rapid technological growth in the United States during this century has resulted in an infrastructure, tightly interconnected by vast systems of sophisticated communications and transportation, integrating industry, government and even other nations. This infrastructure is continually exposed to disruption—or destruction in a catastrophic event—by the full range of disasters that threaten this country. The concurrent urbanization of the United States, particularly since World War II, has substantially increased the numbers of people exposed to a particular threat in a given area.

These points were brought home vividly during 1992, which will probably rank as one of the most devastating in US history. The events of the past year demonstrate the need to prepare for all potential hazards, some common, others newly recognized.

- On the morning of April 13, the heart of Chicago's business district found itself immobilized by the flooding of an old network of tunnels connecting the major buildings of the Chicago Loop. While the flood was limited to the underground tunnel network, it threatened vital power and fiber-optic communications lines that went along the tunnels, along with the electrical power supplies of major Chicago office buildings. Approximately 250,000 workers had to be sent home the first day of the flood, while the downtown subway system was shut down for three weeks. With clean up costs along at a half billion dollars, the Chicago Tunnel Flood points up the increasing threat that faces technological and telecommunications systems.

- California saw several significant earthquakes along the San Andreas fault, causing concern about the possibilities for a major destructive earthquake in the state. Beginning with the Joshua Tree earthquake on April 23 through the Mojave earthquake on July 11, there were quakes from Riverside County in the south all the way to Humbolt County in the north. The largest quake, at Landers, registered 7.4 on the Richter scale.

- The riots that erupted in Los Angeles, Las Vegas, San Francisco and other cities after the "Rodney King Verdict" of April 28, acquitting four Los Angeles police officers from accusations of police brutality, brought the emergency manager's responsibility for civil disturbances to new prominence. The worst riot, in Los Angeles, ranks as the biggest civil disturbance in the nation's history taking 52 lives with $1 billion dollars in damage to property.

- A train derailment dumped 30,000 gallons of benzene and other petroleum additives into the Nemadji River on June 30. The toxic vapor cloud produced from the spill covered an area of more than 1,200 square miles, forcing the evacuation of 25,000 people from Superior, Wisconsin to Duluth, Minnesota.

- Perhaps the most significant aspect of 1992 in terms of natural disasters was the series of hurricanes that battered states on both the Atlantic and Pacific. On August 24, Hurricane Andrew tore across Florida, hitting Louisiana the next day. This Category IV hurricane, causing 15 deaths and billion dollars in damage (an estimated $27 billion in Florida alone), ranks as the most costly natural disaster in U.S. history. Hurricane Andrew was followed by Typhoons Omar and Brian hitting Guam, and Hurricane Iniki which caused over $1 billion dollars of damage to the Hawaiian island of Kauai.

- The year did see a reduction in one major threat: nuclear attack. On October 1, 1992, the United States ratified the Strategic Arms Reduction Treaty (START), the first strategic nuclear arms control treaty to call for an actual reduction in warheads. On January 3, 1993, the Presidents of the United States and Russia signed an follow-on agreement, now referred to as START II, that will cut nuclear arsenals 70 percent from their pre-START levels.

The Threats

For the purposes of this report, there are two basic categories of threats:

Natural threats, the largest single category of repetitive threats to communities and emergency management coordinators, come from weather-, geological-, seismic- or oceanic-related events. They pose a threat to any area of the country; their impact can be localized or widespread, predictable or unpredictable. The damage resulting from natural disasters can range from small to major (depending on whether they strike major or minor population centers). The impact of extremely severe natural disasters can have a long-term effect on the infrastructure of any given location. Natural threats include avalanche, dam failure, drought, earthquake, flood, hurricane/tropical storm, landslide, thunderstorm, tornado, tsunami/seiche, volcano, wildfire and winter storm.

Technological/man-made threats represent a category of events that has expanded dramatically throughout this century with the advancements in modern technology. Like natural threats, they can affect localized or widespread areas, are frequently unpredictable, can cause substantial loss of life (besides the potential for damage to property), and can pose a significant threat to the infrastructure of a given area. In this category are those social threats that primarily come from actions by external, hostile forces against the land, population or infrastructure of the United States, or from domestic civil disturbances. Technological/man-made threats include civil disorder, hazardous materials incidents at fixed facilities and in transport accidents, power failures, radiological incidents at fixed facilities or in-transit accidents, missile attack, nuclear attack, structural fires, telecommunications failures, terrorism, and transportation accidents.

The Nature of Threats

A single threat cannot be viewed as a constant, either in terms of the potential for damage to property, loss of lives or the preparedness measures that must be undertaken to protect the population and infrastructure. For example, the State of Texas experienced 4,110 tornadoes from 1959 to 1989, a significantly higher number than registered for any other State. However, these tornadoes often touched down in rural or sparsely populated areas, causing very limited amounts of damage. Conversely, a single tornado or outbreak of tornadoes in a more urbanized area can cause tremendous losses of life and property, as shown in the following example.

Ohio sustained a significantly lower number of tornadoes than Texas during the same years with a total of 467. Yet, in April 1974 during an unusually severe outbreak of 144 tornadoes in a two day period, the city of Xenia, Ohio, suffered 33 deaths, had 1,200 structures demolished, 1,500 structures damaged and total damage reaching an estimated $70 to $90 million (according to American Insurance Association estimates). If the same outbreak of tornadoes had occurred in an isolated area, the losses would probably have been negligible.

Disaster Synergy

A disaster also cannot be viewed as an isolated event with a predictable kind of damage, i.e., each can trigger a series of other related incidents that can substantially increase the impact of the original disaster event. Such secondary events could, in fact, result in significantly higher death rates or increased damage. The following are some classic examples of the "secondary effects" of a variety of disasters:

- In 1964, the Prince William Sound earthquake in Alaska generated a marine landslide that undermined the Valdez Delta. A total of 122 persons in Alaska, Washington, Oregon, California and Hawaii drowned in the tsunami resulting from the marine landslide.

- The April 1992 Chicago Tunnel Flood is an example of an incident where the immediate physical damage caused by the disaster, while significant, pales behind the commercial and social costs it imposed from the disruption of commerce.

- The approach of Hurricane Andrew required not only standard preparations to protect people and property from harm, but also led to a precautionary shutdown of two nuclear power units of Florida's Turkey Point Power Plant. The destruction caused by the storm not only hurt south Florida residents but also migrant workers who came to find agricultural fields devastated well after Hurricane Andrew had actually hit.

Thus, communities and emergency management coordinators are faced with not only the threats themselves, but also with many other factors that make the process of mitigating against, preparing for and responding to them far more complex.

Disaster Impact

The predictability of a hazardous event or the size of its impact depends on the nature of the particular hazard itself. There is a seasonal association for certain types of natural threats such as tornadoes and hurricanes. Other threats such as earthquakes have no seasonal relationship and predictability is nearly impossible. Technology has simply not progressed to the point where the timing of an earthquake can be predicted with any degree of reliability.

There is also a significant variance in the potential impact of a disaster on a "prepared" jurisdiction *versus* an "unprepared" jurisdiction. For example, the earthquake preparedness and mitigation measures taken in San Francisco and Los Angeles have proven to be significantly effective in reducing the amount of losses from large earthquakes—highrise structures. Although the seismic risk in Charleston, South Carolina, and the New Madrid Seismic Zone (including Missouri, Arkansas, Tennessee, Kentucky and Illinois) is great, the lack of major seismic activity in these areas during this century has lessened the fear of the threat. Consequently, many jurisdictions in these areas have not set up strong earthquake building codes like those in San Francisco and Los Angeles. Thus, the impact of a major earthquake in the New Madrid Seismic Zone or around Charleston, South Carolina, could result in tremendous losses of life and property that could possibly be avoided with more stringent measures for preparedness and mitigation.

Our vulnerability to threats is complicated by the identification of newer threats, some of which were virtually unknown 20 or 30 years ago. Advancements in technology and the increased development and use of chemicals over the past decades have resulted in the rise of a new and wide range of threats. Estimates of the impact of some of these threats are often difficult because of a lack of experience with them or a thorough knowledge of the full range of their impact. For example, the potential for injury and loss from the failure of some of the technical systems we rely on each day has yet to be adequately measured.

The same is also increasing true for other types of threats. Preparing and attempting to mitigate the effects of landslides is becoming an increasing concern in the West, as urban development moves into more areas subject to ground failure. The wildfires that hit the hills of Oakland, California in October 1991 illustrate another hazard that will represent an increasing familiar threat to people and property in the future. The Chicago Tunnel Flood of April 1992, illustrate the vulnerability of our society to technological failures.

There are new changes to our environment that may affect the spectrum of hazards the nation faces. There is concern expressed by some on the potential atmospheric and other environmental changes caused by phenomena such as *acid rain* and the *greenhouse effect* on the United States. A growing consensus believes that weather trends on the African Continent, where most hurricanes that affect the continental United States form, could result in an increase in the frequency and severity of hurricanes hitting the United States mainland during the next decade. The severe hurricane season of 1992 seems to confirm this view.

Preparedness Measures/ Hazard Mitigation Activities

Federal, State and local emergency managers must prepare their communities against the wide range of threats that they face daily, in spite of the many variables involved. No matter what the specific threats are that a community faces, there is one common denominator: *emergency management is like insurance—it may never have to be used, but if it is not available when needed the losses can be staggering.*

The civil defense program provides the primary means by which State and local governments can develop the infrastructure of emergency management personnel, facilities, communications, hardware and systems to prepare for and respond to the full range of disasters that may threaten the population of the United States. State and local emergency management personnel, who are funded by the civil defense program, develop Emergency Operations Plans and procedures to prepare for, respond to and recover from all forms of disaster.

Modern technology has significantly enhanced our ability not only to forecast the impact of some disasters, no matter whether they result from natural, technological/man-made or national security threats, but also to take measures to reduce the potential loss of life and damage to the infrastructure. Our predictive ability to forecast severe storm conditions or the possibility of tornadoes has enhanced the preventive and safety measures that can be taken by the population. The ability to project the path of hurricanes usually allows adequate time to undertake protective measures on structures and evacuations, thereby reducing the loss of life. Spring flooding can frequently be predicted based on the snowfall levels at higher elevations and forecast temperature levels.

However, the degree to which forecasting can contribute to predicting disasters varies. The flash flood in Shadyside, Ohio that swept 26 people to their deaths on June 14, 1990 came without warning. Technology has not progressed to the point where the timing or severity of an earthquake can be predicted with any degree of reliability. In spite of the mitigation measures that can be taken, such as applying strict standards in the construction of buildings, highways and other structures, millions of residents in earthquake-prone areas throughout the country are still vulnerable to a sudden, unexpected occurrence.

Mitigation programs undertaken in response to a wide range of threats do, however, result in measurable numbers of lives saved and property protected, regardless of whether the event can be predicted. Mitigation efforts such as earthquake resistant engineering were critical in reducing the loss of life in the Loma Prieta earthquake. Bridges, roads and buildings that were built according to stringent earthquake standards stood up well during the earthquake. Other structures that had not been built according to strict standards did not fare so well, as was evident from the destruction of the Oakland freeway. Hurricane preparedness activities, including media announcements, the distribution of printed information for residents in threatened areas prior to impact and floodplain management initiatives have gone far in reducing the impact of water/wind-related disasters in coastal and inland areas.

Threats Affecting the United States

There are many threats facing the nation's population and infrastructure. Threats can be widespread or localized, affecting one or more States. Periodic and at times little publicized disasters resulting from floods, tornadoes, landslides and fires take scores of lives and cause hundreds of millions of dollars in property damage annually. The magnitude of the losses of major disasters, such as Hurricane Andrew, when viewed in relationship to the loss of life, property damage, disruption of services and long-term impact on the affected population, serves to heighten the realization of the vulnerability of the United States to such events.

The following sections of this report describe the primary threats that the United States faces and provides general information concerning the dangers posed by them. For the purposes of this study, threats are categorized as being natural hazards or technological/man-made. Each class of threats is broken down further into specific hazards. For each type of hazard, information is provided to define the hazard, its national frequency, regions at risk, season(s) in which it may occur, its effects, the worst recorded event and most relevant recent (largely 1991) statistical information on the hazard.

NATURAL THREATS

Natural threats, the largest single category of repetitive threats to communities and emergency management coordinators, come from weather-, geological-, seismic- or oceanic-related events. They pose a threat to any area of the country; their impact can be localized or widespread, predictable or unpredictable. The damage resulting from natural disasters can range from small to major (depending on whether they strike major or minor population centers). The impact of extremely severe natural disasters can have a long-term effect on the infrastructure of any given location. Natural threats include avalanche, dam failure, drought, earthquake, flood, hurricane/tropical storm, landslide, thunderstorm, tornado, tsunami/seiche, volcano, wildfire and winter storm.

Avalanche

Definition   *A mass of sliding snow in mountainous terrain with large snow deposits on slopes of 20 degrees or more*

National Frequency   Approximately 10,000 avalanches are reported each year. There may be as many as 100 times more that are not observed or recorded. From 1980 to 1985, Alaska recorded 441 avalanches that affected people.

Regions at Risk   The mountain ranges in New Hampshire, Vermont and the Far West have avalanches where the primary risk to people exists in recreational areas that feature climbing and skiing. Transportation corridors along many year-round highways and railroads in the western risk areas experience frequent avalanche activity. In Alaska alone, from 1975 to 1985, 205 avalanche events blocked highways, hitting or disabling 30 vehicles; 274 events blocked railroads, derailing 21 cars. Avalanches closed Colorado highways on 60 days during the winter of 1983-1984. The map in *Figure 1* illustrates the risk severity for snow avalanches by State.

Season(s)   Fall, Winter, Spring.

Effects   An annual average of the effects of avalanches is estimated to be: 140 Americans are caught in avalanches, 65 are buried and 17 are killed. The National Weather Service, though, did not report any deaths or injuries from avalanches in 1991. While there are no national cost figures available, the economic impact of avalanches that damage and destroy public, commercial and private property and forest lands includes the costs for restoration, maintenance and subsequent litigation. The following examples of some costs incurred in specific areas have been taken from the *National Research Council 1990 Report entitled, Snow Avalanche Hazards and Mitigation in the United States, pp. 17-19.*

- Avalanches cost the Washington State Department of Transportation an estimated $330,000 each year. That figure   does not include State salaries and expenses for avalanche   control or plowing and snow removal.

- Costs from damages caused by avalanches in Alaska were estimated to be at least $11.4 million during the years of 1977 through 1986.

Dam Failure

Definition   *Collapse or failure of an impoundment that causes downstream flooding*

National Frequency Dam failures occur several times annually, however, no national average is available.

Regions at Risk   There are over 80,000 dams throughout the States. More than 20,000 of them are classified as posing "high" or "significant" hazards. These designations mean that, if such a dam failed, lives would be lost and extensive property damage would be suffered. *Figure 2* lists some dam and levee failures from 1874-1982 in which lives were lost.

DAM & LEVEE FAILURES IN THE U.S.
1874 - 1982

YEAR	LOCATION	STRUCTURE	DEATHS
1874	Williamsburg, MA	Earth Dam	144
1889	Johnstown, PA	Earth Dam	2,209
1890	Walnut Grove/Prescott, AZ	Dam	150
1894	Mill River, MA	Dam	143
1900	Austin/Austin, PA	Dam	8
1928	St. Francis, CA	Dam (est.)	400-700
1955	Yuba City, CA	Levee	38
1963	Baldwin Hill, CA	Earth Dam	5
1972	Buffalo Creek, WV	Slagheap Dam	125
1972	Rapid City, SD	Dam	200
1976	Newfound, NC	Earth Dam	4
1976	Teton, ID	Earth Dam	14
1977	Toccoa, GA	Earth Dam	35
1982	Estes Park, CO	Earth Dams (2)	3
	TOTAL		**3,528-3,778**

Source: Adapted from U.S. Nuclear Regulatory Commission/
A Risk Comparison.

Figure 2

Season(s)   Dam failures usually occur as a secondary effect of storms or earthquakes.

- Rescue operations cost $74,250 for an avalanche on U.S. Forest Service land in Colorado that killed four people near a ski area on February 18, 1987. Additional undisclosed expenses related to preparation for anticipated litigation were also incurred.

- A March 31, 1981, avalanche in California's Alpine Meadows ski area resulted in seven deaths and caused approximately $1.5 million in property damages. The resulting law suits (not including appeals) cost more than $1,500,000. The cost of the undisclosed out-of-court settlements potentially could have been $14 million.

Worst Event

Definitive data unavailable. The worst period in American history for avalanche-related deaths was during the Colorado gold and silver mining fields from 1880 to 1920 when about 400 people were killed.

Discussion

Avalanches, which are the most frequent forms of lethal mass movement, can be triggered by various means, including earthquakes. They generally occur in the Rockies and other mountains of the western States. There is no centralized reporting of occurrences because most incidents happen in remote, sparsely populated locations and seldom inflict permanent damage. The avalanche threat is becoming more significant because of increased development and recreation in mountainous regions.

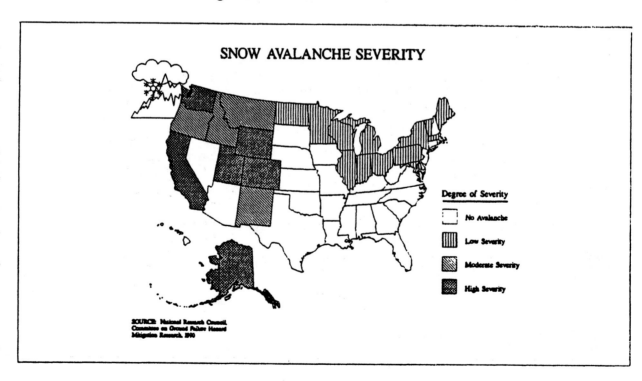

Figure 1

Effects

The primary consequence of the dam failure hazard is loss of life and property damage downstream of the failure. Of the estimated 80,000 dams in the United States, about 95 percent are owned by State and local authorities and private organizations as opposed to the 5 percent owned by the Federal government.

Worst Event

The Johnstown earthen dam collapse and flood on May 31, 1889, resulted in the deaths of more than 2,200 persons.

Discussion

Between 1972 and 1981, the U.S. Army Corps of Engineers had responsibility for the inspection of all non-Federal dams. The responsibility has since been returned to the States. Inspection of Federal dams continues to be the responsibility of the owner agency. The number of unsafe dams in 1981 is shown in *Figure 3*. It is important to note in the Figure, however, that the age of the data does not necessarily mean that the number of dams considered "unsafe" at the time of inspection remains at that level today—some deficiencies may have been corrected while other dams may have become unsafe due to poor maintenance. FEMA is working on a new survey of the condition of the nation's dams, to be completed by early 1993.

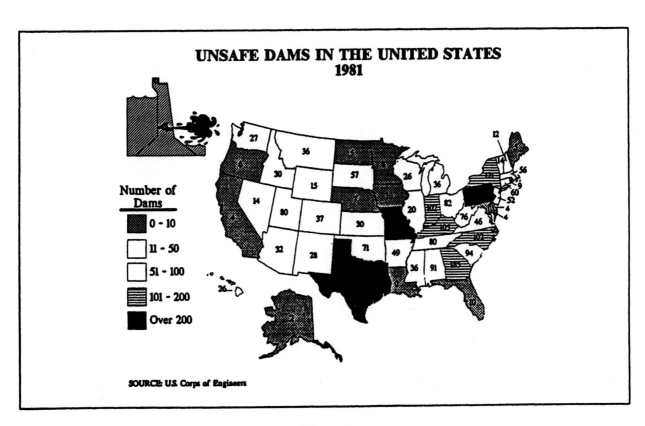

**UNSAFE DAMS IN THE UNITED STATES
1981**

Number of
Dams

■ 0 - 10
□ 11 - 50
□ 51 - 100
▤ 101 - 200
■ Over 200

SOURCE: U.S. Corps of Engineers

Figure 3

Drought

Definition   *A prolonged period without rain*

National Frequency   The frequency is difficult to measure. Droughts can happen any time of the year.

Regions at Risk   The entire country is at risk.

Season(s)   Year round

Effects   Drought in the farm belt devastates crops, resulting in low yields and economic losses. Winds blow away top soil and create dust storms further eroding the fertility of the land. Water tables are lowered. Parched forest lands are more susceptible to wildfires during periods of drought.

Worst Event   "Dust Bowl" of the 1930's in the Southwest

Discussion   Drought gripped much of the West and Midwest during 1987-1991. While beneficial rains in 1991 eased or erased drought conditions in some locations, other areas were not so fortunate. (See *Figure 4* for the changes in affected areas over the year.) Two areas in particular, the Missouri River Basin and California, continued to experience serious drought conditions during Fiscal Year 1991 after several consecutive years of below average precipitation. Reservoir storage in both areas continued to be very low at the beginning of Fiscal Year 1991. The National Weather Service estimated an economic loss totaling $156 million from drought in 1991.

The economic effects of a drought are both direct and indirect. For example, crop losses affect farming income that, in turn, may mean foreclosure of farms because of unserviced debt. Estimating the economic losses attributed solely to drought-related damage is difficult to do and can be misleading when compared from year to year because of constantly fluctuating commodity markets. Also, some areas of the country may suffer drought-related losses while other areas that produce the same crops have record yields, as during the 1989 and 1990 growing seasons.

Misuse of the land and lack of appropriate cultivation practices contributed to the severity of drought effects up until the last 50 years. Research, education and governmental financial aid have done much to restore the land and mitigate the impact of droughts since then. The trend for droughts may worsen in the long term because of the greenhouse effect and cause water shortages for irrigation in the west and for human consumption throughout the country (especially in overdeveloped areas).

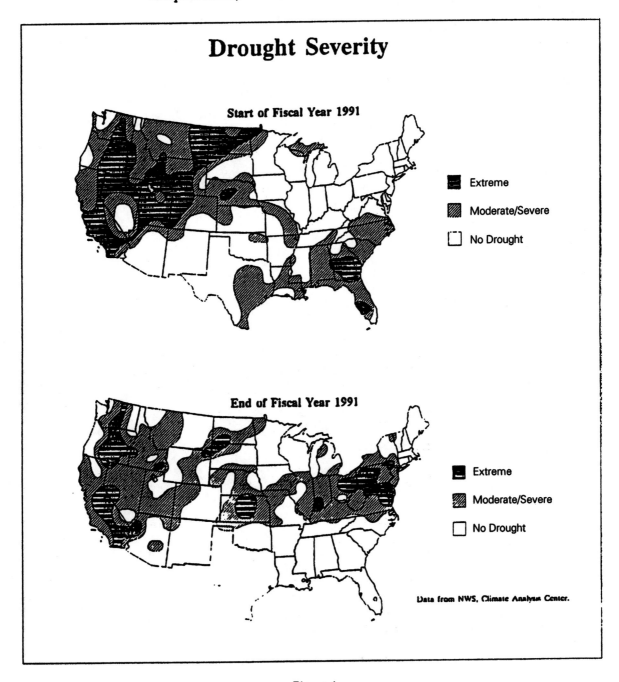

Figure 4

Earthquake

Definition   *A sudden motion of the ground that may cause surface faulting (ground rupture), ground shaking and ground failure*

National Frequency   Each year, there are literally thousands of earthquakes in the United States. Most of these are of such small magnitude that they are not felt by the population.

Regions at Risk   Wide areas of the United States have some vulnerability to earthquakes *(see Figure 5)*. The most frequent earthquake events occur in States west of the Rocky Mountains, although historically the most violent earthquakes have occurred in the central United States. California is especially vulnerable because of its high seismic activity. Other highly vulnerable areas are in Charleston, South Carolina, and the central United States (the New Madrid Seismic Zone), both of which were devastated by earthquakes in the last century.

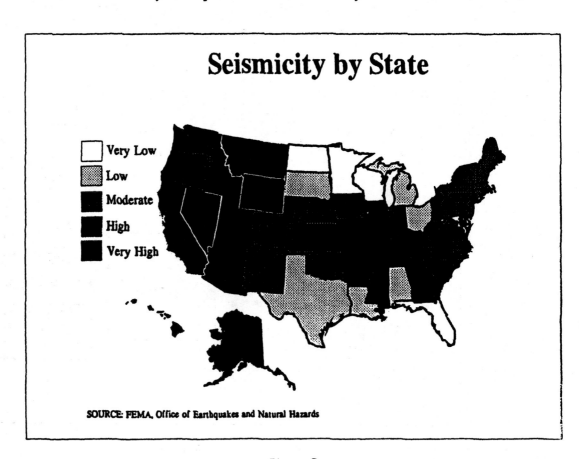

Seismicity by State

Very Low
Low
Moderate
High
Very High

SOURCE: FEMA, Office of Earthquakes and Natural Hazards

Figure 5

Season(s)   Year round

Effects   The greatest danger to life in significant earthquakes comes from falling objects, broken glass and structural failures. Severe earthquakes destroy power and telephone lines and gas, sewer or water mains. These, in turn, may set off fires and/or hinder firefighting or rescue efforts. They may also trigger landslides, rupture dams and generate seismic sea waves (tsunamis).

Worst Event   The worst event for deaths occurred in the 1906 San Francisco quake when 700 lives were lost. The worst event for economic damage was the over $10 billion loss caused by the 1989 Loma Prieta earthquake. *Figure 6* displays the 16 most significant earthquakes in the history of the United States and the number of deaths from each event.

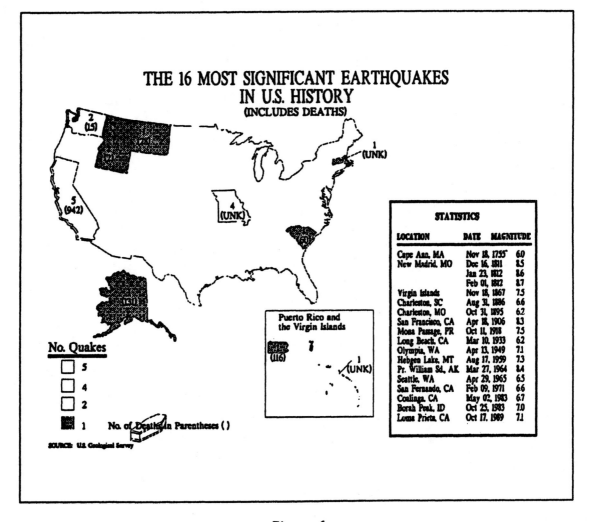

Figure 6

Discussion

Tens of potentially damaging earthquakes of a magnitude equal to 5 or greater on the Richter Scale occur annually in the United States. For example, in a typical year such as 1982, 70 earthquakes of a magnitude equal to 5 or greater on the Richter scale occurred throughout the country. Of these, there were 45 in Alaska, 22 in the contiguous 48 States and 3 in Hawaii. Great magnitude earthquakes (equal to 8 or greater on the Richter Scale), which are more infrequent, occur in the United States on an average about once every 12 years.

Earthquakes occur in virtually all 50 States, Puerto Rico and the Virgin Islands. They happen most frequently in California, Alaska and the Caribbean in the grid of faults, chains of volcanoes and mountains and deep oceanic trenches that are the boundaries between the great crustal plates that form the Earth's outer shell. Intraplate earthquakes—shocks within the interior of the giant crustal plates—are less common occurrences, but they can be equally destructive. Intraplate earthquakes are more typical of the types of earthquakes that occur in the eastern United States.

While earthquakes are relatively infrequent in the eastern States, an earthquake the magnitude of Loma Prieta could cause significantly more damage in the eastern States than it did in California. Because of unique factors relating to the length of time seismic waves take to diminish in the East, the ground shaking in eastern earthquakes extends over much larger areas than it does in western earthquakes of comparable magnitude. For example, the distributions of intensities of the 1811 New Madrid, Missouri, earthquake and the 1886 Charleston, South Carolina, earthquake were substantially greater than those of the 1906 San Francisco, California, earthquake and the 1971 San Fernando, California, earthquake.

Landslides, lateral spreads, differential settlements and ground cracks induced by earthquake ground shaking are a principal cause of damage and casualties. In the 1906 San Francisco, California, earthquake, lateral spreads and ground settlement were responsible for considerable damage in the city. This damage included the breaking of several water pipelines that, in turn, left the city largely defenseless against the conflagration that followed.

Earthquake magnitude is a measure of the strength of an earthquake, or the strain energy released by it, as calculated from the instrumental record made by the event on a calibrated *seismograph.* Seismographs record a zig-zag trace that shows the varying amplitude of ground oscillations beneath the instrument. Sensitive seismographs, which greatly magnify these ground motions, can detect strong earthquakes from sources anywhere in the world. The time, location and magnitude of an earthquake can be determined from the data recorded by seismograph stations.

The Richter magnitude scale was developed in 1935 by Charles F. Richter of the California Institute of Technology as a mathematical device to compare the size of earthquakes. The magnitude of an earthquake is determined from the logarithm of the amplitude of waves recorded by seismographs. Adjustments are included in the magnitude formula to compensate for the variation in the distance between the various seismographs and the epicenter of the earthquakes.

On the Richter Scale, magnitude is expressed in whole numbers and decimal fractions. For example, a magnitude of 5.3 might be computed for a moderate earthquake, and a strong earthquake might be rated as magnitude 6.3. Because of the logarithmic basis of the scale, each whole number increase in magnitude represents a tenfold increase in measured amplitude. As an estimate of energy, each whole number step in the magnitude scale corresponds to the release of about 31 times more energy than the amount associated with the preceding whole number value.

Earthquakes with magnitudes of about 2.0 or less are usually called microearthquakes. They are not commonly felt by people and are generally recorded only on local seismographs. Events with magnitudes of about 4.5 or more—there are several thousand such shocks annually—are strong enough to be recorded by sensitive seismographs all over the world.

Floods

Definition

Four types of floods are included in this discussion.

- *Riverine—periodic overflow of rivers and streams*
- *Flash—quickly rising small streams after heavy rain or rapid snowmelt*
- *Urban—overflow of storm sewer systems, usually due to poor drainage, following heavy rain or rapid snowmelt*
- *Coastal—flooding along coastal areas associated with severe storms, hurricanes or other events*

National Frequency

The frequency is undetermined, but there are many floods each year.

Regions at Risk

Floods occur in every State and territory.

Season(s)

Flooding can happen any time of the year, but predominates in the Spring.

Effects

The National Weather Service attributed a total of 61 deaths and 56 injuries due to flooding in 1991. Property damage and agricultural losses for 1991 were estimated to be over $847 million. The annual death toll from floods has averaged 146 over the past 20 years. The average annual figure for economic damage, derived from losses during the years of 1981 through 1990, stands at $2.2 billion. The map in *Figure 7* shows the areas of the US with the greatest flood problems. Other effects from floods include crop damage and soil erosion. Flooding can also trigger secondary events such as power failure and landslide. In spite of risk reduction mitigation efforts for floodplain management, increasing numbers of households are at risk and increased damage is projected for the future.

Worst Event

The worst recorded event (loss of lives) was the 1889 flood in Johnstown, Pennsylvania, in which more than 2,200 lives were lost. (The flood itself was actually caused by the failure of a dam upstream from Johnstown. This flood is a classic example of the "secondary effects" that can occur from another event.) The worst

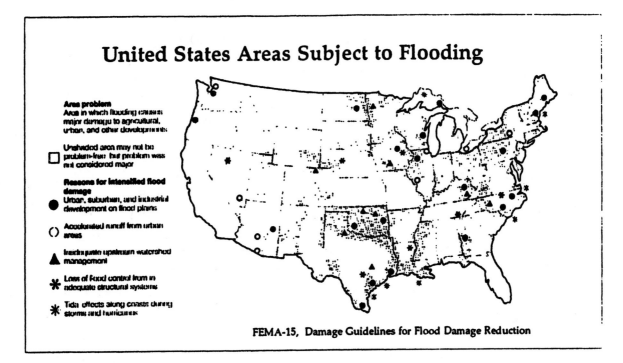

United States Areas Subject to Flooding

Area problem
Area in which flooding causes major damage to agricultural, urban, and other developments.

☐ Unshaded area may not be problem-free; but problem was not considered major

Reasons for intensified flood damage

● Urban, suburban, and industrial development on flood plains

() Accelerated runoff from urban areas

▲ Inadequate upstream watershed management

✱ Loss of flood control from inadequate structural systems

✱ Tidal effects along coasts during storms and hurricanes

FEMA-15, Damage Guidelines for Flood Damage Reduction

Figure 7

economic losses were incurred in the 1972 floods that resulted from Hurricane Agnes ($4 billion) and the 1973 spring flood of the Mississippi River system ($1.2 billion).

Discussion

Flooding, perhaps the most pervasive natural hazard in the United States, occurs from a variety of causes. Floods often accompany hurricanes and tornadoes. While some floods develop over a period of days, "flash floods" can result in raging waters in a matter of minutes.

In an attempt to alleviate flood losses, Congress established the National Flood Insurance Program with the passage of the National Flood Insurance Act of 1968. The intent was to mitigate future damage and provide protection for property owners against potential losses through an insurance mechanism that was not formerly available. Over 2.5 million insurance policies have been issued under this program, and claimants have received $2.5 billion for 350,000 insurance losses since 1978. Claim payments of $365 million covered flood damage caused by Hurricane Hugo in South Carolina. Communities participating in the National Flood Insurance Program are required to adopt and implement measures to reduce future flood losses in Special Flood Hazard Areas.

Hurricanes/Tropical Storms

Definition *A large cyclonic storm accompanied by high winds, extreme rainfall and storm surge*

National Frequency The national annual average for hurricane incidents within the continental United States, based on figures from 1871 to 1989, is 1.9. During the same period, Florida experienced the largest number of hurricanes of any State, 57. Texas was second with 37. During the last 10 years, the Western Pacific Insular Areas have experienced 14 hurricanes. An average of 29 tropical storms or hurricanes occur each year in the West Pacific Ocean.

Regions at Risk Vulnerable areas in the United States include the territories in the Caribbean, the coast from Texas to Maine and tropical areas of the western Pacific Ocean, including Hawaii. (Typhoons are the Pacific Ocean versions of hurricanes.) *Figure 8* depicts the number of hurricanes by State during the period 1871-1989.

Season(s) Summer and Fall. Hurricanes and tropical storms occur seasonally (June through November) with August and September being the peak months.

Effects The consequences of hurricane winds and storm surge, which are often accompanied by other devastating events such as tornadoes, include loss of life, coastal erosion, coastal and inland flooding, structural failures, felled trees that cause other damage, power failures and significant economic disruption. In 1991, hurricanes and tropical storms were blamed for 13 storm-related deaths, 208 injuries and an estimated $1.164 million dollars in damage. The 20-year annual average rate of hurricane-related deaths is estimated to be 17 by the National Weather Service.

Worst Event The worst event happened in Galveston, Texas, in 1900 when 6,000 lives were lost. Hurricane Andrew will probably rank as the costliest hurricane, with 1992 estimates going up to $20 billion. (See *Figure 9* for a list of the 10 costliest U.S. hurricanes, ranked by insured losses.)

Discussion Hurricanes are cyclonic storms with counterclockwise winds of 74 miles per hour or higher. The coastal areas that receive the full brunt of hurricane winds and storm surge sustain the most damage. Since hurricanes dissipate quite rapidly to less than

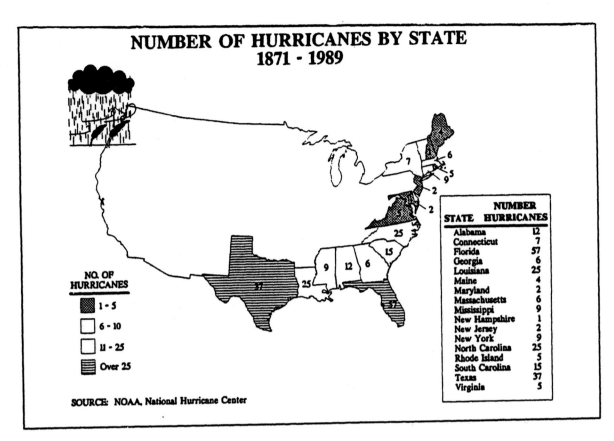

NUMBER OF HURRICANES BY STATE
1871 - 1989

NO. OF
HURRICANES

■	1 - 5
□	6 - 10
□	11 - 25
▤	Over 25

SOURCE: NOAA, National Hurricane Center

STATE	NUMBER HURRICANES
Alabama	12
Connecticut	7
Florida	57
Georgia	6
Louisiana	25
Maine	4
Maryland	2
Massachusetts	6
Mississippi	9
New Hampshire	1
New Jersey	2
New York	9
North Carolina	25
Rhode Island	5
South Carolina	15
Texas	37
Virginia	5

Figure 8

THE 10 COSTLIEST U.S. HURRICANES
(Estimated Insured Losses)

HURRICANE	YEAR	DAMAGE
Andrew (FL, LA, MS)	1992	$10,700,000,000
Hugo (VI, PR, SC, NC)	1989	$4,200,000,000
Iniki (HI)	1992	$1,600,000,000
Frederic (MS, AL, FL)	1979	$752,510,000
Alicia (TX)	1983	$675,520,000
Elena (FL, AL, MS, LA)	1985	$543,300,000
Betsy (FL, LA)	1965	$515,000,000
Gloria (NC, VA, MD, DE, PA)	1985	$418,750,000
Celia (TX)	1970	$309,950,000
Camile (LA, MS, AL, FL)	1969	$165,300,000

Source: Insurance Information Institute

Figure 9

hurricane strength after they make landfall, inland areas receive less severe damage, usually from flooding associated with the exceptionally heavy rains commonly associated with the remaining storm system.

Figure 10 contains data on the deadliest hurricanes, those causing 25 deaths or more from 1900 on.

DEADLIEST U.S. HURRICANES
(Hurricanes of more that 25 deaths)

HURRICANE	YEAR	CATEGORY	NUMBER OF DEATHS
Texas, Galveston	1900	4	6,000
Florida (Lake Okeechobee)	1928	4	1,836
Florida (Keys/S. Texas)	1919	4	600–900
New England	1938	3	600
Florida (Keys)	1935	5	408
Audrey (LA & TX)	1957	4	390
Northeast U.S.	1944	3	390
Louisiana (Grand Isle)	1909	4	350
Louisiana (New Orleans)	1015	4	275
Texas (Galveston)	1915	4	275
Camille (MS & LA)	1969	5	256
Florida (Miami)	1926	4	243
Diane (Northeast U.S.)	1955	1	184
Florida (Southeast)	1906	2	164
Mississippi/Alabama/ Pensacola, Florida	1906	3	134
Agnes (Northeast U.S.)	1972	1	122
Hazel (SC & NC)	1954	4	95
Betsy (FL & LA)	1965	3	75
Carol (Northeast U.S.)	1954	3	60
Southeast Florida, Louisiana, Mississippi	1947	4	51
Hugo (SC, NC, PR & VI)	1989	5	26

Figure 10

Landslides

Definition

Downward and outward movement of slope-forming materials composed of natural rock, soils, artificial fills or combinations of these materials. The moving mass may be preceded by any of three principal types of movement: falling, sliding or flowing, or by their combinations.

National Frequency

Precise data are not available. Reporting of landslides is not a standard practice, and it is difficult to distinguish the effects of landslides from incidents that may trigger them.

Regions at Risk

According to the report of the Committee on Ground Failure Hazards of the National Research Council: "Landsliding is widely distributed in the United States and is not restricted to a few localized areas. Many different physiographic and climatic regions are subject to landslides, and in much of the United States landsliding is a dominant process of landscape alteration." The same report said that: "Landslides are indigenous to much of the Appalachian Highlands, particularly southwestern Pennsylvania, southeastern Ohio and northern West Virginia. More than two million mappable landslides are estimated to have occurred in the Appalachian Highlands from New England to the Gulf coastal plain. These include landslides in the portions of the highlands that extend into New England, New York, Maryland, Kentucky, Virginia, Tennessee, North Carolina, South Carolina, Georgia and Alabama."

See *Figure 11* for a map of the regions at risk from landslides in the United States.

Season(s)

Year round.

Effects

At least 25 people are thought to die in landslides every year. The annual economic loss from landslides is estimated at $1 to $2 billion. According to the National Research Council report mentioned above, "The loss of life from landsliding is comparable to the total loss of life from floods, earthquakes and hurricanes (Krohn and Slosson, 1976)." Economic losses are extensive, including not only the replacement and repair of damaged facilities but associated costs relating to lost productivity, disruptions to utility and transportation systems and losses of revenue for affected communities.

Worst Event   In terms of sheer volume (2.8 billion cubic meters), the collapse of the northern part of the cone of the Mt. St. Helens volcano immediately before the May 18, 1980, eruption is the world's largest landslide in historical terms (because of evacuation and other preparedness measures taken beforehand, only 5-10 people were killed by the landslide). The May 1983 landslide at Thistle, Utah, probably is the most expensive, with $200 million in damages attributed to landslides alone.

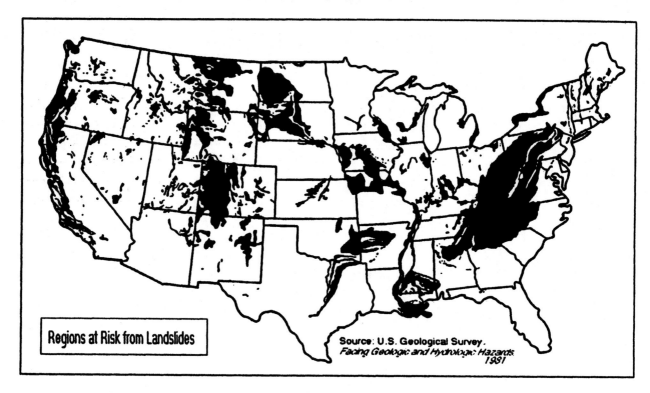

Regions at Risk from Landslides

Source: U.S. Geological Survey.
Facing Geologic and Hydrologic Hazards
1981

Figure 11

Discussion   Landslides can occur either very suddenly or slowly. They can be triggered during earthquakes, heavy rainstorms or rapid snowmelt, volcanic eruptions, storm generated ocean waves or by other landslides. Landslides can also be triggered by freeze-thaw and shrink-swell cycles, root wedging, animal burrows, natural erosion or deposition or the thaw of ice-bearing soils such as permafrost. While most landslides are single events, more than one-third of the cases are associated with heavy rains or the melting of winter snows.

Although the term *landslide* is generally assumed to mean any slide of rock or soil down a mountainous or hilly location, the term encompasses several different types of earth movements.

For example, lateral shifts, even in soil that appears nearly flat to the naked eye are, in reality, landslides. Such movement is often caused by heavy saturation or liquefication of the soil following heavy rains or snowmelt, but it can also be the result of an earthquake. Classic examples of lateral shifts occurred in Sylmar, California, during the 1971 San Fernando earthquake. Another type of landslide can come from the "rotational" movement of land. During the earthquake in Alaska in 1964, for example, acreage in some areas moved as much as 11 feet, yet the buildings standing on the land were undamaged. (It is believed that liquefied soil beneath the earth supported the buildings and absorbed much of the shaking from the earthquake.)

In the past two decades, the expansion of the population into seismic risk areas (including relatively flat terrain) and/or steeply sloping terrain has contributed to the increase of damaging landslides. Building residential and other structures and developing irrigated landscape areas in such terrain alter soil or hillside patterns and aggravate the instability of many slopes. Such development can also reactivate older landslides or create conditions for new landslides.

Thunderstorm/Lightning

Definition

Thunderstorms are generated by temperature imbalances in the atmosphere, bringing heavy precipitation, strong winds, hail, thunder and lightning. A Severe Thunderstorm is one with winds of more than 57 miles per hour or one producing hail of 3/4 inch or more in diameter.

National Frequency

There are at least 100,000 thunderstorms occurring every year in the United States.

Regions at Risk

Few areas of the United States are free from thunderstorms and their attendant risks (see *Figure 12* for estimate of annual number of thunderstorm days). The area with greatest occurrence extends eastward from Wyoming/Colorado/New Mexico and includes most of the central and southern sections of the country. Florida is an area of extremely high frequency. Along the Pacific coast, thunderstorms and lightning are rare.

Thunderstorm Days in the U.S.

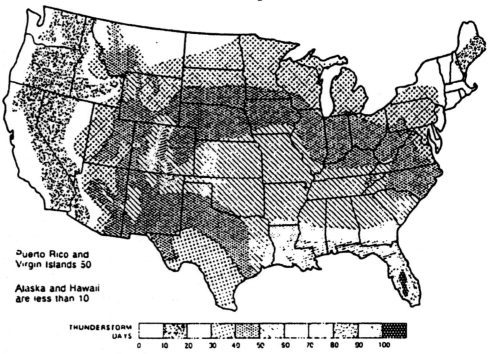

Puerto Rico and
Virgin Islands 50

Alaska and Hawaii
are less than 10

Figure 12

Season(s)

Thunderstorm activity starts in the Spring, with storms becoming more frequent throughout the Summer.

Effects

The locally heavy rains, damaging winds, hail and lightning that accompany thunderstorms frequently produce direct damage and flash flooding creating annual losses in the hundreds of millions of dollars. More people are killed every year from lightning than from tornadoes or hurricanes. Lightning strikes can also threaten aviation and electronic equipment. In 1991, lightning from thunderstorms killed 73 and created $25.1 million in damage. Deaths resulting from thunderstorm winds totaled 32 with $293 million in damage. Property losses from hail totaled $411.8 million in 1991.

Worst Event

The most dramatic disasters resulting from thunderstorms have occurred in air transport. In July 1982, 146 people were killed in Kenner, Louisiana as a result of a plane crash caused by a downburst from a thunderstorm. In December 1963, 38 people were killed when their plane was struck by lightning near Elkton, Maryland.

Discussion

A thunderstorm can produce death and damage in many ways. Flash floods can result from the locally heavy rains that are associated with a thunderstorm. The lightning that accompanies a thunderstorm, occurring at a thunderstorm's most violent stage, is very destructive to buildings, causes most forest fires, and kills more people than any other weather phenomenon. If a thunderstorm's precipitation takes the form of hail, lumps of ice that form during the life of the storm, crops can be devastated. Hail can also cause heavy damage to aircraft, automobiles, roofs and windows.

One particularly dangerous aspect of the violent downdrafts associated with thunderstorms is a feature called a *microburst*, or downburst. These are intense concentrations of sinking air that fan out on striking the earth's surface, producing damaging "straight" winds, and sometimes blowing dust, particularly in the southwestern United States. Thunderstorms that have downbursts typically produce several in succession of varying strengths and sizes, creating horizontal winds of upwards of 100 miles or more. Frequently, damage that is attributed to tornadoes, including downed trees and powerlines, broken windows and wind-caused structural damage to buildings, is actually caused by the straight winds of a downburst. Major air disasters in Kenner, Louisiana (1982) and Dallas/Fort Worth (1985) have been attributed to thunderstorm downbursts.

Finally, severe thunderstorms can lead to the creation of tornadoes under certain circumstances. (See following section on *Tornadoes* for description.)

Tornado

Definition *A small radius cyclonic windstorm*

National Frequency The yearly national average of incidents (taken from 1959-1988 data) is 783. The average annual frequency per State is 16 with a high for Texas of 132 and less than 3 in 14 States.

Regions at Risk Tornadoes are risks in all States but are more frequent in the Midwest, Southeast and Southwest. The States of Mississippi, Kansas, Arkansas, Oklahoma, Illinois, Indiana, Iowa, Missouri, Nebraska, Texas, Louisiana, Florida, Georgia, Alabama and South Dakota are at greatest risk. (See *Figure 13* for a national summary of the 1959-1988 tornado occurrences and *Figure 14* for the 1991 tornado activity.)

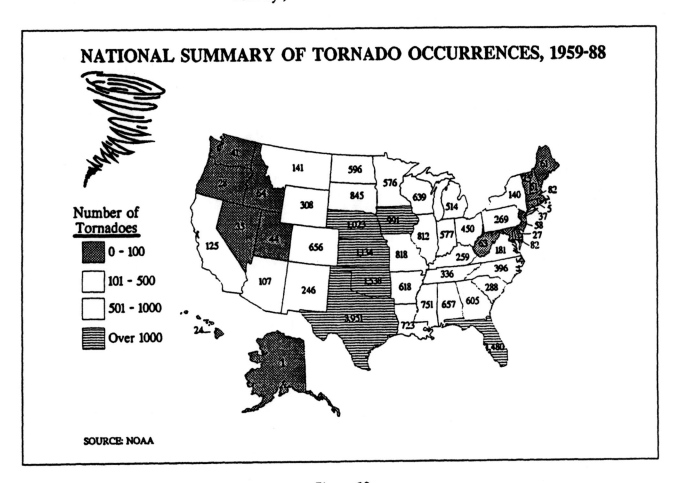

Figure 13

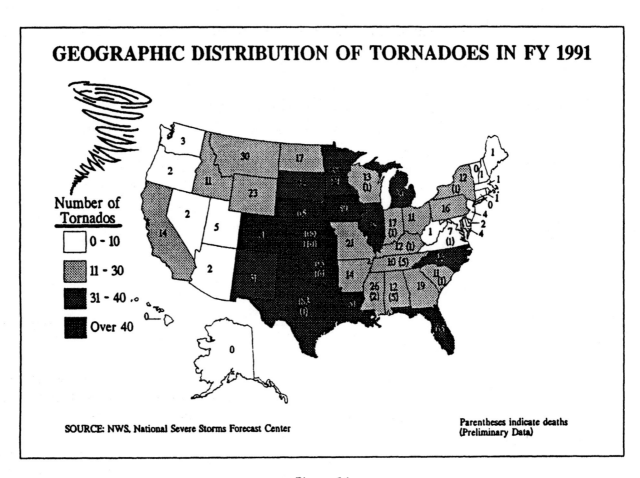

Figure 14

Season(s)	Tornadoes can occur year-around. While the normal tornado season extends from March to August, the peak months are from April through June.
Effects	The National Weather Service recorded 39 deaths and 854 injuries due to tornadoes, with a 20-year average annual rate of 69 deaths. The costs of tornado-related damage reached $798 million in 1991.The annual rate of economic damage for the eight fiscal years 1983-1990 is around $590 million. Tornadoes cause secondary events such as power failure and fires. (See *Figure 15* for a summary of tornado deaths during the period 1959-1988.)
Worst Event	The worst event in this century occurred on March 18, 1925, when eight tornadoes in Missouri, Illinois, Indiana, Kentucky, Tennessee and Alabama caused 689 deaths. The worst November on record was in 1988 when 121 tornadoes, mainly concentrated

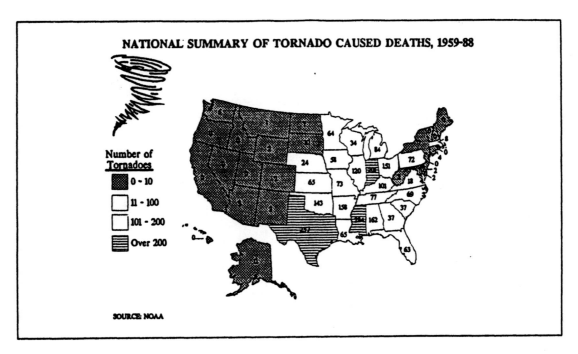

Figure 15

in four major outbreaks, struck 15 south-central States. (The annual tornado average for November is 23.) A total of 14 lives were lost and damages were more than $108 million.

Discussion

While they are relatively short-lived in duration, tornadoes are intensely focused, making them one of the most destructive natural hazards. With winds of 150 miles per hour or more at their centers, tornadoes can destroy almost everything in paths that can range from 200 yards to one mile wide. Although tornadoes normally travel for up to 10 miles, tornado tracks of 200 miles have been reported.

More tornadoes occur in the United States than anywhere else in the world. They generally develop from thunderstorms and sometimes as the result of hurricanes. The weather conditions that tend to generate this phenomenon are unseasonably warm and humid earth surface air, cold air at middle atmospheric levels and strong upper-level jet stream winds. The instability of weather patterns during the "transitional" Spring and Fall seasons, when warm- and cold-air systems often converge violently, make these times of the year particularly dangerous for tornado activity.

In the first half of this century, the number of tornadoes recorded per year was less than 200. Since 1953, the numbers have ranged from 421 to 1,102 per year. The increase results from several factors not necessarily related to weather changes. Increased population density means that there are more people to detect and report tornadoes that touch down in areas that were formerly isolated. In addition, significant improvements in technology, communications and military and weather service tracking have improved both the detection and reporting of tornadoes.

Tsunami/Seiche

Definition

Tsunami: A water wave or a series of waves generated by an impulsive vertical displacement of the ocean or other body of water usually due to earthquakes, volcanoes or landslides

Seiche: A long wave set up on an enclosed body of water such as a lake or reservoir

National Frequency

Between 1900 and 1990, coasts in the United States have been struck by 151 confirmed tsunamis, for an average frequency of 1.67 per year. During this time, a damaging tsunami occurred every 3.6 years on the average.

Regions at Risk

Hawaii, the highest risk area, averages one tsunami every year with a damaging occurrence every 7 years. Alaska, also at high risk, averages a tsunami every 1.75 years and a damaging event every 7 years. The West Coast and American Samoa experience a damaging tsunami every 18 years on the average. Although Guam, the Commonwealth of the Northern Marianas (Saipan) and the other Western Pacific Insular entities record a tsunami every 3 years, they are at low risk because the waves cause almost no damage. Also at low risk are Puerto Rico, the Virgin Islands and the East Coast where tsunamis are recorded every 13 to 18 years. Historically, however, at least one tsunami has caused damage and deaths in Puerto Rico and the Virgin Islands. The tsunami risk table (developed by the National Geophysical Data

TSUNAMI RISK AREAS
Frequency Per Year 1900 - 1990

AREA	TOTAL	DAMAGING	RISK
Hawaii	1.00	0.14	High
Alaska	0.57	0.14	High
West Coast	0.5	0.06	Moderate
American Samoa	0.67	0.06	Moderate
Pacific Islands	0.33	0.01	Low
Puerto Rico/ Virgin Islands	0.06	0.01	Low
East Coast	0.08	0.01	Low

Figure 16

Center) in *Figure 16* lists the 1900-1990 frequency rate.

Season(s)   Year round

Effects   History records at least 470 fatalities and several hundred million dollars in property damage in the United States and its territories. Tsunamis can trigger the secondary effects of flooding and landslides.

Worst Event(s)   On April 1, 1946, a tsunami with wave heights of 55 feet above sea level struck Hawaii, killing 159 people and causing property damage estimated at $26 million. Generated by an earthquake near the Aleutian Islands in Alaska, the tsunami had a wave length of about 100 miles and traveled at 490 miles per hour. Deaths from this tsunami were also recorded in Alaska and the West Coast.

A tsunami following the Prince Rupert Sound (Alaska) earthquake in 1964 directly affected the three West Coast States and Alaska, resulting in 123 deaths and damage totaling $98 million.

Figure 17 summarizes the damage from the five major tsunamis that have occurred within the past 50 years.

Discussion   While tsunamis and seiches are commonly considered secondary effects of major earthquakes, they are frequently responsible for much of the damage attributed to an earthquake. As one study noted:

DAMAGE FROM MAJOR TSUNAMIS
(1940 - 1990)

Date/Source	Hawaii	Alaska	West Coast	Samoa
April 1, 1946 Aleutian Islands	$26,000,000 159 deaths	Some 5 deaths	Moderate 1 death	
November 4, 1952 Kamchatka, USSR	$1,000,000	Slight		Minor
March 9, 1957 Aleutian Islands	$5,000,000	Severe	Minor	Minor
May 22, 1960 S. Chile	$24,000,000	Minor	$1,000,000	Minor
March 28, 1964 Gulf of Alaska	$15,000	$86,000,000 107 deaths	$12,000,000 16 deaths	

Figure 17

Most of the loss of life and damage to property during the Alaska earthquake of 1964 was caused by waves that inundated coastal communities. Some of the waves were of the tsunami type, some were seiches, and some were caused by submarine sliding including slides from the margins of deltas.

The term "tsunami," a Japanese word meaning "harbor wave," has become the accepted name for this phenomenon. Although tsunamis are often called tidal waves, the latter term is incorrect because tsunamis are not caused by the tidal action of the moon and the sun.

The waves triggered by an earthquake or volcano travel outward in all directions from the generating area, traveling at speeds of 300 to 600 miles per hour in the deep and open ocean. The distance between successive crests can be as much as 300 to 400 miles. In deep water, the height of the waves may be no more than 1-2 feet and may pass a surface vessel unnoticed. However, upon reaching shallower waters around islands or on a continental shelf, the speed of the advancing wave diminishes, its length decreases and its height increases greatly (possibly to more than 60 feet) as the water piles up along the shoreline. The advancing turbulent wave front of a tsunami may crash inland, sweeping all before it, sometimes beaching boats and ships thousands of feet inland.

Seiches, long waves created in enclosed bodies of water, are usually caused by unusual tides, winds or currents, but in certain circumstances are produced by earthquake ground motion. Such seiche waves can be destructive to facilities along the water's shoreline, or inland, may damage sewage and water storage basins. Seiching occurred in several areas during the 1964 Alaskan earthquake. At one end of a lake, a seiche caused water to run inland for at least 366 feet with initial runup heights of 30 feet. The Alaskan earthquake produced seiching as far away as Michigan, along with well agitation to the Gulf of Mexico, along with surges that caused some damage to Mississippi River barge moorings.

Volcano

Definition

An eruption from the earth's interior producing lava flows or violent explosions issuing rock, gases and debris

National Frequency

Among the known risk areas, volcanic eruptions occur more frequently in Hawaii.

Regions at Risk

The primary areas affected include the Pacific Rim States of Hawaii, Alaska, Washington, Oregon and California and the Commonwealth of Northern Marianas in the Western Pacific. Montana and Wyoming are also at risk, but to a much lesser extent.

Season(s)

Year round

Effects

Violent volcanic outbursts are characterized by clouds of poisonous gasses, rivers of lava and volcanic ash that can spread over wide areas. Major eruptions can result in heavy layers of ash covering widespread land areas, as witnessed following the eruption of Mt. St. Helens. Volcanic activity can also trigger tsunamis, landslides, floods (from the damming effects of slides or lava) and fires.

Worst Event

The eruption of Mount St. Helens in southwestern Washington on May 18, 1980, caused 60 deaths and approximately $1.5 billion in damage.

Discussion

All of the areas in the United States where volcanic action has occurred in the last 10,000 years are located west of the Rocky Mountains and thus could pose potential future hazards *(see Figure 18).*

Besides the Mount St. Helens event, other recent eruptions have occurred in Alaska's Mount Augustine in 1976 and 1986 and Mount Redoubt in 1989 and 1990. Hawaii's Kilauea and Mauna Loa have been relatively active in recent years. For the past seven years, Kilauea has posed a continuous threat to the surrounding population. Mauna Loa, on the same island, has been less active with a major eruption in 1950 and ones of smaller magnitude in 1975 and 1984. The Commonwealth of Northern Marianas has three active volcanos. Mt. Pagan erupted in 1981.

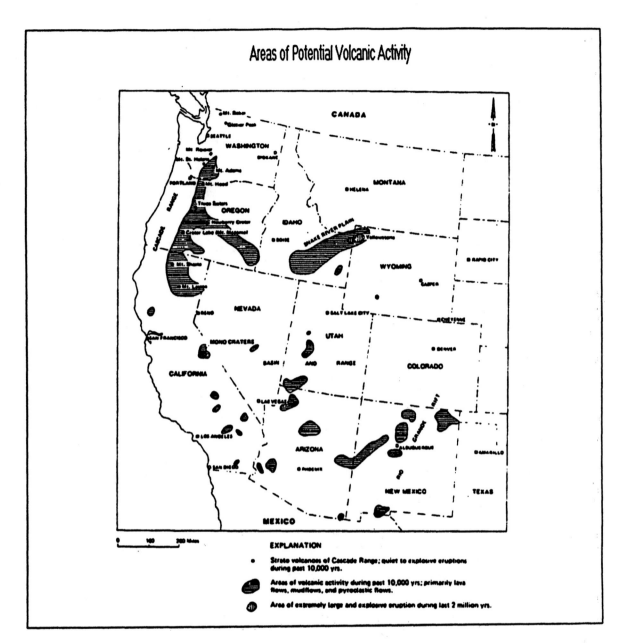

Figure 18

About 500 volcanoes have had recorded eruptions within historical times. Most volcanoes occur at the boundaries of the earth's
crustal plates, such as the famous "Ring of Fire" that surrounds
the Pacific Ocean Plate. Of the world's active volcanoes, about 60
percent are along the perimeter of the Pacific. (Source: *Earthquakes, Volcanoes, and Tsunamis—An Anatomy of Hazards, by
Karl V. Steinbrugge. Skandia America Group, 1982. pp. 259-274.)*

Wildfire

Definition

Any instance of uncontrolled burning in grasslands, brush or woodlands

National Frequency

According to the U.S. Forest Service, 1990 saw a total of 122,763 wildfires, resulting in 5,454,773 acres burned. *Figure 19* shows the wildfires that occurred between 1984 and 1990.

Regions at Risk

All wooded, brush and grassy areas—especially those in Kansas, Mississippi, Louisiana, Georgia, Florida, the Carolinas, Tennessee, California, Massachusetts and the National forests in the western States.

Season(s)

Wildfires occur most often in the Spring, Summer and Fall.

Effects

The annual death and economic damage rates have not been determined. Secondary events of wildfires would be soil erosion and subsequent landslides following heavy rains.

Worst Event

The worst single event in terms of deaths was the 1871 wildfire in Wisconsin where 1,182 people died. The worst single wildfire season in six decades, in terms of response effort, occurred in 1988 with Federal expenditures of $538 million for combating fires in widespread areas of the West where 6,000 soldiers and marines and nearly 4,000 temporary workers assisted the 20,000 professional firefighters on the line. The wildfires in the hills of Oakland, California are probably the worst in terms of property loss, with the fire resulting in $1.5 *billion* in damages.

Discussion

The Summer and Fall of 1991, wildfires were common in the Western states, including California, Montana, Colorado, Oregon and Washington. Perhaps the most dramatic were the October wildfires that swept through an area of over 1,800 acres in the hills of Oakland and Berkeley, California. Fires killed 26 people, injured 148 and left 5,000 people homeless. The destruction of almost 2,000 homes and apartments resulted in property damage of $1.5 billion, one of the largest disasters to hit the State. These fires dramatize the threat that wildfires pose to both urban and rural areas.

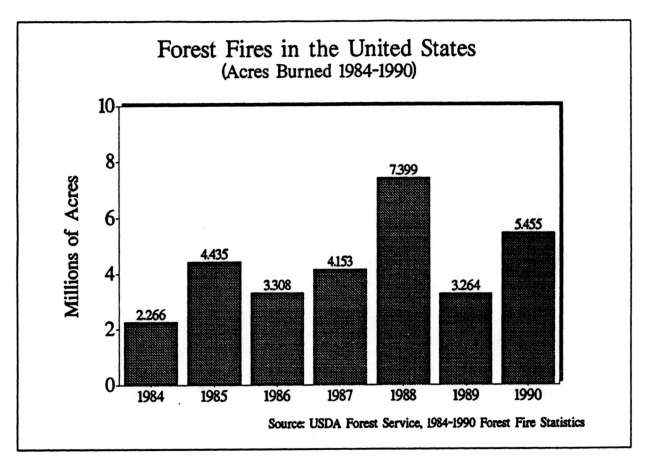

Figure 19

Winter Storm (Severe)

Definition

Ice storm, blizzard and extreme cold. Vulnerable areas would be subject to heavy snowfall, combined snow and high winds or ice storms.

National Frequency

None has been determined. The winter storm season varies widely depending upon the area's latitude, altitude and proximity to moderating influences.

Regions at Risk

Almost the entire United States except Hawaii and the Territories are at risk. The level of risk depends on the normal severity of local winter weather. Winter storms known as "northeasters" cause extensive coastal flooding, erosion and property loss in the northeastern and middle Atlantic States.

Season(s)

Winter, although some may occur in the late Fall and early Spring.

Effects

Between 1988 and 1991, the National Weather Service recorded a total of 372 deaths that could be attributed to snow, ice storms and extreme cold weather, an average of 93 deaths per year. In 1991, winter snows and blizzards were responsible for the deaths of 37 people, with injuries to 350 nationwide. Ice storms killed 8 and created economic damage estimated at almost a half billion dollars nationwide.

In the aftermath of winter storms, the weight of snow can cause structural failures; for example, in 1978 the roof of the Hartford Civic Center in Connecticut collapsed following back-to-back blizzards. The spring thaw of heavy winter snowfalls and river ice jams can cause floods. The estimated damage from flooding resulting from melting ice jams is more than $200 million a year.

Worst Event

The worst event was an 1888 East Coast blizzard when 400 deaths were recorded.

Discussion

Some areas of the country tend to be more susceptible than others to severe winter storms. Generally, the regions where harsh winters are common are more prepared for severe winter weather. Those areas where such weather is rare are more likely to experience disruptions when winter storms impact.

TECHNOLOGICAL/MAN-MADE THREATS

Technological/man-made threats represent a category of events that has expanded dramatically throughout this century with the advancements in modern technology. Like natural threats, they can affect localized or widespread areas, are frequently unpredictable, can cause substantial loss of life (besides the potential for damage to property), and can pose a significant threat to the infrastructure of a given area. In this category are those social threats that primarily come from actions by external, hostile forces against the land, population or infrastructure of the United States, or from domestic civil disturbances. Technological/man-made threats include civil disorder, hazardous materials incidents at fixed facilities and in transport accidents, power failures, radiological incidents at fixed facilities or in-transit accidents, missile attack, nuclear attack, structural fires, telecommunications failures, terrorism, and transportation accidents.

Civil Disorder

Definition Any incident, the intent of which is to disrupt a community to the degree that police intervention is required to maintain public safety. Terrorist attacks, riots, strikes that lead to violence and demonstrations resulting in police intervention and arrests are included in this category.

National Frequency Undetermined

Regions at Risk Nationwide

Season(s) Civil disorders may occur at any time.

Effects The effects of this threat can vary based upon the type of event and its severity and range. Loss of life and property as well as disruptions in services such as electricity, water supply, public transportation, communications, etc., could result from civil disorder. *Figure 20* lists the insured losses from past major civil disturbances in the U.S. Certain types of facilities are more vulnerable than others during civil disorders. These include Federal, State and local government buildings, universities, military bases, abortion clinics, nuclear power facilities and correctional facilities.

Most Costly Civil Disturbances
(Insured Losses Adjusted to 1992 Dollars)

Disturbance	Date	Cost (92 Dollars)
Los Angeles	April 28 - May 1, 1992	$ 775 Million
Los Angeles	August 11-17, 1965	$183 Million
Detroit	July 23, 1967	$16 Million
Miami	May 17-19, 1980	$103 Million
New York City	July 13-14, 1977	$90 Million
Newark	July 12, 1967	$59 Million
Baltimore	April 6-9, 1968	$53 Million
Chicago	April 4-11, 1968	$49 Million
Washington, D.C.	April 4-9, 1968	$45 Million
New York City	April 4-11, 1968	$15 Million

Source: Insurance Information Institute

Figure 20

Discussion   A civil disorder is an incident of collective violence interfering with the peace, security, and normal functioning of the community. They are public in character although, like institutional disorders, they may take place in a restricted setting. Although on occasion they begin with surprising suddenness and develop with alarming speed and intensity, mass disorders are always outgrowths of their particular social context. Indications of such occurrences, though often ignored at the time, can be clearly detected by hindsight. Civil disorders can develop out of legitimate expressions of protest, lawfully organized and conducted. Many such are symptomatic of deep-seated tensions in community relationships; when a precipitating event occurs, these tensions erupt into violence. The immediate, official response to disorder must be to restore order and allow the normal functioning of the community; only a long-range strategy can remove the root causes of disorder and ensure that it will not recur when emergency constraints have been lifted.

Until 1992, the likelihood of disturbances comparable to those that occurred in the 1960s appeared low. However, the riots that erupted in Los Angeles, Las Vegas, San Francisco and other cities after the "Rodney King Verdict" of April 28, acquitting four Los Angeles police officers from accusations of police brutality, brought the issue of civil disorder to new prominence. The worst disturbance, the riot in Los Angeles, ranks as the biggest civil disturbance in the nation's history taking 52 lives with over $1 billion dollars in damage to property.

Even if the 1992 civil disturbances are considered an aberration, communities are faced every year with incidents at political demonstrations and special public events which tax the capabilities of local law enforcement organizations. Local communities should plan to establish links with State and Federal sources of support in case of overwhelming crisis.

Hazardous Materials Incident - Fixed Facility

Definition

Uncontrolled release of hazardous materials from a fixed site

National Frequency

In 1988, 6.2 billion pounds of environmental releases and offsite transfers of chemical wastes were reported by 19,762 manufacturing facilities which submitted 79,343 individual chemical release reports. While more facilities (5 percent) submitted more forms (7 percent), total releases and transfers decreased 11 percent from 1987 to 1988. Facilities in the Gulf Coast, Great Lakes and mid-Atlantic States and California had the largest number of releases. The Rocky Mountain and Great Plains States generated smaller amounts. Ten states accounted for over half of the total releases and transfers. Facilities in Louisiana reported the largest amount of releases (12 percent of the national total) with those in Texas coming in a close second.

Regions at Risk

All areas of the U.S. where hazardous materials facilities exist are at risk to this hazard. Jurisdictions with hazardous materials fabrication, processing, storage sites, hazardous waste treatment storage or disposal sites are at risk.

Season(s)

Year round

Effects

The designated chemicals cover a wide range of toxicity and many have minimal or no effects on humans in small doses. Further, release does not necessarily mean there was exposure to humans. In accordance with data maintained by the U.S. Coast Guard's National Response Center, there were 279 reports of hazardous material releases at fixed facilities which injured 537 people and killed 15 in 1990 (as of December 13). The 4-year annual averages are 280 for incidents, 637 for injuries and 24 for deaths (*Figure 21*).

Worst Event

An incident, which included a release of radioactive material, occurred at the Kerr-McGee plant in Oklahoma in 1986, resulting in one death and the hospitalization of 100 people. In addition, 1,000 people were contaminated in Erwin, Tennessee, at a nuclear fuel plant in 1979.

Discussion

The principal reporting of these incidents falls under the terms of the Emergency Planning and Right to Know Act of 1986 which requires reporting to the Environmental Protection Agency (EPA) releases of 308 specific chemicals in 20 chemical categories. This input serves as the basis for the Toxics Release Inventory maintained by the EPA. The different types of releases include:

- emissions of gases or particles to the air;
- wastewater discharges into rivers and other bodies of water;
- solid waste disposal in on-site landfills;
- injection of wastes into underground wells;
- transfers of wastewaters to public sewage plants; and
- transfers of wastes to off-site facilities for treatment or storage.

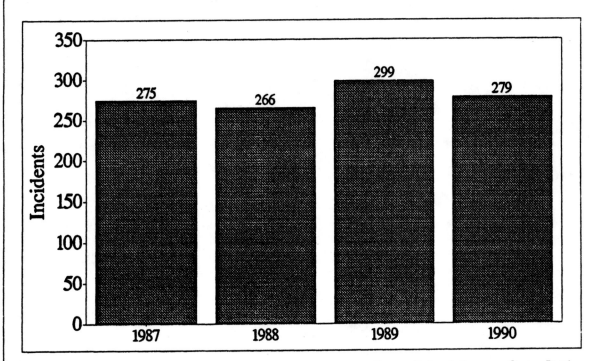

Hazardous Material Releases/Spills at Fixed Facilities
(As Reported to the National Response Center)

Source: National Response Center Database

Figure 21

Hazardous Materials Incident - Transportation

Definition Uncontrolled release of hazardous materials during transport

National Frequency Between 1982 and 1991, there were an annual average of 6,774 hazardous materials transportation incidents. In 1991, there were 9,069 incidents.

Regions at Risk Areas at risk would be along highways, rail lines, pipe lines, rivers and port areas. Because major highways run through virtually all local jurisdictions, every section of the country is at risk.

Season(s) There is no season for these incidents but, since highway-related incidents account for 83 percent of the total, factors such as weather conditions do influence the patterns of occurrence.

Effects In 1991, there were 10 deaths and 436 injuries as a result of hazardous materials transport incidents. The damage caused was estimated to cost over $38 million. These raw figures do not reveal losses that may go over a year, like the economic losses of the Sacramento River fishing industry after a 1991 chemical spill into the river, or the disruptions caused by evacuations, as in the 1992 Nemadji river spill.

Worst Event Definitive data unavailable

Discussion There are a variety of Federal and State mechanisms for reporting incidents involving the transportation of hazardous materials. The major source of data related to interstate transportation incidents is the U.S. Department of Transportation (DOT). Data from this source for the years 1982 through 1991, shown in *Figure 22*, clearly indicate that the great majority of incidents occurred in highway transportation and that such incidents were responsible for the preponderance of resultant deaths and injuries.

HAZARDOUS MATERIAL INCIDENTS BY TRANSPORTATION MODE
(TOTALS, 1982 - 1991)

MODE OF TRANSPORTATION	NUMBER OF INCIDENTS	ASSOCIATED DEATHS	ASSOCIATED INJURIES	ESTIMATED DAMAGES
Air	1,607	0	190	$1,825,288
Highway	55,172	106	2,006	$156,178,344
Rail	9,906	1	538	$64,540,964
Water	103	1	36	$1,065,244
Freight Forwarder	923	0	56	$234,171
Other	29	0	2	$10,425
Totals	67,740	108	2,828	$223,854,436

Source: Department of Transportation

Figure 22

Missile Attack

Definition

Attack by "any missile which does not rely upon aerodynamic surfaces to produce lift and consequently follows a ballistic trajectory when thrust is terminated." (JCS Publication 1, Dictionary of Military and Associated Terms) Ballistic missiles are divided into the classes of short-range (less than 600 nautical miles), medium-range (600 to 1500 miles), intermediate-range (1500 to 3000 miles), and intercontinental (3,000 to 8,000 miles) missiles.

National Frequency

No domestic incident has occurred. Ballistic missiles have been used against U.S. interests abroad.

Regions at Risk

All areas of the U.S. are potentially at risk from those nations with an intercontinental ballistic missile capability and a hostile intent to use them.

Season(s)

An attack could occur at any time of the year.

Effects

While most ballistic missiles have limited payloads, the force that accumulates from their travel can still lead to considerable destruction of military targets and urban areas. The addition of chemical, biological or nuclear warheads to ballistic missiles can make their use even more devastating.

Discussion

In the past, the use of ballistic missiles was largely associated with nuclear attack. In recent years, however, the worldwide proliferation of ballistic missiles led it to become an issue in conventional warfare. Libya fired missiles at the Mediterranean US military base at Lampedusa in 1986. Iraq's dramatic use of the Scud (a direct descendant of the World War II era V-2 missile) in the 1991 Gulf War led to several American military deaths. Iraq's use of its Scud missiles has also provided a lesson to other small nations in the relative ease of use and concealment capabilities of ballistic missiles.

Figure 23 lists the nations that currently have some sort of deployed missile capability. (Some countries with notable developmental efforts, like India's *Agni* ballistic missile project, are not on the list.) Few countries, besides the declared nuclear powers, currently have the capability to send missiles that can reach US territory. Still, as military analyst Edward N. Luttwak notes: *"a country that can manufacture missiles with a range of say, 300 kilometers will not generally encounter great difficulties in producing ballistic missiles with a range of 600 kilometers and may well be*

Land-Based Surface to Surface Missile Inventories
(Excludes Coastal Defense Forces)

	ICBMs (5550 to 14,800 Km)	IRBMs (2750 to 5550 Km)	MRBMs (1100 to 2750 Km)	SRBMs (‹ 1100 Km)
US	●			●
Belgium				●
France		●		●
Germany				●
Italy				●
Netherlands				●
United Kingdom		●		●
Bulgaria				●
Czechoslovakia				●
Hungary				●
Poland				●
Romania				●
Serbia/Montenegro				●
Russia**	●			●
Belarus**	●			●
Ukraine**	●			●
Kazakhstan**	●			●
Tajikistan*				●
Turkmenistan*				●
Uzbekistan*				●
Pakistan				●
Afghanistan				●
China	●		●	●
Japan				●
North Korea				●
South Korea				●
Egypt				●
Iran				●
Israel			●	●
Libya				●
Saudi Arabia			●	
Syria				●
Yemen				●

* Forces currently under joint Republic/Commonwealth of Independent States control
** Strategic nuclear forces currently under the centralized control of the Commonwealth of Independent States

Source: IISS, The Military Balance 1992-1993

Figure 23

able to acquire missiles with a range of 6,000 kilometers - without having to overcome the enormous barriers, both political and operational, that constitute such a secure fire wall between tactical and strategic airpower." In any event, a number of nations already have, or will soon get, the ability to reach the territory of US allies in Europe, the Middle East and Asia.

There have been efforts to restrict the proliferation of missile technology through the establishment of the Missile Technology Control Regime. There is enough indigenous technical capability in the Third World, however, to ensure that some will try to develop intercontinental missiles over the next decade to reach the US.

A more ominous missile threat could come from the move to develop air-breathing cruise missiles. Cruise missiles could offer Third World countries a cheaper and more flexible alternative to the acquisition of ballistic missiles. If the terrain data needed by cruise missiles became easily available through commercial geographic information firms, the major obstacle to the widespread development of cruise missiles would be eliminated.

Nuclear Attack

Definition

Any hostile action taken against the United States by foreign forces which results in destruction of military and/or civilian targets through use of nuclear weapons.

National Frequency   No U.S. occurrence.

Regions at Risk

Any area of the U.S. is potentially at risk from either direct blast effects or secondary effects from fire, radioactive fallout and electromagnetic pulse.

Season(s)

An attack could occur at any time of the year.

Effects

The effects of a nuclear attack, even one limited to just a few targets in the US, would be catastrophic and far reaching. Millions of lives could be at risk to the effects of blast overpressure, fire, direct radiation and radioactive fallout. The loss of property and infrastructure would be catastrophic, causing national repercussions far beyond the limited area directly affected.

Discussion

There has been a considerable reduction in recent years in the nuclear attack threat facing the nation, due to the establishment of a number of arms control agreements. The July 1991 signing of the Strategic Arms Reduction Treaty (START), marked the first US/Soviet arms control agreement that actually *reduced* the number of strategic nuclear weapons held by each side. In October 1991, the Presidents of both the United States and Soviet Union promised to eliminate unilaterally their stocks of short-range tactical nuclear weapons.

When the Soviet Union suddenly fell apart in December 1991, there was some concern about what would happen, not only to the arms control treaties the U.S.S.R. agreed to, but also to the vast arsenal of conventional and nuclear weapons now left to 15 individual republics. Still, it appears that events will work to keep the threat of a nuclear attack against the United States at an extremely low level for some time.

At its initiation, the Commonwealth of Independent States, the successor republics to the former Soviet Union, agreed to adhere to the arms control treaties that the Soviet Union entered into. They also agreed to send all of the tactical nuclear weapons on their territory to Russia, with the intent of eventually having the Russians destroy them. By

May 1992, this effort to transfer these weapons had been completed. In a protocol to the START treaty signed on May 24, 1992 in Lisbon, the nuclear-capable republics of the Ukraine, Kazakhstan and Belarus announced their willingness to give up nuclear weapons on their territory by 1999, and enter into the Nuclear Non-Proliferation Treaty as non-nuclear states renouncing the development of nuclear weapons.

The follow-up to the START treaty, now called START II, will make even more dramatic changes in strategic nuclear inventories of the U.S. and those of the former Soviet Union. Beginning at the completion of the START I reductions, START II makes major cuts in both the number of warheads and in the means they are delivered. By the year 2003 (or earlier if the U.S. provides financial aid to the Russians to dispose of weapons) the number of strategic nuclear warheads on both sides will be cut by two-thirds from pre-START levels. The START II treaty was signed by Presidents Bush and Yeltsin on January 3, 1993 and will take effect after the provisions of the START I treaty are completed. The United States ratified the START I treaty on October 1, 1992.

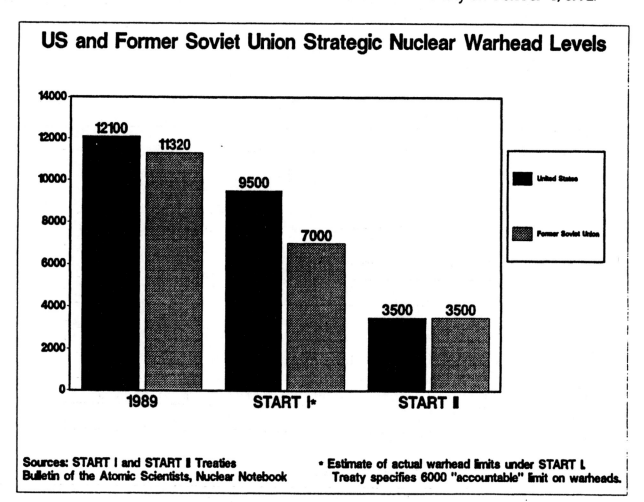

Figure 24

Figure 24 illustrates the considerable reduction in nuclear arsenals that the START treaties will bring. The implementation of the START I treaty will bring about a thirty percent cut in warheads. (While START I limits the signatories to 6000 "accountable" warheads, inclusion of those warheads not covered by the treaty brings the totals to approximately 9,500 warheads for the U.S. and 7,000 for those in the former Soviet Union. By the full implementation of the START II treaty, warhead levels will be at least 70 percent below those of a decade earlier. Besides the cut in warheads, the treaty's elimination of multi-warhead intercontinental land-based missiles will represent a major reduction in the strategic nuclear threat faced by the United States.

While the likelihood of the United States suffering a massive, coordinated nuclear attack diminishes as a possibility, a more limited nuclear attack threat still remains. *Figure* 25 lists estimates of the nuclear arsenals of the world's declared nuclear powers. Looking at the list, it is clear that while most of these nuclear arsenals are much smaller than that of the US, there are several that could inflict significant damage on the country through a strategic nuclear attack.

Estimated Strategic Nuclear Delivery Systems — 1992

	ICBMs	IRBMs	SLBMs	Bombers
Russia	1040		832	67
Ukraine	176			41
Kazakhstan	104			40
Belarus	54			
France		18	64	60
China	8	60	12	120
Britain			32	

Source: IISS, The Military Balance 1992-1993

Figure 25

Power Failure

Definition

Interruption or loss of electrical service for an extended period of time. An extended period of time would be long enough to require emergency management organization response to needs for food, water, heating, etc., caused by loss of power.

National Frequency

The North American Electric Reliability Council reports 30 incidents of electrical system disturbances, load reductions or unusual occurrences; 21 of them leading to an actual loss of customer service.

Effects

A summary of potential effects includes loss of power to hospital and medical care facilities which could cause life-threatening situations for patients because necessary medical care equipment would be inoperable (in the absence of working backup generators); massive traffic stoppages due to failures of traffic lights; spoilage of food; lack of heating/air conditioning for many residences/businesses; work interruptions since equipment cannot be used; curtailment of financial and commercial activity from the loss of major databases for security trading and credit checks; lack of potable water and polluted water because of inoperable water and sewage treatment facilities. The cost for repair to power systems and restoration of electricity as well as the economic and societal damage caused by a long-term blackout would be enormous. As an example, the 25-hour black out in New York City in 1977 cost approximately $345 million.

Worst Event

On November 9, 1965, a power failure in an Ontario plant blacked out parts of eight northeastern States and two provinces of Canada. More recently, recovery efforts in South Carolina were seriously hampered by widespread loss of electric power following Hurricane Hugo in September 1989.

Discussion

There are two classes of power failures: failures internal to the power distribution system such as occurred in New England in 1965 and failures from external causes such as severe storms.

The devastating effect on power systems by major natural disasters can cause widespread outages over a long period of restoration and recovery. Hurricanes affect distribution systems more than generation and transmission equipment with damage to power lines from falling trees, flooding and flying debris. Earthquakes can destroy both distribution systems and generation and transmission equipment. There is also a possible threat from geomagnetic storms arising from solar disturbances. A very strong geomagnetic storm on March 13, 1989 damaged voltage control equipment in Quebec, resulting in the collapse of nearly the entire system for a nine hour blackout. The same storm damaged several transformers in the United States, including a step-up unit at the Salem Nuclear Plant in New Jersey, which forced a six week shut down of the entire plant. There were three geomagnetic disturbances in 1991, but they did not lead to major damage to electrical systems.

Besides the natural threats, there is the possibility of power failure from sabotage. In recent years, there have been attacks against electric utilities in West Virginia, Kentucky, Colorado, California, Arizona and Puerto Rico. While most utilities have the ability to recover quickly from isolated acts of vandalism, a sophisticated group, using information found in public sources, could make a coordinated, multi-site attack on community power production with devastating effect. The effort to replace damaged equipment could take months. Some of the largest transformers can take up to a year to manufacture and, weighing up to 500 tons, must rely on a small number of rail cars capable of transporting them to the site of power generation.

Radiological Incident - Fixed Facility

Definition

Uncontrolled release of radioactive material at a commercial nuclear power plant or other reactor facility

Regions at Risk

Areas at risk are normally designated as: (1) within the *plume emergency planning zone* of such facilities (jurisdictions located within a 10-mile radius of a nuclear power plant) or (2) within the *ingestion emergency planning zone* (jurisdictions within a 50-mile radius of a nuclear power plant). About 38 states are affected, in particular the eastern half of the contiguous 48 States and the West Coast States. *Figure 26* shows the location of commercial nuclear reactor sites in the United States as of 1991.

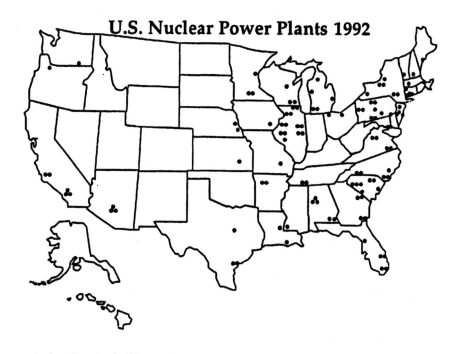

Figure 26

Season(s)

Year round

Effects

An incident could cause the release of radioactive materials into the atmosphere. Three dominant exposure modes to people have been identified: (a) whole body (bone marrow) exposure from external gamma radiation, (b) thyroid exposure from inhalation or ingestion of radioiodines and (c) exposure from ingestion of radioactive materials.

Worst Event

The nuclear power plant accident that occurred at the Three Mile Island Nuclear Power Plant in Pennsylvania on March 28, 1979, was the worst to date in the United States. While this incident caused no deaths, officials considered the possibility of evacuating 650,000 citizens within a 20-mile radius of the plant which is near Harrisburg.

Discussion

As a result of the incident at Three Mile Island, major changes were instituted in the regulation of the nuclear power industry. FEMA was given the responsibility for review and approval of State and local radiological emergency plans and preparedness for jurisdictions located near commercial nuclear power plants. *Figure 27* depicts events that occurred at nuclear reactor facilities during the period 1987-1991.

NUCLEAR REACTOR FACILITY EVENTS
1987-1991

Class of Event	Year 1987	1988	1989	1990	1991
Unusual Event	231	212	197	151	170
Alert	9	6	13	10	9
Site Area Emergency	0	1	0	1	2
General Emergency	0	0	0	0	0

Source: NRC, NUREG-1272

Figure 27

Structural Fires

Definition   Uncontrolled burning in residential, commercial, industrial or other properties in rural or developed areas

National Frequency   The National Fire Protection Association estimated that 640,500 structural fires occurred in the nation during 1991.

Regions at Risk   All areas are at risk to personal injury or property damage due to fire.

Season(s)   Year round, with the residential fire rate in January being twice that of the summer months

Effects   During 1991, there were 4,465 civilian fire deaths, 21,850 injuries, costing an estimated $8.3 billion dollars in fire-related losses. As summary of the year's worst events is presented in *Figure 28.*

Worst Multiple-Death Fires in U.S.— 1991

Date	Location	Type	Deaths
October 20	California	Oakland Wildfire	26
September 3	North Carolina	Chicken Processing Plant	25
February 1	California	Aircraft Collision	22
September 11	Texas	Aircraft	14
March 4	Colorado	Retirement Home	10
February 16	Connecticut	Three-Family Dwelling	10
December 9	Illinois	Apartment Building	10
June 17	South Carolina	Chemical Plant	9
May 1	Louisiana	Chemical Plant	8

Source: National Fire Protection Association

Figure 28

Worst Event   The "Chicago Fire" of 1871, which killed 1,152 people, burned 17,450 buildings and caused damages of $168 million, ranks as one of the worst urban fires in the country's history. A summary of the nation's worst fire disasters is given in *Figure 29.*

Worst Multiple-Death Fires in U.S. History

Date	Place	Deaths
April 27, 1865	S.S. Sultana (Mississippi River)	1,547
October 8, 1871	Great Chicago Fire	1,152
June 15, 1904	S.S. General Slocum (New York)	1,030
December 30, 1903	Iroquois Theater (Chicago)	602
October 12, 1918	Cloquet, MN	559
April 18, 1906	San Francisco Earthquake	500
November 28, 1942	Coconut Grove (Boston)	492
April 16, 1947	Texas City, TX	468
September 1, 1894	Hinkley, MN	413
June 30, 1900	Hoboken, NJ Pier	326

Source: Insurance Information Institute

Figure 29

Discussion

According to the FEMA United States Fire Administration (USFA), the fire problem in the United States is of major proportions and, comparatively, is one of the worst in the world in terms of relative populations. As reported by the United Nations World Health Organization in 1983, the United States, with 27 fire deaths per million persons per year, had the third highest ranking of the countries for which statistics were available. Only Scotland (32 deaths per million) and Canada (31 deaths per million) ranked higher. Nations reporting the lowest number of deaths included Germany/Spain (each with nine deaths per million), Italy (with seven deaths per million) and Switzerland (with five deaths per million).

Fire fatalities tend to be distributed according to population density, i.e., those States with the largest populations tend also to have the greatest number of fire fatalities. For example, ten States accounted for *52 percent* of the 5,514 recorded fires for 1987. While it is useful to know by State where the greatest number of fire deaths occur, it is perhaps even more useful to know in which States people face the greatest *personal risk* of death by fire. As the map in *Figure 30* illustrates in the checkered pattern, the areas with the worst fire death rates per million population during 1987 were the Southeast and the

States of Alaska, Maine, West Virginia and Delaware. While the States in the vertical and diagonal striped areas of the map have lower death rates than those in the checkered areas, they have fire death rates higher than most of the developed nations in Europe and the Far East. *Any one of these States would have the highest or the second highest death rate in the world if it were a separate country.*

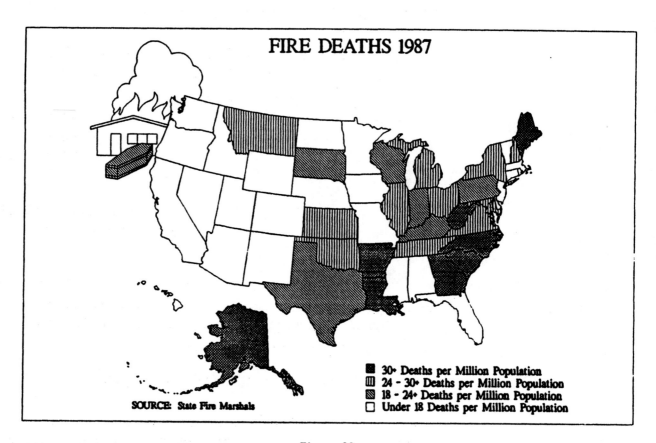

Figure 30

Terrorism

Definition

Terrorism is the unlawful use of force or violence against persons or property to intimidate or coerce a government, the civilian population, or any segment thereof, in furtherance of political or social objectives.

The FBI categorizes two types of terrorism in the United States:

- *Domestic terrorism* involves groups or individuals whose terrorist activities are directed at elements of our government or population without foreign direction.
- *International terrorism* involves terrorist activity committed by groups or individuals who are foreign-based and/or directed by countries or groups outside the United States or whose activities transcend national boundaries.

National Frequency

From the years 1983 through 1991, the Federal Bureau of Investigation (FBI) identified a total of 110 terrorist incidents that occurred in the United States (See *Figure 30*).

Regions at Risk

Nationwide. In recent years, the largest number of terrorist strikes occurred in the Western States and Puerto Rico. Attacks in Puerto Rico accounted for about 60 percent of all terrorist incidents between 1983 and 1991 that occurred on US territory.

Season(s)

A terrorist incident can occur at any time of the year.

Effects

A terrorist attack can take several forms, depending on the technological means available to the terrorist, the nature of the political issue motivating the attack, and the points of weakness of the terrorist's target. Among the possibilities are:

- **Bombing.** Most terrorist incidents in the US have involved bombing attacks, including detonated and undetonated explosive devices, tear gas, pipe and fire bombs and a rocket attack.
- **Airline Attack.** Despite efforts to improve airline security in the United States, some note that US airport security still falls short of necessary standards. Common practices such as curbside check-in of airline baggage and free access of non-passengers to airports create a considerable potential for airline related terrorist incidents to occur.

- While the introduction of more competition into the communications industry over the past decade has some benefits for the nation, there are also potential drawbacks. Different vendors frequently rely on incompatible operating systems, thus preventing one from serving as a backup for another. There is also the fact that the increased competition for telecommunications services based on lowest price diminishes the ability of vendors to spend more money on tight security.

- The development of firms establishing their own telecommunications networks could cause problems. Private telecommunications networks may not have the same degree of redundancy and security that the earlier national system had. Private telephone links are more likely to rely on the vagaries of commercial power, unlike the monopoly phone system of the past. Private networks will also rely more on standard "open" software systems that are more vulnerable to computer attack.

- Finally, as computer software becomes more complex, the likelihood of software bugs appearing in new software programs for telecommunications operations increases.

The vulnerability of the society to some form of telecommunications failure is inevitable. As the National Research Council notes: *"It is impossible to build systems that are guaranteed to be invulnerable to a high-grade threat, that is, a dedicated and resourceful adversary capable of and motivated to organize an attack as an industrial rather than an individual or small group enterprise."* Still, there is a considerable amount of work currently going on to establish security standards, as in the Defense Department's *Trusted Computer System Evaluation Criteria*, and the development of Computer Emergency Response Teams to deal with the consequences of telecommunications failure.

Telecommunications Failure

Definition

The failure of data transfer, communications or processing brought about by: 1) physical destruction of computers or communications equipment, or 2) a performance failure of software needed to run such equipment, either through bad design or sabotage.

National Frequency

Standards for reporting telecommunications failures are still being established. Since the beginning of 1990, there have been at least three major disruptions of long distance telephone service reported. In the summer of 1991, there were also a number of regional failures in telephone communications. In the matter of computers and computer networks, attacks against them have started to become common in the past two years, but there is no formal list of reported attacks.

Effects

Because of the dependence of firms and organizations on electronic access to data and the need to rely on computers to manage complex operating systems, any telecommunications failure can bring significant costs. The consequences of a telecommunications failure include:

- The reduction in, or perhaps complete termination of, business functions.

- A loss in business revenues.

- Increases in the cost of doing business.

- Intangible costs entailed in the loss of business image and customers, or even the possibility of making legal or regulatory violations as a result of the failure.

There are a number of examples of how the single fact of a telecommunications failure can lead to far-reaching effects. In November 1985, a computer problem at the offices of the Bank of New York prevented it from completing an exchange of government securities. This not only cost the bank $1.5 million after taxes, but the delay forced the bank to borrow $24 billion from the Federal Reserve System. The long-distance telephone failure that occurred in New York on September 17, 1991 led air traffic controllers at Newark, LaGuardia and JFK airport to halt flights, resulting in cancellation of 458 flights and affecting 31,000 passengers.

Worst Event

Definitive data are not available. However, among the most significant were the long-distance failure of January 16, 1990, when AT&T lost an estimated $75 million in revenue just from an inability to place calls. The costs in lost commerce from the nine-hour loss of service is assumed to reach hundreds of millions of dollars. The most disruptive computer attack was the Internet Worm in November 1988, which within a few hours had infected 6,200 research and government computers, including one at the Lawrence Livermore National Laboratory.

Discussion

Telecommunications hardware is not only subject to physical threats like flood and fire, but also to a number of electronic threats. Lightning can damage telecommunications equipment either through conduction of its direct current or an induced current from coupling or electromagnetic radiation, typically delivered through power lines. There are other sources of electromagnetic radiation like radars, radio and television broadcast antennas, motors, generators, arc welders, nuclear bursts and even other computers. Electrostatic discharge, a personal irritant on dry winter days to most people, can be devastating to electronic equipment. A measure of the potential problem is the estimate that the electronics industry suffers losses of up to $5 billion annually in both direct and indirect costs arising from the effects of electrostatic discharge on equipment reliability.

Computer software is another source of telecommunications failure. A number of the disruptions in long-distance and regional phone service was caused by installation of new, inadequately tested computer software packages. Weaknesses in software security also allow vandals, criminals and terrorists to gain access to important computer databases and control systems.

As the operation of modern society becomes more dependent on computerized databases and instant communications at intercontinental distances, a failure of telecommunications will have a much more devastating effect. Once electronic systems have been established in an organization, it becomes almost impossible to make a temporary return to manual procedures when systems fail. And there are trends that make the possibility of telecommunications failures much more common than they were in the past, including:

- Technological developments have allowed communications links to carry much more traffic on fewer lines. Network switches have also grown smaller while they increase their capacity. Both trends could limit the ability of the country to recover from a telecommunications failure. This reduction in the number of telecommunications links limits the number of alternative routes that could be used if one should fail. A trend towards greater centralization of communications switches will mean that the physical destruction of one center will cause more disruption than those of the past.

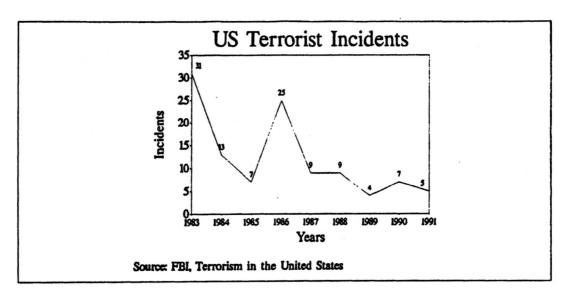

Figure 31

- **Chemical/Biological Attack.** Terrorists can use chemical or biological weapons to either extort or deliberately try to kill in order to further political goals. Toxins or even some radiological materials, like the water-soluble plutonium chloride, could become a credible threat to municipal water supplies.

- **Infrastructure Attack.** A group of terrorists could coordinate an attack against utilities and other public services. Modern society's dependence on automation allows the terrorist to target computers as a means of causing chaos. The recent revelation that Dutch computer hackers were able to successfully gain access to Defense Department computers at 34 different sites is an illustration of the immediacy of the danger.

The effects of the threats posed by terrorism can vary significantly in relationship to the size and scale of the event and its associated severity. At a minimum, disruptions can include property damage, disruptions in services such as electricity, water supply, public transportation, communications, etc., and loss of life.

Worst Event

One death and 19 injuries were attributed to domestic terrorism in 1986. No deaths or injuries have been recorded since then.

Discussion

Compared to other countries, there have been only a limited number of terrorist incidents that have occurred within the borders of the United States. Still, as the RAND Corporation's chronology of international terrorism notes, while North America has one of the lowest number of terrorist incidents, the United States stands as the number one target of international terrorist actions. And, as *Figure 32* illustrates, the past two decades have witnessed a general increase in re-

Trends in International Terrorism

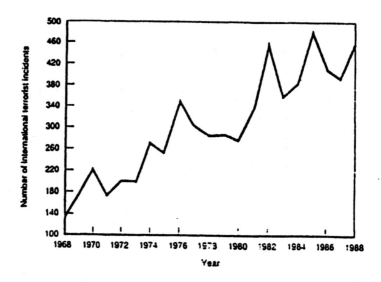

Figure 32

corded terrorist incidents in the world. Terrorists overseas, like Yu Kikumura of the Japanese Red Army, have already started to look for opportunities to make their point on American territory. Inevitably, increasing numbers of America's local emergency managers will have to face the task of dealing with the consequences of terrorist actions.

Besides a possible increase in the frequency of terrorist incidents, each incident is likely to become more difficult to manage. Terrorists have started to become more technically accomplished in recent years. Among the terrorists participating in the 1988 hijacking of a Kuwait Airlines jet was a trained pilot. The Chukakuha of Japan provided an example of high-tech terrorism in November 1985 by simultaneously cutting the communications and control cables of the Japanese National Railroad at 30 different locations. Thirteen million rail passengers and 30,000 tons of freight were stranded at an estimated cost of 2 billion yen. In the future, such attempts to attack the nation's infrastructure are expected to become more common.

While the FBI recorded only five terrorist incidents in 1991, it still noted that:

> *Despite this positive trend, we cannot conclude that the threat of terrorism in the United States has been eliminated. Throughout the world, the political and social events and conditions which spawn terrorism still remain. Also, there exists an infrastructure in the United States which could support either domestic or international terrorism.*

Transportation Accidents

Definition   An incident involving air or rail travel resulting in death or injury

National Frequency According to the National Transportation Safety Board, large commercial scheduled airlines registered four fatal accidents in 1991, with a total of 50 fatalities. For scheduled airlines, there was a slight increase in the ratio of accidents per 100,000 flight hours for the year (see *Figure 33*). Commuter aircraft were responsible for 77 fatalities in eight fatal accidents. In general aviation, the Safety Board reports a total of 2,143 accidents, with a record low 745 general aviation fatalities 1991.

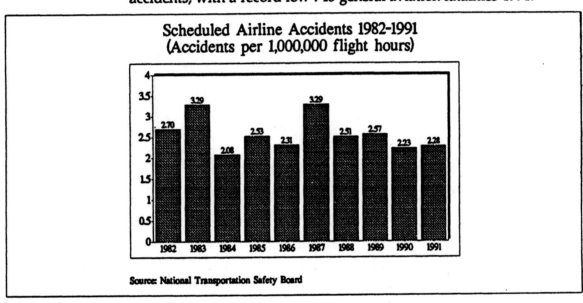

Source: National Transportation Safety Board

Figure 33

Accident reports maintained by the Federal Railroad Administration reveal that there were 25,911 train accidents/incidents in 1991, continuing the decline in accidents over recent years (see *Figure 34*). There has also been a decline in casualties per miles traveled, dropping from 49.40 casualties per million train miles in 1986, down to 42.75 casualties per million miles in 1991. Train accidents and incidents during 1991 were estimated to have caused losses totaling $222 million dollars.

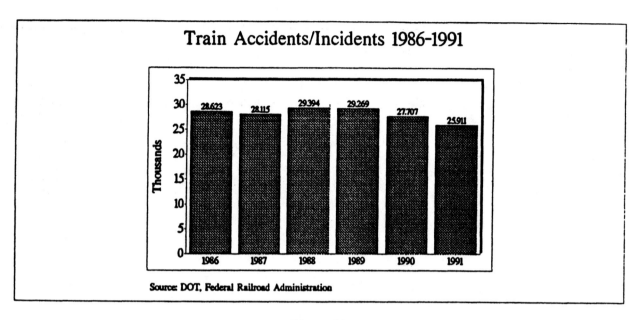

Source: DOT, Federal Railroad Administration

Figure 34

Regions at Risk   All areas of the country are at risk to transportation incidents. Risk areas would be around airports with Federal Aviation Administration control towers or with traffic flow heavy enough to pose a hazard and passenger rail lines. The greatest risk involves those local jurisdictions with airports, rail lines and major highway systems.

Season(s)   Year round

Effects   Effects can include loss of life, associated property losses and fire.

Worst Event   This accident occurred on May 25, 1979, at Chicago's O'Hare Airport when an American Airlines DC-10 lost its left engine upon take-off and crashed seconds later, killing all 272 people aboard and 3 on the ground.

Discussion   There are two circumstances in air transport which trigger a disaster response: an airliner crashing in a populated area, such as happened over Cerritos, California, in 1986 as the result of a collision with a private aircraft and a takeoff or landing accident such as occurred in Washington, D.C., in 1982 and Sioux City, Iowa, in 1989.

Apart from the actual rescue operations, the Washington, D.C., crash highlighted two problems. First, there was a multi-jurisdictional response and a lack of coordination capability, even to the extent there were no common radio frequencies for communications. Second, while this rescue operation was underway, there was another fatal accident involving a subway train which placed an added severe strain on the District of Columbia's disaster response resources.

In terms of loss of life, there have been two serious railroad accidents in the past 20 years. The first was in Chicago in 1972 when one commuter train plowed into the back of another, causing 45 deaths and over 200 injuries. (A saving factor can be attributed to the location of the accident—in the backyard of a major hospital which had participated in a disaster drill the preceding day.) The second occurred in Chase, Maryland, in 1987 when a train derailment resulted in the death of 16 people.

RANKING OF THE THREATS

In its direction to FEMA, the Committee stated that it:

"...understands that certain natural and manmade disasters threaten communities with a varying degree of severity and frequency..." and specifically requested that the study, "...rank the principal threats to the population according to region and any other factors deemed appropriate."

However, it is important to note that any ranking of the threats to communities and emergency management coordinators is potentially misleading because of: (1) the wide variations that can occur with the application of different criteria to the same threat, (2) the significant differences that can occur from the impact of a particular threat on a region and the individual States within that region, (3) the fact that threats in one region are not necessarily applicable to another region, (4) variances in the types of data collected on each threat and (5) the lack of available data in some cases with which to develop a reasoned ranking. As anthropologist Mary Douglas noted: *"A risk is not only the probability of an event but also the probable magnitude of its outcome, and everything depends on the value that is set on the outcome. The evaluation is a political, aesthetic, and moral matter."*

Still, there is some use to trying to determine the comparative threats presented by the hazards facing the nation. By using different criteria of loss to rank hazards, a general picture of the most severe threats to the nation can be created. In the study below, the nation's threats are ranked by:

- The reports from local jurisdictions on the threats they face.
- The average annual loss of life caused by each type of hazard.
- The severity of the death toll caused by the worst instance of each type of disaster.
- The number and types of disasters requiring a Presidential declaration to provide Federal recovery assistance.
- The economic loss caused by each hazard.

Figure 35 illustrates the results of using these different methods of ranking hazards. The lack of a consistent pattern of results between the various methods of ranking shows the difficulties in arriving at a single definition of what are actually the most dangerous hazards facing the communities across the nation.

THREAT RANKINGS BY VARIOUS CRITERIA

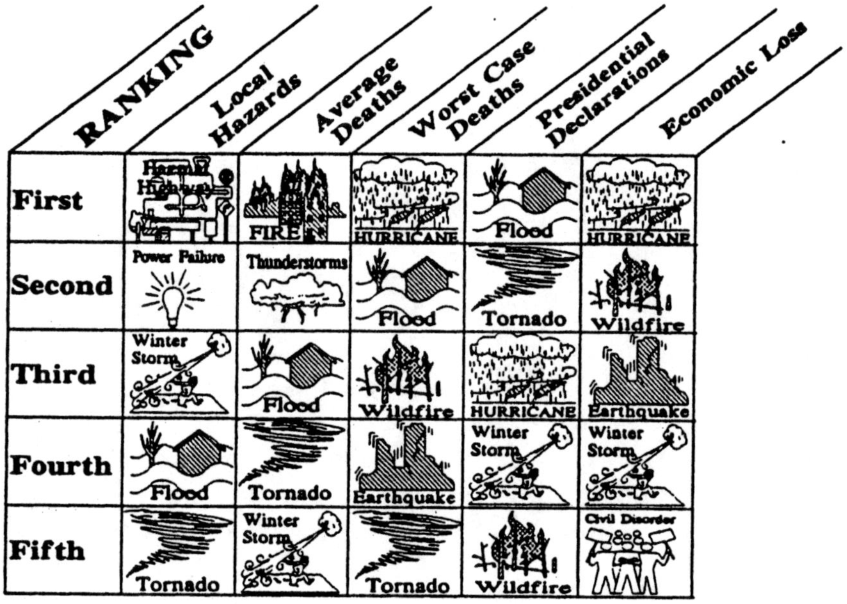

Figure 35

Local Hazard Identification

In a survey periodically conducted by FEMA, local emergency managers themselves identify the hazards that threaten their communities. They report on the hazards that could potentially strike their community. *Figure 36* ranks the 26 hazards listed in the FEMA 1992 survey by the number of communities that cited them as threats. *Hazardous Materials Incident — Highway* was mentioned the most as a possible threat. Second most mentioned was *Power Failure*. The next most mentioned hazards were *Winter Storm, Flood, and Tornado.*

Annual Deaths

If the ranking was to be based on the average annual number of deaths alone, the rankings would change dramatically. Even though the data on deaths are relatively incomplete (data are only available on one-third of the hazards on an annual basis and one-half on a worst case basis), the top five threats based on the number of deaths for 1991 would be: *(1) urban fires—4,465 deaths, (2) thunderstorms—105 deaths, (3) floods—61 deaths, (4) tornadoes—39 deaths, (5) winter storms—37 deaths.*

Potential Hazards
Identified by Local Emergency Managers
(Ranked by Number of Responses)

1. Hazardous Materials Incident — Highway
2. Power Failure
3. Winter Storm
4. Flood
5. Tornado
6. Drought
7. Radiological Incident — Transportation
8. Hazardous Materials Incident — Fixed Facility
9. Urban Fire
10. Hazardous Materials Incident — Rail
11. Wildfire
12. Hazardous Materials Incident — Pipeline
13. Civil Disorder
14. Earthquake
15. Air Transport Incident
16. Dam Failure
17. Hazardous Materials Incident — River
18. Rail Transportation Incident
19. Hurricane/Tropical Storm
20. Subsidence
21. Radiological Incident — Fixed Facility
22. Nuclear Attack
23. Landslide
24. Avalanche
25. Volcano
26. Tsunami

Source: FEMA, CPG 1-35,
Capability Assessment and
Hazard Identification Program
for Local Governments, 1992

Figure 36

**Worst Case
Deaths**

The difference is even more dramatic when compared to a ranking based on the **worst-case deaths.** Based on this data, the rankings would be as follows: *(1) hurricanes—6,000 deaths from the Galveston, Texas hurricane in 1900, (2) floods—2,209 deaths from the Johnstown, Pennsylvania flood in 1889, (3) wildfires—1,182 deaths from a wildfire in Wisconsin in 1871, (4) earthquakes—700 deaths from the San Francisco, California earthquake in 1906, (5) tornadoes—with 689 deaths in 1925.*

**Presidential
Declarations**

An examination of Presidential disaster declarations, as a measure of the most severe disasters over a ten year period gives the following ranking of hazards. *Severe storms and flooding (153 declarations)* would rank first in terms of hazards to the nation's communities. *Tornadoes* and their associated effects would rank second, with a total of *63 declarations* over the period. *Hurricanes and typhoons (a combined total of 17 declarations)* ranks third. *Severe winter weather (8 declarations)* and *fires (6 declarations)* rank fourth and fifth respectively. *(See Figure 37).*

PRESIDENTIAL DISASTER DECLARATIONS
January 1983 through December 1992

Hazard	No. of Declarations
Severe Storms & Flooding	153
Tornadoes	63
Hurricanes/Typhoons	50
Severe Winter Weather	17
Fires	8
Earthquakes	6
Other	3
Total	300

Source: FEMA, Office of Disaster Assistance

Figure 37

Economic Loss

And finally, if rankings are prepared on the basis of economic loss alone, the list changes yet again. While there are a number of estimates on the annual loss, they come from disparate sources with wildly varying degrees of accuracy. Relying on these annual loss estimates for a comparison between hazards would be misleading. There can be a estimate of the losses from actual disasters, though, providing an accurate comparison between damage caused in the nation's most devastating incidents. *Figure 38* gives an estimate of the largest cases of insured losses caused by disasters. In terms of economic loss, the greatest hazards are caused by *(1) hurricanes, (2) wildfire, (3) earthquakes, (4) winter storms, and (5) civil disorder.*

Ten Most Costly Insured Disasters

Date	Disaster	Estimated Insured Loss
August 1992	Hurricane Andrew	$10.7 Billion
September 1989	Hurricane Hugo	$4.2 Billion
September 1992	Hurricane Iniki	$1.6 Billion
October 1991	Oakland, CA Wildfire	$1.2 Billion
October 1989	Loma Prieta Earthquake	$960 Million
December 1983	Winter Storms (41 States)	$880 Million
April 1992	Los Angeles Riots	$775 Million
September 1979	Hurricane Frederic	$753 Million
August 1983	Hurricane Alicia	$676 Million
July 1990	Denver, CO Storms	$625 Million

Source: Insurance Information Institute

Figure 38

Summary

This review of the greatest dangers facing the nation shows that it is difficult to develop a single list enumerating the relative threat posed by each hazard compared to all others. Still, a sense of priorities does emerge. Natural hazards, particularly the meteorological ones, dominate in the review. Fire and hazardous material incidents also consistently show up in the rankings as major threats.

Floods represent an ever-present threat to people and property in every State of the nation. The average annual figure for economic damage from floods, derived from losses during the years 1981-1990, is *2.2 billion*. Perhaps the most pervasive of the natural hazards, floods affect all regions of the country to varying degrees. The Upper Northwest, including Washington, Oregon, Alaska, Idaho, Montana and Wyoming, has the lowest percentage of flood-prone areas, totaling 0-5 percent of the total land area of these States. The midwestern region, comprised of the States of North Dakota, South Dakota, Nebraska, Iowa, Missouri, Kansas, Illinois, Indiana, Wisconsin, Minnesota, Michigan, Ohio and Kentucky, has 0-20 percent of its total land area prone to flooding. The same ratio, 0-20 percent, applies to the western region, which includes the States of California, Nevada, Arizona, Utah, Colorado, New Mexico and Hawaii. The States in the southern region

(North Carolina, South Carolina, Georgia, Alabama, Florida, Tennessee, Arkansas, Louisiana, Mississippi, Oklahoma and Texas) have the highest percentage of flood-prone land areas, a total of 0-30 percent.

Hurricanes and tropical storms represent some of the most devastating catastrophes in our nation's history. They are of particular concern to all southern and eastern coastal States from Texas to Maine. During the period 1871-1989, *185* hurricanes and tropical storms hit the coastal areas from North Carolina to Texas; 33 hurricanes and tropical storms affected the coastal region stretching from Virginia to Maine. More than *13,000* people have lost their lives in hurricanes from Texas to the northeast in the years of 1900-1989. Property losses from major hurricanes during that time exceeded $43 *billion*.

The long-term effects of major hurricanes are particularly serious. The high winds that hurricanes trigger can cause enormous timber losses. Massive storm surges that result from the forces of cyclonic winds on the ocean below can substantially change the geography of a severely hit coastal area. In addition, hurricanes are classic examples of the types of disasters that can trigger "secondary effects" such as tornadoes and flooding which, together with storm surges, can cause extensive damage. Because of the frequently erratic paths of hurricanes, inland States from Oklahoma on a northeastward path to Ohio, Pennsylvania, New York and the New England States can sustain significant damage from the downgraded remnants of hurricanes.

Tornadoes present a threat to all regions of the country, but the southern and midwestern States are particularly susceptible to them. During the period 1959-1988, a staggering *11,343* tornadoes struck the southern region, including the States of North Carolina, South Carolina, Georgia, Alabama, Florida, Tennessee, Arkansas, Louisiana, Mississippi, Oklahoma and Texas. During the same period, *9,234* tornadoes struck the Midwestern region, comprised of the States of North Dakota, South Dakota, Nebraska, Iowa, Missouri, Kansas, Illinois, Indiana, Wisconsin, Minnesota, Michigan, Ohio and Kentucky. In the remaining areas of the country, 513 tornadoes struck the southwestern States, including California; 1,091 affected the northeastern and mid-Atlantic States and 583 occurred in the upper northwestern States. Although many tornadoes hit sparsely populated, rural areas, they are a serious threat to many States and cause scores of deaths and millions of dollars in property damage on an annual basis.

Winter storms are a common occurrence every year in various areas of the country. Still, they result in deaths and injuries in the hundreds, along with economic losses of hundreds of millions of dollars. The ice storm that struck western and northern New York in March 1991, creating losses at well over $100 million, is perhaps the most costly natural disaster in the history of New York State.

Earthquakes are a particularly serious threat. While mitigation measures such as building codes can be implemented to reduce the potential damage from an earthquake, some preparedness general are particularly difficult because of the lack of warning prior to an occurrence. In terms of the potential for significant loss of life and damages totaling in the billions of dollars (particularly in urbanized areas), major earthquakes pose a serious threat to the population in risk areas—especially to those populations in the high-risk areas of California and associated risk areas in the western United States.

Fire, based on its frequency of occurrence, areas affected, and the toll it takes in lives and property every year, could be the number one threat facing the American population today. As noted earlier, the annual average of reported fires in the United States during the years 1983-1987 were 2,300,000, which resulted in an average of *5,900 civilian fire deaths, 29,000 civilian injuries and $7.8 billion in losses from fire each year.*

Hazardous materials transportation incidents are a newer threat that is becoming a major challenge to the nation's emergency managers. The country's roads and railways see thousands of hazardous material incidents every year, occasionally resulting in some deaths. The direct costs of such incidents, along with the indirect costs that arise from transportation disruption and the need for people to evacuate from a hazardous materials scene, make this one of the most significant hazards the nation now faces.

Floods, hurricanes, tornadoes, winter storms, earthquakes, fires and hazardous material incidents represent the primary threats facing communities and emergency management coordinators. This by no means diminishes the magnitude of the many other threats discussed in this report. All hazards must be addressed in the effort to adequately protect the nation's people and property from the threats they face.

THE RELATIONSHIP OF FEMA PROGRAMS TO THREATS

Emergency management consists of organized analysis, planning, decision making, assignment and coordination of available resources for mitigation, preparedness, response and recovery to save lives and protect property from the effects of any emergency, whether from natural, technological/man-made sources. In order to fulfill their responsibilities to manage and conduct essential functions, State and local governments must have operational capabilities that will survive any kind of catastrophic emergency. The aim is to ensure the ability to direct, control, manage and coordinate emergency operations within and among jurisdictions in cooperation with all government entities—Federal, State and local. To achieve this goal, all jurisdictions need integrated, in-place capabilities built on people, communications and hardware, systems and plans that will enable them to prepare for and respond to all emergencies, including catastrophic disaster, from any source.

Agency Mission   FEMA is responsible for ensuring the establishment and development of policies and programs for emergency management at the Federal, State and local levels. This includes developing a national capability to mitigate against, prepare for, respond to and recover from the full range of emergencies .

In view of the broad range of threats the population and industry of the United States face, FEMA is also responsible for ensuring that plans are in place as part of an integrated, all-hazard emergency management program. While the nature of some emergencies (e.g., earthquakes, hurricanes, tornadoes, radiological emergencies) does require certain hazard-specific procedures and activities, the goal of the Agency is to ensure the establishment of an integrated, all-hazards emergency management capability.

The Agency has a wide range of programs available to provide financial and technical assistance to State and local governments. The purpose of these programs is to help State and local emergency managers coordinate their governments' mitigation, preparedness, response and recovery activities for protecting the population from the numerous hazards that threaten their communities.

**Preparedness:
State and Local
Support Programs**

The State and Local Programs and Support Directorate is responsible for developing and maintaining an effective emergency management and response capability designed to mitigate against and reduce the effects of civil emergencies upon life and property. The Directorate develops and oversees programs that enhance State and local government capabilities to prepare for, respond to and recover from emergencies. This responsibility includes preparedness planning and mitigation activities for earthquakes, dam safety, hurricanes, floods (except for those programs authorized by the National Flood Insurance Act of 1968, as amended, which are the responsibility of the FEMA Federal Insurance Administration), tornadoes, radiological and hazardous material accidents and all other types of emergencies.

**The Civil Defense
Program**

In accordance with the Federal Civil Defense Act of 1950, as amended, the civil defense program provides the basic elements to build an emergency management capability at the State and local levels—an infrastructure of personnel, hardware, facilities, communications and systems that will provide State and local governments with integrated, all-hazard emergency management capability. As stated in Section 2 of the Civil Defense Act:

> *It is the policy and intent of Congress to provide a system of civil defense for the protection of life and property in the United States from attack and natural disasters.*

EMERGENCY
MANAGERS

The civil defense program provides funding for up to 50 percent of the salaries of State and local emergency managers and fully funds population protection planners, radiological defense officers and facility surveyors in each State. The preparedness planning undertaken by these individuals has application to the full spectrum of threats.

Although the radiological defense program was primarily designed to provide equipment for determining radiation levels following a nuclear attack, the same equipment is available for use in peacetime radiological emergencies.

State Emergency Operating Centers, for which up to 50 percent of the funding is provided through the civil defense program, are focal points for coordinated State-level disaster response activities throughout the Nation and are the foundation of the developing survivable crisis management system. In addition, the lessons learned from their use in natural disasters allows State and local governments to be better prepared in the event of attack from conventional, nuclear, chemical or biological weapons.

Listed below are some examples of how the civil defense program is used to cover all hazards:

- Through the National Warning System (NAWAS), approximately 7,000 warnings and tests were issued in 1991 alone.

- The Emergency Broadcast System (EBS) was developed in the civil defense program as a means for the President to talk to the general population during times of national emergency; yet, the EBS stations report that Governors and mayors use it over 1,000 times a year in response to natural and technological emergencies.

- Emergency Operating Centers (EOC's) usually are activated on a daily basis by State and local governments during natural disaster response operations to provide effective population protection and crisis management.

- The protection provided to counter the effects of electromagnetic pulse on State and local EOC's, civil defense emergency communications systems and equipment and EBS stations ensures their survivability because it also protects against the effects of lightning and power transients that occur during natural disasters.

- Plans developed by Emergency Management Assistance planners funded under the civil defense program at the State and local levels are used in a community's response to a disaster. Lessons learned by implementing these plans are of great importance in developing subsequent planning guidance and evaluations.

- Civil defense-sponsored testing/exercising proved invaluable to Sioux City, Iowa, by making possible that city's rapid response to the tragic plane crash that occurred in 1989. As Bev Costello, the Iowa State Training Manager noted in an October 1989 letter to the Superintendent of the FEMA Emergency Management Institute, "The direct impact of the FEMA exercise requirements is that we were very well prepared to respond [to the airline crash] and, in fact, responded accordingly because most of the responders had experience working together...*I found it interesting that the considerations not rehearsed were precisely the areas where problems arose*" (emphasis added).

The civil defense program reduces the vulnerability of the American people, not just to attack, but to the full range of hazards they face. Combined with the other FEMA emergency management programs, the civil defense program is an integral component of and provides the basic infrastructure for a State and local emergency management capability. Currently, FEMA, along with other Federal agencies and

State and local emergency managers, is conducting an examination of the resource requirements of the civil defense program. This civil defense requirements study will be completed in 1993.

Natural Hazard Programs

FEMA's natural hazards programs include the following elements: (1) National Earthquake Hazards Reduction, (2) Hurricane Preparedness, (3) Dam Safety.

The purpose of the *National Earthquake Hazards Reduction Program* is to reduce the risk to lives and property. This is accomplished through a comprehensive, multi-agency program of scientific research, mitigation, preparedness and response planning and public education. FEMA, as the lead agency, has the statutory responsibility to plan, coordinate and recommend goals, priorities and budgets for earthquake activities among the principal agencies authorized under the Earthquake Hazards Reduction Act of 1977, as amended. The agencies include the United States Geological Service, the National Science Foundation and the National Institute for Standards and Technology.

EARTHQUAKE

The primary activities of the program are to:

- develop improved seismic design and construction practices for adoption by Federal agencies, State and local governments and the private sector;
- provide financial and technical assistance to State and local governments to implement comprehensive earthquake hazard reduction programs;
- develop public education and awareness programs; and
- plan for and coordinate an adequate Federal capability to respond to a catastrophic earthquake.

The goal of the *Hurricane Preparedness Program* is to reduce the loss of life and property damage from hurricanes in high-risk populations. FEMA, as the chair of the Interagency Coordinating Committee on Hurricanes, coordinates ongoing hurricane-related planning and mitigation activities of the U.S. Army Corps of Engineers, the National Weather Service, the National Hurricane Center and the Office of Ocean and Coastal Resource Management.

HURRICANE

The primary functions performed include: (1) conducting population preparedness projects which assist State and local governments in developing and implementing evacuation plans for coastal areas and (2) and property protection projects, which assist State and local governments in developing and implementing hazard mitigation plans for coastal areas.

The objective of the *Dam Safety Program* is to enhance the safety of the Nation's dams, thereby protecting lives and property. FEMA exercises dual responsibilities through its Dam Safety Program to (1) coordinate Federal dam safety activities and (2) coordinate and implement activities designed to encourage States to implement strong dam safety programs.

DAM SAFETY

FEMA chairs the Interagency Committee on Dam Safety (ICODS) and coordinates non-Federal dam safety with the Association of State Dam Safety Officials. Training for dam safety officials has been enhanced by the development of "Training Aids for Dam Safety (TAD)." TAD was created, funded, developed and disseminated under FEMA's leadership. Technical assistance is provided through the publication, revision and distribution of technical assistance materials developed by ICODS and others. In addition, FEMA activities help to bring the dam safety message to State and local officials and the private sector by sponsoring State public awareness workshops, informational videos, brochures and other materials.

Technological Hazard Programs

FEMA's programs to help State and local emergency managers prepare for the technological hazards they face include: (1) Radiological Emergency Preparedness, (2) Hazardous Materials and (3) Chemical Stockpile Emergency Preparedness Program.

As a result of a Presidential Directive in 1979, FEMA was assigned the lead Federal role for radiological emergency planning and response. Under FEMA's *Radiological Emergency Preparedness Program*, the goal is to enhance integrated emergency planning and response for all types of peacetime radiological emergencies by the State, local and Federal governments. The primary emphasis is directed to planning and preparedness for commercial nuclear power plants, nuclear fuel cycle and material license holders, Department of Defense and Department of Energy facilities and transportation accidents.

RADIOLOGICAL EMERGENCY

Much of the program's effort is directed towards protecting the health and safety of citizens living in the Emergency Planning Zones that are established around each commercial nuclear power plant in the United States. There are 75 commercial nuclear power plant sites nationwide involving planning and preparedness activities of 460 State, local and tribal governments. Approximately 3 million people live within the Emergency Planning Zones around these sites.

Key activities pertaining to offsite radiological emergency planning and preparedness include evaluation of emergency response and utility plans, review of public emergency information materials, review and testing of utility alert and notification systems, periodic exercises to test emergency response plans and periodic program activities such as drills, plan updates and public meetings.

FEMA's primary regulatory responsibilities includes the provision of FEMA findings on the adequacy of offsite planning and preparedness to the Nuclear Regulatory Commission. FEMA findings are used by the Nuclear Regulatory Commission in making licensing determinations.

HAZARDOUS MATERIALS

The mission of the *Hazardous Materials Program* is to provide technical and financial assistance to State and local governments. In addition, FEMA coordinates and cooperates with the private sector in developing, implementing and evaluating hazardous materials emergency preparedness programs for State and local governments. The mission is accomplished through five separate functional elements—planning, training, exercising, information exchange and intergovernmental coordination/cooperation.

FEMA develops and distributes planning and preparedness guidance to State and local governments in cooperation with the 13 member agencies of the National Response Team. Hazardous materials training courses and course materials are developed and financial assistance is provided to State and local governments in support of State derived course development and delivery. FEMA supports State and local governments in the design, implementation and evaluation of hazardous materials exercises used for assessing the adequacy and effectiveness of existing planning and training programs. FEMA also cooperates with the Department of Transportation in the maintenance of electronic bulletin boards to provide the latest information on hazardous materials planning, training, exercises and conferences to State and local governments and the private sector.

The Department of Defense Authorization Act of 1986 (PL 99-145) mandated the destruction of the Army's stockpile of unitary chemical weapons, which was stored at eight sites in the continental United States. The law directed the Secretary of Defense to provide for the "maximum protection of the environment, the general public, and the personnel who will be involved in the destruction of the chemical agents and munitions."

Based on a Memorandum of Understanding between FEMA and the United States Army, FEMA assists State and local jurisdictions surrounding these eight sites in preparing for incidents related to the storage and destruction of the Army's unitary chemical weapons stockpile through its *Chemical Stockpile Emergency Preparedness Program (CSEPP) (Figure 39)*. The program provides technical assistance to these jurisdictions with comprehensive planning, exercises, training and emergency public information. In addition, FEMA serves as the conduit for Army funds to these jurisdictions through its Comprehensive Cooperative Agreement process.

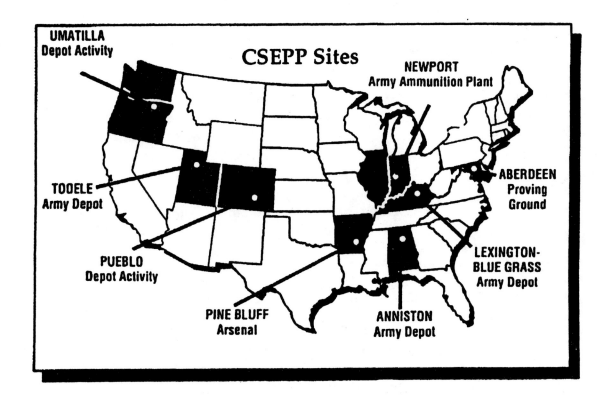

Figure 39

The National Urban Search and Rescue System

FEMA's initiation of the National Urban Search and Rescue (US&R) System represents a new type of effort in building State and local emergency capabilities. The US&R program combines the benefits of the National Earthquake Hazards Reduction Program with the responsiveness of the Stafford Act. Under this program, grants will be made available to State and local jurisdictions that display a certain level of US&R response capability. These grants are used to enhance their existing capabilities through equipment acquisition and additional training programs, while simultaneously providing the Federal government with an immediately deployable response capability to respond to disasters that require US&R support within the United States.

To ensure standardization of the Federal US&R response, FEMA has developed a 56-person task force structure by which all applicants must configure their resources. These task forces are multi-functional, configured into four specialized teams of search, rescue, medical and technical. For the past four years, FEMA has awarded equipment grants to 25 State-consolidated and local sponsored task forces totaling over $3 million dollars . There are also nine other task forces that will participate in the US&R System by adhering to its developmental guidelines and offering themselves for Federal deployment.

Response: Federal Response Plan

The Federal government also provides aid in catastrophic disasters where the emergency response capabilities of State and local governments are overwhelmed. In a major disaster, the Robert T. Stafford Disaster Relief and Emergency Assistance Act allows the President to "direct any Federal agency, with or without reimbursement, to utilize its authorities and the resources granted to it under Federal law (including personnel, equipment, supplies, facilities, and managerial, technical, and advisory services) in support of State and local disaster assistance efforts."

There are instances where emergency response assistance may be obtained from Federal government agencies without a Presidential declaration of a major disaster or an emergency. For example:

- Search and Rescue Assistance may be provided by the U.S. Coast Guard or U.S. Armed Forces in search and rescue operations to evacuate disaster victims and transport supplies and equipment.
- Flood Protection Assistance can be provided by the U.S. Army Corps of Engineers, which has the authority to assist in flood-fighting and rescue operations and to protect, repair and restore federally constructed flood-control works threatened, damaged or destroyed by a flood.
- Fire Suppression Assistance may be authorized by the President to provide aid, including grants, equipment, supplies and personnel to a State for the suppression of a forest or grassland fire on public or private lands that threatens to become a major disaster.

FEDERAL RESPONSE

Still, a major disaster may require a broad spectrum of Federal assistance to immediately support State and local emergency response operations. The formal process of coordinating Federal support to States and localities in an overwhelming emergency is outlined in the *Federal Response Plan*. The Plan describes the basic mechanisms and structures that Federal government will use in mobilizing department and agency resources to augment State and local response efforts.

In the Plan, Federal support is organized according to a series of Emergency Support Functions (ESFs). Each ESF is headed by a primary or lead Federal agency, with other agencies providing support as necessary to carry out the function. Primary agencies for an ESF are established on the basis of having the most resources and capabilities in the particular functional area. *Figure 40* lists the current ESFs and their primary agencies under the current Federal Response Plan.

FEDERAL RESPONSE PLAN
EMERGENCY SUPPORT FUNCTIONS

EMERGENCY SUPPORT FUNCTION	PRIMARY AGENCY
1. Transportation	Department of Transportation
2. Communications	National Communications System
3. Public Works and Engineering	Department of Defense
4. FireFighting	Department of Agriculture
5. Information and Planning	Federal Emergency Mangement Agency
6. Mass Care	American Red Cross
7. Resources Support	General Services Administration
8. Health and Medical Services	Department of Health and Human Services
9. Urban Search and Rescue	Department of Defense
10. Hazardous Materials	Environmental Protection Agency
11. Food	Department of Agriculture
12. Energy	Department of Energy

Figure 40

Activation

In an emergency, the FEMA Director may direct the activation of the Plan on a partial or full basis. Under a Presidential declaration of disaster, the FEMA Director will also appoint a Federal Coordinating Officer on behalf of the President for each declared State to coordinate the overall delivery of Federal assistance to State governments managing the response to a disaster.

Regional Operations

At the Regional level, the FEMA Regional Director will set up a Regional Operations Center (ROC) and establish links with affected States as an interim measure.

Shortly thereafter, an Emergency Response Team (ERT) is established for the disaster. Made up of FEMA personnel and regional representatives of Plan ESFs, the ERT is the interagency group providing administrative, logistical and operational support to the regional response activities. An advance element of the ERT will assess the impact of the disaster situation, collect damage information and set up response operations in the field.

National Operations.

A national support structure is also established in order to support Federal disaster response operations in the field. A Catastrophic Disaster Response Group (CDRG) is set up. Made up of the heads of Federal agencies responding to the disaster, the CDRG resolves any broad resource or operational issues arising from the response. The CDRG is supported by an Emergency Support Team (EST). The EST mirrors the structure of the ERT in the field, providing national support as needed.

The Federal Response Plan is the means by which the Federal government can provide a gradual, organized and coordinated means of meeting the needs of States and local governments overwhelmed by a major disaster or emergency. *Figure 41* is a list of the agencies with assigned roles in the current Federal Response Plan.

Federal Response Plan — Agencies Involved

Department of Agriculture	Agency for International Development
Department of Commerce	American Red Cross
Department of Defense	Environmental Protection Agency
Department of Education	Federal Communications Commission
Department of Energy	Federal Emergency Management Agency
Department of Health and Human Services	General Services Administration
Department of Housing and Urban Development	Interstate Commerce Commission
Department of the Interior	National Aeronautics and Space Administration
Department of Justice	National Communications System
Department of Labor	Nuclear Regulatory Commission
Department of State	Office of Personnel Management
Department of Transportation	Tennessee Valley Authority
Department of the Treasury	U.S. Postal Service
Department of Veterans Affairs	

Figure 41

**Recovery:
The Disaster Relief
Program**

The Disaster Relief Program is designed to supplement the efforts and available resources of State and local governments and voluntary relief organizations. The President's declaration of a "major disaster" or an "emergency" authorizes Federal assistance under the Robert T. Stafford Disaster Relief and Emergency Assistance Act and triggers other Federal disaster relief programs.

Two primary forms of Federal disaster assistance can be made available under a Presidential declaration of a major disaster: (1) assistance to individuals and (2) assistance to State and local governments.

**Individual
Assistance**

One of the most important objectives after any disaster is to inform individuals of the assistance available and to assist them in the application and delivery process. Information outlining available aid programs is disseminated by FEMA through radio, television, newspapers and the mass distribution of pamphlets, as well as "outreach" teams and toll-free telephone "hotlines." This *"Individual Assistance"* may include:

- temporary housing until alternative housing is available for disaster victims whose homes are uninhabitable;

- minimum essential repairs to owner-occupied residences in lieu of other forms of temporary housing so that families can return quickly to their damaged homes;

- disaster unemployment assistance and job placement assistance for those unemployed as a result of a major disaster;

- individual and family grants of up to $11,500 to meet disaster-related necessary expenses or serious needs when those affected are unable to meet such expenses or needs through other programs or other means;

- legal services to low-income families and individuals;

- crisis counseling and referrals to appropriate mental health agencies to relieve disaster-caused mental health problems; and

- assistance through the Cora Brown Fund to victims of natural disasters for those disaster-related needs that have not been or will not be met by government agencies or other organizations that have programs to address such needs.

Individual Assistance

Although the following forms of assistance are not FEMA programs, FEMA, as the lead agency for Federal disaster assistance, coordinates the aid provided by other Federal agencies under Presidential declarations of major disasters or emergencies:

- loans to individuals, businesses and farmers for repair, rehabilitation or replacement of damaged real and personal property and some production losses not fully covered by insurance;

- agricultural assistance, including technical assistance; payments covering a major portion of the cost to eligible farmers who perform emergency conservation actions on farmland damaged by a disaster and provision of federally owned grain for livestock and herd preservation;

- veteran's assistance, such as death benefits, pensions, insurance settlements and adjustments to home mortgages held by the Veterans Administration if a VA-insured home has been damaged;

- tax relief, including help from the Internal Revenue Service in claiming casualty losses resulting from the disaster and State tax assistance; and

- waiver of penalty for early withdrawal of funds from certain time deposits.

Public Assistance

Assistance to State and local governments is provided as soon as practicable following the President's declaration of a major disaster. Project applications submitted by States and eligible political subdivisions of States for "*Public Assistance*" may be approved to fund a variety of projects, including:

- clearance of debris, when in the public interest or on public or private lands or waters;

- emergency protective measures for the preservation of life and property;

- repair or replacement of streets, roads and bridges;

- repair or replacement of water control facilities (dikes, levees, irrigation works and drainage facilities);

- repair or replacement of public buildings and related equipment;

- repair or replacement of public utilities;

- repair or restoration of public facilities damaged while under construction;

- repair or replacement or recreational facilities and parks; and

- repair or replacement of eligible private nonprofit educational, utility, emergency, medical and custodial care facilities, including those for the aged or disabled, and facilities on Indian reservations.

Public Assistance

Other forms of assistance that may be made available under a Presidential declaration of a major disaster include:

- community disaster loans from FEMA to communities that may suffer a substantial loss of tax and other revenues and can demonstrate a need for financial assistance in order to perform their governmental functions;

- certain forms of hazard mitigation assistance from FEMA under its own authorities and with other Federal agencies through the interagency hazard mitigation team process;

- funding of mitigation projects through the Hazard Mitigation Grant Program, which can fund up to 50 percent of the project;

- use of Federal equipment, supplies, facilities, personnel and other resources (other than the extension of credit) from various Federal agencies; and

- repairs to Federal-aid system roads when authorized by the Department of Transportation.

Mitigation: FIA/USFA

Finally, FEMA provides support to States and localities in their effort to mitigate the occurrence and effects of disasters. Besides the hazard mitigation aid already mentioned above, Federal mitigation programs also address our most frequently occurring disasters—flood and fire.

The Federal Insurance Administration

The FEMA Federal Insurance Administration directs Federal programs dealing with flood insurance and the Unified National Program for Floodplain Management.

Congress established the National Flood Insurance Program (NFIP) with the passage of the National Flood Insurance Act of 1968. The program was broadened and modified in the Flood Disaster Protection Act of 1973.

Before the passage of the National Flood Insurance Act of 1968, national response to flood disasters consisted of constructing flood control works and providing disaster relief to flood victims. Flood losses were not reduced nor was unwise development discouraged. No insurance companies provided flood coverage for the public, and building techniques to reduce flood damage were overlooked. In creating the National Flood Insurance Program, Congress provided a program for mitigating future damage from floods and an insurance mechanism for the public to obtain protection from flood losses.

The National Flood Insurance Program, which is administered by FEMA's Federal Insurance Administration, enables property owners to purchase flood insurance. It is designed to provide an insurance alternative to disaster assistance as a means of meeting escalating costs for repairing flood damage.

Local communities participate in the NFIP through an agreement with the Federal government. Under this agreement, the Federal government makes flood insurance available as a financial protection against actual flood losses if the community implements and enforces measures to reduce future flood risks to new construction in special flood hazard areas. To date, there are nearly 18,000 communities participating in this program.

FLOOD INSURANCE

When a community joins the NFIP, it adopts and enforces minimum floodplain management standards. FEMA works closely with States and local communities to identify flood hazard areas and flooding risks. The floodplain requirements are designed to prevent new development from increasing the flood threat and to protect new and existing buildings from anticipated floods.

In 1981, FEMA developed the "Write Your Own" program to reinvolve the private-sector insurance companies in the NFIP. The goals of the "Write Your Own" program are:

- to increase the NFIP policy base and the geographic distribution of policies,
- to improve service to NFIP policy holders through the infusion of insurance industry knowledge and
- to provide the insurance industry with direct operating experience with flood insurance.

The Community Rating System (CRS), created by FEMA in 1990, provides a new incentive for activities that reduce flood losses and support the sale of flood insurance. Any community that participates in the NFIP may apply for CRS classification to receive flood insurance premium rate credits for its residents. To qualify for these credits, the community must demonstrate that its implementation activities for floodplain management and public information exceed the minimum NFIP requirements.

United States Fire Administration

The mission of the FEMA United States Fire Administration (USFA) is (1) to enhance the Nation's fire prevention and control activities, (2) to reduce significantly the Nation's loss of life from fire and (3) to achieve a reduction in property loss and non-fatal injury due to fire. The FEMA National Fire Academy provides educational programs at the FEMA training facility located in Emmitsburg, Maryland, and through off-campus outreach courses.

The United States Fire Administration offers a wide range of programs to both fire service professionals, emergency managers and the public. These include:

FIRE DATA

- The National Fire Incident Reporting System, which operates in conjunction with the National Fire Information Council. The USFA coordinates this fire data collection and analysis program on a voluntary basis with most States and a number of metropolitan areas. This system allows USFA to track fire safety trends and measures any change in the numbers of fire casualties.

- The Management Application Project and the *Arson Information Management Systems Project* expand the data capabilities of the National Fire Incident Reporting System with computer software packages that manage fire data.

ARSON INFORMATION

- Community Volunteer Fire Prevention grants to 21 States and the District of Columbia fund local fire prevention and education projects.

- The Firefighters Integrated Response Equipment System improves the design and performance of structural firefighters' clothing and equipment. Firefighter suits are being developed and tested to withstand hazardous chemicals and toxic gases. Field tests and studies to determine the effects of smoke and other environmental and behavioral characteristics on firefighters are being conducted.

TECHNICAL SUPPORT

- The USFA works with the Children's Television Workshop to develop fire safety materials for use by educators, focusing on fire safety for pre-school children by using Sesame Street materials. The USFA also runs a series of educational teleconferences yearly for fire service and emergency management audiences throughout the country on subjects ranging from flammable gases and liquids to residential sprinklers, stress management and public affairs. In addition, the USFA

Fire Education

maintains an Arson Resource Center as an information clearinghouse on arson data for use by students of the National Fire Academy, emergency management personnel and the public.

Summary

The FEMA program of developing a Federal-State-Local infrastructure of emergency managers is essential to ensure that the nation is properly protected from the hazards they face. Regardless of whether the programs listed above are provided in the form of financial assistance, technical assistance or guidance, they provide the primary system within the Federal government to assist State and local governments in developing a readiness capability against threats. They cover the full range of emergency management activities—mitigation, preparedness, response and recovery—required against the full range of emergencies.

In 1992, FEMA used the Comprehensive Cooperative Agreement (CCA) process to distribute more than $129 million in direct assistance to State and local governments in 1992. As *Figure 42* shows, these programs provided support to State and local governments across the full range of threats.

FUNDING PROVIDED TO STATES THROUGH FEMA'S COMPREHENSIVE COOPERATIVE AGREEMENT PROCESS

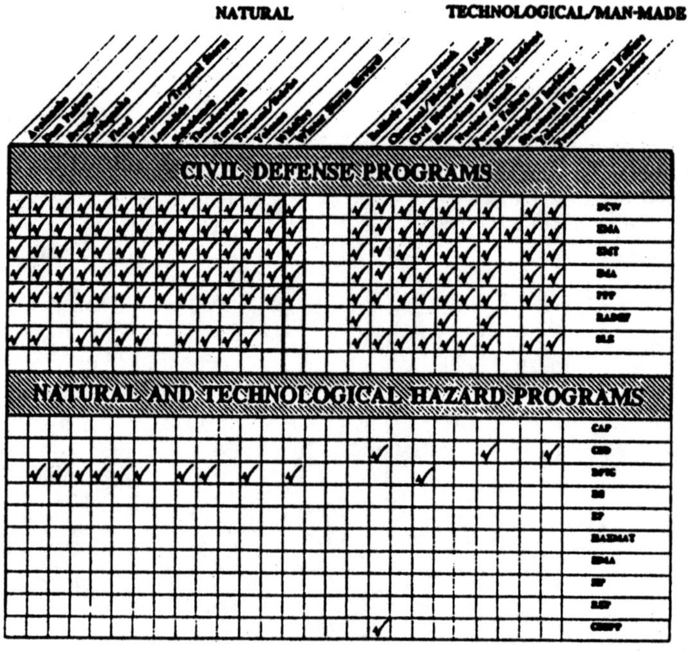

Figure 42

The importance of all elements of the FEMA program were never more apparent than in 1992. In Florida, an estimated 700,000 people were safely evacuated, and 80,000 sheltered, from areas endangered by Hurricane Andrew. This effort, possible only because of the emergency plans and personnel supported by FEMA, greatly reduced the potential death toll from the hurricane. In the disasters that occurred, the Federal Response Plan coordinated the immediate response to prevent suffering. During the year, over 7 million meals were served, over 18,000 people received medical treatment, and tons of ice, plastic sheeting and other supplies were provided to meet immediate needs. In recovery, over a quarter of a million families applied for FEMA assistance to get back on their feet.

The effort to protect the nation's people and property against disaster will gain in importance over the next few years. As *Figure* 43 illustrates, the recent trend has seen more and more disasters occurring. Increases in population and development, changes in our environment and the emergence of new threats means that the nation's emergency managers will have increasing challenges in the future.

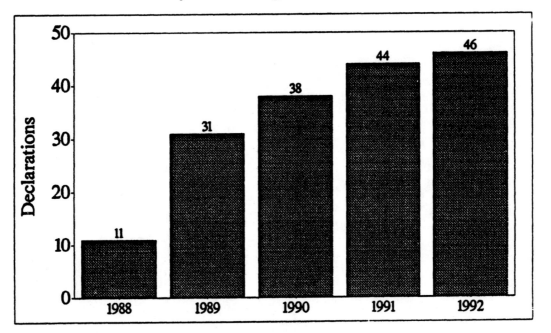

PRESIDENTIAL DISASTER DECLARATIONS

Number of Declarations by Year
January 1988 through December 1992

Source: FEMA, Office of Disaster Assistance

Figure 43

BIBLIOGRAPHY

NATURAL HAZARDS

AVALANCHE

Committee on Ground Failure Hazards Mitigation Research, Division of Natural Hazard Mitigation, Commission on Engineering and Technical Systems, National Research Council. *Snow Avalanche Hazards and Mitigation in the United States*. Washington DC: National Academy Press, 1990.

DAM SAFETY

Federal Emergency Management Agency. *National Dam Safety Program: A Progress Report*. Washington, DC: Government Printing Office, 1986.

Federal Emergency Management Agency. *State Non-Federal Dam Safety Programs-1985*. Washington, DC: Government Printing Office, 1985.

Tschantz, Bruce A. *1989 Report on Review of State Non-Federal Dam Safety Programs*. Knoxville, TN: University of Tennessee, August 1989.

DROUGHT

U.S. Department of Commerce, National Oceanic and Atmospheric Administration. *Brief Bibliography: Drought*. Washington, D.C.: August 1989.

U.S. Army Corps of Engineer/Office of Hydrology, National Weather Service. *U.S. Army Corps of Engineers Annual Flood Damage Report to Congress for Fiscal Year 1991*. Washington, D.C., February 1992.

EARTHQUAKE

Coffman, Jerry L. and Carl A. von Hake (eds). *Earthquake History of the United States*. U.S. Department of Commerce, National Oceanic and Atmospheric Administration: Boulder, CO, 1989.

Federal Emergency Management Agency. *Earthquakes: A National Problem*. Washington, D.C.

U.S. Geological Survey. *Lessons Learned from the Loma Prieta, California, Earthquake of October 17, 1989*. Circular 1045.

U.S. Geological Survey. *The 15 Most Significant Earthquakes in U.S. History*. Department of Interior: March 1989.

U.S. Department of the Interior, Geological Survey. *Earthquake Information Bulletin.* Washington, D.C.: Government Printing Office, 1983.

FLOOD

Federal Emergency Management Agency. *Design Guidelines for Flood Damage Reduction. FEMA-15.* Washington, D.C., December 1981.

Federal Emergency Management Agency. *National Flood Insurance Program: A Cost-Effective Plan for Flood Studies Maintenance.* Washington, D.C.: Government Printing Office, February 1989.

Federal Emergency Management Agency. *Flood Insurance Program: Flood Studies and Surveys Historical Statistics.* Washington, D.C.: Government Printing Office, September 1989.

Federal Emergency Management Agency. *Flood Insurance Program: Risk Studies Completion and Full Program Status.* Washington, D.C.: Government Printing Office, September 1984.

Federal Emergency Management Agency. *Flood Insurance Study: Guidelines and Specifications for Study contractors.* Washington, DC: Government Printing Office, September 1985.

Federal Emergency Management Agency. *Answers to Questions About the National Flood Insurance Program.* Washington, DC: Government Printing Office, October 1989.

Federal Emergency Management Agency. *Federal Insurance Administration: Communities Participating in the National Flood Insurance Program.* Washington, DC, August 1988.

Thompson, Stephan A. and Gilbert F. White, "A National Floodplain Map." *Journal of Soil and Water Conservation,* September-October 1985.

U.S. Army Corps of Engineers/Office of Hydrology, National Weather Service. *U.S. Army Corps of Engineers Annual Flood Damage Report to Congress for Fiscal Year 1991.* Washington, D.C., February 1992.

HURRICANE

Federal Emergency Management Agency. *Perspectives on Hurricane Preparedness: Techniques in Use Today.* Washington DC: Government Printing Office, October 1984.

Gray, William M. *Appendix A: Multi-Decadal Trends in Atlantic Intense Hurricane Activity with Implications for Increased US Landfall of Intense Hurricanes in the 1990s.* Department of Atmospheric Science, Colorado State University, November 1989.

Hebert, Paul J. and Glenn Taylor. *The Deadliest, Costliest, and Most Intense United States Hurricanes of this Century (and Other Frequently Requested Hurricane Facts)*. NOAA Technical Memorandum NWS NHC 18, June 1985.

Libby, Sam. "Weathering A Storm." *The Hartford Courant.*, 14 December 1989, Section E, p. 1.

"Stronger Storms Predicted." *Asheville Citizen Times*, 12 November 1989, p. 27A.

U.S. Department of Commerce, National Oceanic and Atmospheric Administration. *Brief Bibliography: Hurricanes.* Washington, DC: July 1989.

LANDSLIDE

28th International Geological Congress. *Landslides: Extent and Economic Significance.* Washington, DC: US Geological Survey, 1989.

Brabb, Earl E. and Robert H. Fickies. *Landslide Inventory Map of New York.* New York: New York State Museum, 1989.

Brabb, E.E., G.F. Wieczorek, and E.L. Harp. *Map Showing 1983 Landslides in Utah.* U.S. Geological Survey: Department of the Interior, 1989.

Brabb, Earl E. and Fred Taylor. *Map Showing Landslides in California that have Caused Fatalities or at Least $1,000,000 in Damages from 1906 to 1984.* U.S. Geological Survey: Department of the Interior, 1988.

Brabb, Earl E. "On the Line: Losing by a Landslide," *U.S. Geological Survey*, 1985.

Committee on Ground Failure Hazards, Commission on Engineering and Technical Systems, and National Research Council. *Reducing Losses from Landsliding in the United States.* Washington, DC: National Academy Press, 1985.

Department of the Interior. *Estimating the Costs of Landslide Damage in the United States.* Geological Survey Circular 832.

Department of the Interior. *Feasibility of a Nationwide Program for the Identification and Delineation of Hazards from Mud Flows and Other Landslides.* Open-File Report 85-276.

Federal Emergency Management Agency. *Landslide Loss Reduction: A Guide for State and Local Government Planning.* FEME 182/August 1989.

Fleming, Robert W. and Robert L. Schuster, "Economic Losses and Fatalities Due to Landslides," *Bulletin of the Association of Engineering Geologists,* Volume XXIII, pp. 11-22.

Geological Survey. *Goals and Tasks of the Landslide Part of a Ground-Failure Hazards Reduction Program.* Washington DC: Government Printing Office, Circular 880.

International Symposium on Landslides. *Innovative Approaches to Landslide Hazard and Risk Mapping.* Toronto, Canada, 1984.

Keefer, David K. "Landslides Caused by Earthquakes," *Geological Society of America bulletin,* Volume 95, April 1984, pp 406-421.

Kockelman, William. "Some Techniques for Reducing Landslide Hazards," *Bulletin of the Association of Engineering Geologists,* Volume XXIII, Number 1, February 1986, pp 29-53.

Swanston, Douglas N. and Robert L. Schuster, "Long-Term Landslide Hazard Mitigation Programs: Structure and Experience from Other Countries," *Bulletin of the Association of Engineering Geologists,* Volume XXVI, 1989, pp 109-133.

Steinbrugge, Karl V. *Earthquakes, Volcanoes, and Tsunamis.* New York, NY: Skandia America Group, 1982.

Symposium on Landslides. *Landslides: Extent and Economic Significance.* Washington, DC: International Geological Congress, 1989.

THUNDERSTORM

Brinkmann, Waltraud A. *Severe Local Storm Hazard in the United States: A Research Assessment.* Boulder, CO: Institute of Behavioral Sciences, University of Colorado, 1975.

Erickson, Jon. Violent Storms. Blue Ridge Summit, PA: TAB Books, 1988.

U.S. Department of Commerce, National Oceanic and Atmospheric Administration, National Weather Service. *Thunderstorms and Lightning.* Washington, DC: June 1985.

TORNADO

Fujita, T. Theodore. *U.S. Tornadoes: Part 1: 70 Year Statistics.* Chicago: University of Chicago, 1987.

Grazulis, T.P. *Violent Tornado Climatography, 1880-1982.* St. Johnsbury, VT: Environmental Films Inc., 1984.

Kessler, Edwin (ed). *Volume 1: The Thunderstorm in Human Affairs.* Washington, D.C.: National Oceanic and Atmospheric Administration, 1981.

U.S. Department of Commerce, National Oceanic and Atmospheric Administration, *Brief Bibliography: Tornado.* Washington, DC: May 1989.

Vigansky, Henry N. *National Summary of Tornadoes, 1987.* Washington, DC: National Oceanic and Atmospheric Administration, 1987.

TSUNAMI/SEICHE Bolt, B.A., W.L. Horn, G.A. MacDonald, R.F. Scott. *Geological Hazards.* New York: Springer-Verlag, 1977.

McCulloch, David S. *Slide-Induced Waves, Seiching and Ground Fracturing Caused by the Earthquake of March 27, 1964 at Kenai Lake, Alaska.* Geological Survey Professional Paper 543-A. Washington, DC: U.S. Government Printing Office, 1966.

Lander, James F. and Patricia A. Lockridge. *United States Tsunamis 1690-1988 (Including United States Possessions).* Boulder, CO: National Geophysical Data Center, 1989.

VOLCANO Bailey, R.A., P.R. Beauchemin, F.P. Kapinos, and D.W. Klick. *The Volcano Hazards Program: Objectives and Long-Range Plans.* Reston, VA: U.S. Department of Interior, 1983.

Bridge, David, John H. Latter, Lindsay McClelland, Christopher Newhall, Lee Siebert, and Tom Simkin. *Volcanoes of the World.* Stroudsburg, PA: Smithsonian Institution.

McClelland, Lindsay, Elizabeth Nielsen, Tom Simkin, Thomas Stein, and Marjorie Summers. *Global Volcanism 1975-1985.* Washington, DC: Smithsonian Institution.

Steinbrugge, Karl V. *Earthquakes, Volcanoes, and Tsunamis.* New York, NY: Skandia America Group, 1982.

WILDFIRE United States Department of Agriculture, Forest Service. *1984-1990 Forest Fire Statistics.* Washington, DC, January 1992.

TECHNOLOGICAL/MAN-MADE HAZARDS

BALLISTIC MISSILE ATTACK

Carus, W. Seth. *Ballistic Missiles in Modern Conflict*. New York: Praeger Publishers, 1991.

Donnelly, Warren H., James E. Meilke, John D. Moteff, Warren W. Lenhart, Robert D. Shuey, and Rodney A. Snyder. *Missile Proliferation: Survey of Emerging Missile Forces*. Congressional Research Service: October 1988.

International Institute for Strategic Studies. *The Military Balance 1991-1992*. London: Brassey's, Autumn 1991.

Nolan, Janne E. *Trappings of Power: Ballistic Missiles in the Third World*. Washington, DC: The Brookings Institution, 1991.

Walmer, Max. *An Illustrated Guide to Strategic Weapons*. New York: Prentice Hall Press, 1988.

CHEMICAL AND BIOLOGICAL ATTACK

Carnes, S.A. *Site-Specific Emergency Response Concept Plans for the Chemical Stockpile Disposal Program: A Comparative Summary*. Oak Ridge National Laboratory: October 1989.

Douglass, Joseph L., Jr. and Neil C. Livingstone. *America the Vulnerable: The Threat of Chemical/Biological Warfare*. Lexington, MA: D.C. Heath and Company, 1987.

The Senate Committee on Government Affairs and its Subcommittee, The Permanent Subcommittee on Investigations. *DCI Testimony on Chemical and Biological Weapons*. Washington, DC: February 1989.

HAZARDOUS MATERIALS

Environmental Protection Agency. *The Toxics-Release Inventory: A National Perspective*. Washington, DC: June 1989.

Environmental Protection Agency. *Toxics in the Community: 1988 National and Local Perspectives*. Washington, DC,: Government Printing Office, September 1990.

Federal Emergency Management Agency. *Digest of Federal Training in Hazardous Materials*. Washington, DC: Federal Emergency Management Agency, July 1987.

Speight, G.R. Commander, U.S. Coast Guard., Letter. 8 March 1990.

**NUCLEAR
ATTACK**

"Nuclear Notebook," *Bulletin of the Atomic Scientists*, various issues.

U.S. Department of State, Arms Control and Disarmament Agency. *Treaty Between the United States of America and the Russian Federation on the Further Reduction and Limitation of Strategic Offensive Arms.* January 3, 1993.

U.S. Department of State, Bureau of Public Affairs. *START: Treaty Between the United States of America and the Union of Soviet Socialist Republics on the Reduction and Limitation of Strategic Offensive Arms.* Dispatch Supplement Vol. 2, No. 5. October 1991.

POWER FAILURE

North American Electric Reliability Council. *1984 System Disturbances.* Princeton, NJ: North American Electric Reliability Council, 1985.

North American Electric Reliability Council. *1986 System Disturbances.* Princeton, NJ: North American Electric Reliability Council, 1987.

North American Electric Reliability Council. *1987 System Disturbances.* Princeton, NJ: North American Electric Reliability Council, 1988.

North American Electric Reliability Council. *1988 System Disturbances.* Princeton, NJ: North American Electric Reliability Council, 1989.

North American Electric Reliability Council. *1991 System Disturbances.* Princeton, NJ: North American Electric Reliability Council, 1992.

Hearing before the Senate Committee on Governmental Affairs. *Physical Vulnerability of Electric Systems to Natural Disasters and Sabotage.* Office of Technology Assessment, June 1990.

U.S. General Accounting Office. *Efforts Underway to Improve Federal Electrical Disruption Preparedness.* GAO/RCED-92-125. Washington, DC: April 1992.

RADIOLOGICAL HAZARDS

Federal Emergency Management Agency and U.S. Nuclear Regulatory Commission. *Criteria for Preparation and Evaluation of Radiological Emergency Response Plans and Preparedness in Support of Nuclear Power Plants-Criteria for Utility Offsite Planning and Preparedness.* Washington, DC: Government Printing Office, March 1987.

Federal Emergency Management Agency. *Report to the President: State Radiological Emergency Planning and Preparedness in Support of Commercial Nuclear Power Plants.* Washington, DC: Government Printing Office, June 1980.

Federal Emergency Management Agency. *Federal Emergency Management Agency's Radiological Emergency Preparedness (REP) Program.* Washington, DC: Federal Emergency Management Agency, 1988.

Federal Emergency Management Agency. *Guide for the Evaluation of Alert and Notification Systems for Nuclear Power Plants.* Washington, DC: Government Printing Office, 1985.

Federal Emergency Management Agency and U.S. Nuclear Regulatory Commission. *Criteria for Preparation and Evaluation of Radiological Emergency Response Plans and Preparedness in Support of Nuclear Power Plants.* Washington DC: Government Printing Office, 1987.

Federal Emergency Management Agency. *Guidance for Developing State and Local Radiological Emergency Response Plans and Preparedness for Transportation Accidents.* Washington, DC: Federal Emergency Management Agency, 1991.

U.S. Nuclear Regulatory Commission. *AEOD 1988 Annual Report on Power Reactors.* Washington, DC: U.S. Nuclear Regulatory Commission, June 1989.

U.S. Nuclear Regulatory Commission. *AEOD 1989 Annual Report on Power Reactors.* Washington, DC: U.S. Nuclear Regulatory Commission, July 1990.

U.S. Nuclear Regulatory Commission. *AEOD 1991 Annual Report on Power Reactors.* Washington, DC: U.S. Nuclear Regulatory Commission, July 1992.

U.S. Nuclear Regulatory Commission. *Report to Congress on Abnormal Occurrences July-September 1989.* Washington, DC: Government Printing Office, January 1990.

STRUCTURAL FIRE "NDPA Reports: U.S. Fire Deaths at 70 Year High in 1988," *Fire Control Digest,* September 1989, pp 1-3.

"U.S. Disaster Aid: Hits Decade Low," *Fire Control Digest,* January 1989, pp 1-3.

Federal Emergency Management Agency. *Fire in the United States: Deaths, Injuries, Dollar Loss, and Incidents.* Washington, DC: Government Printing Office, 1987.

Federal Emergency Management Agency. *Fire in the United States: 1983-1987 and Highlights for 1988.* Washington, DC: Government Printing Office, 1990.

Sundt, Nicholas A. *Budgetary Levels and Flexibility: the 1988 Fire Season and Beyond.* Washington, D.C.: U.S. Forest Service, 1989.

TELE-COMMUNICATIONS FAILURE
Cooper, James Arlin. *Computers and Communications Security: Strategies for the 1990s.* New York: McGraw-Hill Book Company, 1989.

Denning, Peter J. (ed). *Computers Under Attack: Intruders, Worms, and Viruses.* New York: ACM Press, 1990.

Lee, Leonard. *The Day the Phones Stopped: The Computer Crisis — The What and Why of It and How we Can Beat It.* New York: Donald I. Fine, 1991.

Matisoff, Bernard S. *Handbook of Electrostatic Discharge Control (ESD): Facilities Design and Manufacturing Procedures.* New York: Van Nostrand Reinhold Company, 1986.

National Research Council. *Computers at Risk: Safe Computing in the Information Age.* Washington, DC: National Academy Press, 1991.

National Research Council. *Growing Vulnerability of the Public Switched Networks: Implications for National Security Emergency Preparedness.* Washington, DC: National Academy Press, 1989.

Neumann, "Illustrative Risks to the Public in the Use of Computer Systems and Related Technology," *ACM Software Engineering Notes,* Vol 17, No. 1, Pages 23-38.

U.S. Congress, U.S. House of Representatives, Committee on Science, Space, and Technology, Subcommittee on Investigations and Oversight. *Bugs in the Program: Problems in Federal Government Computer Software Development and Regulation.* Subcommittee Staff Study. Washington, DC: U.S. Government Printing Office, April 1990.

U.S. Congress, Office of Technology Assessment. *Critical Connections: Communications for the Future.* OTA-CIT-407. Washington, DC: U.S. Government Printing Office, January 1990.

TERRORISM

Bolz, Frank Jr., Kenneth J. Dudonis and David P. Shultz. *The Counter-Terrorism Handbook: Tactics, Procedures and Techniques.* New York: Elsevier, 1990.

Brock, Jack L., Jr. *Hackers Penetrate DOD Computer Systems.* Testimony before the Subcommittee on Government Information and Regulation, Committee on Government Affairs, United States Senate. GAO/T-IMTEC-92-5. Washington, DC: U.S. Government Accounting Office, November 20, 1991.

Federal Emergency Management Agency. *Planning for and Dealing with the Consequences of Terrorism in Local Communities: An International Perspective.* Conference Report, Senior Executive Policy Center, April 30 - May 3, 1984

Gardela, Karen and Bruce Hoffman. *The RAND Chronology of International Terrorism for 1987.* R-4006-RC. Santa Monica: RAND Corporation, 1991.

Gardela, Karen and Bruce Hoffman. *The RAND Chronology of International Terrorism for 1988.* R-4180-RC. Santa Monica: RAND Corporation, 1992.

Kupperman, Robert and Jeff Kamen. *Final Warning: Averting Disaster in the New Age of Terrorism.* New York: Doubleday, 1989.

Kupperman, Robert and David M. Smith. *Coping with Biological Terrorism.* Processed. August 22,1991.

Livingstone, Neil C. and Terrell E. Arnold (eds). *Beyond the Iran-Contra Crisis: The Shape of U.S. Anti-Terrorism Policy in the Post-Reagan Era.* Lexington, MA: D.C. Heath and Company, 1988.

National Advisory Committee on Criminal Justice Standards and Goals. *Disorders and Terrorism: Report of the Task Force on Disorders and Terrorism.* Washington, DC, 1976.

National Governor's Association. *Domestic Terrorism.* Washington, DC: National Governor's Association, 1978.

President's Commission on Aviation Security and Terrorism, *Report to the President.* Washington, DC: U.S. Government Printing Office, May 15, 1990.

Rubin, Barry (ed). *Terrorism and Politics.* New York: St. Martin's Press, 1991.

St. John, Peter. *Air Piracy, Airport Security, and International Terrorism: Winning the War Against Hijackers.* New York: Quorum Books, 1991.

U.S. Congress, Office of Technology Assessment. *Technology Against Terrorism: The Federal Effort.* OTA-ISC-481. Washington, DC: U.S. Government Printing Office, July 1991.

U.S. Congress, Senate Committee on Governmental Affairs. *Terrorism: Interagency Conflicts in Combatting International Terrorism.* Hearings, July 15, 1991. Washington, D.C.: Government Printing Office, 1992.

U.S. Department of Justice. *Terrorism in the United States 1987.* Terrorist Research and Analytical Center, Federal Bureau of Investigation, December 1987.

U.S. Department of Justice. *Terrorism in the United States 1988.* Terrorist Research and Analytical Center, Federal Bureau of Investigation, December 1988.

U.S. Department of Justice. *Terrorism in the United States 1989.* Terrorist Research and Analytical Center, Federal Bureau of Investigation, December 1989.

U.S. Department of Justice. *Terrorism in the United States 1990.* Terrorist Research and Analytical Center, Federal Bureau of Investigation, 1991.

U.S. Department of Justice. *Terrorism in the United States 1991.* Terrorist Research and Analytical Center, Federal Bureau of Investigation, 1992.

U.S. General Accounting Office. *Aviation Security: Corrective Actions Underway, but Better Inspection Guidance Still Needed.* Report to the Chairwoman, Government Activities and Transportation Subcommittee, Committee on Government Operations, House of Representatives. GAO/RCED-88-160. Washington, DC: General Accounting Office, August 1988.

U.S. General Accounting Office. *Aviation Security: FAA Needs Preboard Passenger Screening Performance Standards.* Report to the Secretary of Transportation. GAO/RCED-87-182. Washington, DC: General Accounting Office, July 1987.

TRANSPORTATION ACCIDENTS

Federal Railroad Administration, Office of Safety. *Certain Fatalities Investigated by the Federal Railroad Administration Third Quarter 1987.* Washington, DC: Government Printing Office, September 1989.

Federal Railroad Administration, Office of Safety. *Certain Fatalities Investigated by the Federal Railroad Administration Fourth Quarter 1987.* Washington, DC: Government Printing Office, October 1989.

Federal Railroad Administration, Office of Safety. *The Baltimore and Ohio Railroad Company (CSX Transportation/Chessie System).* Washington, DC: Government Printing Office, July 1986.

Federal Railroad Administration, Office of Safety. *Accident/Incident Bulletin, No. 160, Calendar Year 1991.* Washington, DC: Department of Transportation, July 1992.

Federal Railroad Administration, Office of Safety. *Accident/Incident Bulletin, No. 158, Calendar Year 1989.* Washington, DC: Department of Transportation, June 1990.

National Transportation Safety Board. *Annual Review of Aircraft Accident Data: U.S. Air Carrier Operations.* Washington, DC: Government Printing Office, 1986.

National Transportation Safety Board. *Safety Information.* Washington, DC: Government Printing Office, January 1990.

National Transportation Safety Board. *News Release SB 91.03.* Washington, DC January 17, 1991.

RANKING OF THE THREATS

Douglas, Mary and Aaron Wildavsky. *Risk and Culture: An Essay on the Selection of Technical and Environmental Dangers.* Berkeley, CA: University of California Press, 1982.

Insurance Information Institute, *The Fact Book 1993: Property/Casualty Insurance Facts.* New York, 1993.

"Risk," *Daedalus,* Fall 1990.

Slovic, Paul. "Perception of Risk," *Science,* Vol. 236, 17 April 1987.

RELATIONSHIP OF FEMA PROGRAMS TO THE THREATS

Federal Emergency Management Agency. *CCA General Program Guidance.* CPG 1-3. Washington, DC, June 1987.

Federal Emergency Management Agency. *Federal Response Plan.* Washington, DC, April 1992.

Federal Emergency Management Agency. *A Guide to Federal Aid in Disasters.* Washington, DC, June 1990.

Federal Emergency Management Agency. *Civil Defense: A Report to Congress on National Disaster Preparedness.* Washington, DC, March 1992.

Glossary

alternate site

A designated location, remote from the facility, that is used to process data and/or conduct critical business functions in the event of a disaster.

blizzard warnings

Issued when sustained winds of a least 35 mph are accompanied by considerable falling and/or blowing snow.

business continuity planning

A planning effort designed to develop preparedness activities for the continued operation of critical business functions in the event of a disaster.

cold site

A facility that has no resources or equipment designed for activities such as computer operations, telephone operations, and general organizational functions. Any required resources and equipment must be installed in this facility to duplicate the critical business functions of a business.

command

The act of directing, ordering, and/or controlling resources by virtue of explicit legal, agency, or delegated authority.

command post

The location at which primary command functions are executed.

critical business records

Records and documents which, if damaged or destroyed, would cause considerable disruption to the facility because of the cost of replacing the records, loss of efficiency, or lost business.

critique

An evaluation of the actions of personnel during an emergency situation. A critique is not to place blame; it is intended to provide information on areas of the plan and training in need of improvement.

decontamination

The process of removing harmful materials (hazardous materials) from personnel, protective clothing, and equipment.

direct losses

Losses that are measured in terms of dollars lost as the result of the emergency.

disaster recovery

The restoration, through the implementation of planned procedures, of critical business functions following a disaster that disrupts services and facilities.

emergency

Any event which threatens to, or actually does, inflict damage to property or people.

emergency action plan

A written document, developed in accordance with regulatory guidelines, that provides guidance to employees and employers during an emergency situation.

emergency operations center

A site (usually a safe distance from the emergency scene) from which management personnel exercise direction and control in an emergency situation.

emergency planning

The process of developing procedures and practices for the handling of emergency situations.

Emergency Planning and Community Right-to-Know Act

Commonly referred to as SARA Title III, this act requires the development of comprehensive hazardous materials emergency response plans by every community. These plans are developed by the Local Emergency Planning Committee (LEPC).

emergency response team (ERT)

A generic term used to identify a group of personnel assembled for the purpose of responding to emergency situations. ERTs must receive specialized training for emergency activities. (An ERT may be trained to respond to only one type of emergency, such as a fire or a medical emergency, or it may have multiple capabilities, such as the ability to respond to fire, hazardous materials, medical, and confined space emergencies.)

ERT

See Emergency Response Team.

Federal Emergency Management Agency (FEMA)

The agency responsible for directing federal efforts related to preparedness for, mitigation of, response to, and recovery from emergencies encompassing the full range of natural and manmade disasters.

FEMA

See Federal Emergency Management Agency.

flood plain

Level land that may be submerged by floodwaters.

hazardous material

Any substance or material in any form or quantity which poses an unreasonable risk to safety and health, the environment, or property.

hazard and risk management assessment

A comprehensive assessment of a business's potential for and its projected ability to handle an emergency situation and remain in business.

HAZWOPER

Hazardous Waste Operations and Emergency Response, a federal OSHA regulation (29 CFR 1910.120), which deals with the response to and handling of hazardous materials emergency incidents.

heavy snow warning

Indicates that snowfalls of at least 4 inches in 12 hours or 6 inches in 24 hours are expected.

high wind watch

Indicates sustained winds of at least 40 mph, or gusts of 50 mph or greater, which are expected to last for at least one hour.

hot site

An alternate facility that is supplied with the equipment and resources needed to allow a business to conduct critical operations following a disaster.

hurricane warning

A weather advisory issued by the National Weather Service which alerts people in coastal areas that may feel the full effects of a hurricane within 24 hours.

hurricane watch

A weather advisory issued by the National Weather Service which alerts people in the coastal areas that the hurricane may impact and informs those within the watch area to listen for further advisories and be ready to take precautionary actions.

incident action plan

The strategic goals, tactical objectives, and support requirements for the incident. All emergency incidents require an action plan. For simple incidents, the action plan is not usually in written form. Large or complex incidents will require that the action plan be documented in writing.

ICS

See incident command system.

incident command system (ICS)

An incident management system with a common organizational structure responsible for the management of assigned resources to effectively accomplish the stated objectives pertaining to an incident.

incident debriefing

The process of reviewing an emergency incident to inform personnel about any health hazards that might result from the incident, identify any equipment damaged or unsafe conditions that exist, assign information-gathering responsibilities to be used in the critique, and summarize the activities performed by personnel during the emergency.

indirect losses

Losses, resulting from an emergency incident, that may be difficult to measure in terms of dollars, such as human suffering, lost business, and loss of trained employees.

LEPC

See Local Emergency Planning Committee.

Local Emergency Planning Committee (LEPC)

A planning body appointed by the State Emergency Response Commission (SERC) under the requirements of SARA Title III. It is responsible for the development of a comprehensive hazardous materials emergency response plan for the community.

material safety data sheet (MSDS)

Chemical information form, generally prepared by the manufacturer of a hazardous chemical, indicating the hazards—both chemical and physical—that can be anticipated when using the material.

MSDS

See Material Safety Data Sheet.

mutual aid agreements

Agreements among companies and government agencies to assist one another, within defined limits, during major emergencies.

National Fire Protection Association (NFPA)

An international nonprofit organization that develops fire protection and safety related standards and codes.

NFPA

See National Fire Protection Association.

Occupational Safety and Health Administration (OSHA)

The federal agency responsible for the development and enforcement of worker safety regulations.

OSHA

See Occupational Safety and Health Administration.

personal protective equipment

Equipment used to provide protection to personnel when working in or near hazardous environments.

PPE

See personal protective equipment.

SARA

See Superfund Amendments and Reauthorization Act of 1986.

SERC

See State Emergency Response Commission.

severe thunderstorm

A weather advisory, issued by the National Weather Service, which alerts to the possibility of frequent lightning and/or damaging winds of greater than 50 mph, hail 3/4 inch or more in diameter, and heavy rain.

severe thunderstorm watch

A weather advisory issued by the National Weather Service which alerts to the possibility of tornadoes, thunderstorms, frequent lightning, hail, and winds of greater than 75 mph.

State Emergency Response Commission (SERC)

A committee appointed by the governor of each state as part of the requirements of SARA Title III. The SERC oversees the development of the local emergency response plans developed by the Local Emergency Planning Committees (LEPC).

Superfund Amendments and Reauthorization Act of 1986 (SARA)

This act amended and reauthorized the Comprehensive Environmental Response, Compensation, and Liability Act of 1980 (CERCLA) and added two very important components: (1) Title I, which led to the issuance of Hazardous Waste Operations and Emergency Response (HAZWOPER) by OSHA, and (2) Title III which is the Emergency Planning and Community Right-to-Know Act.

technological hazard

Includes a range of hazards resulting from the manufacture, transportation, and use of such substances as radioactive materials, chemicals, explosives, flammables, pesticides, and disease-causing agents.

tornado warning

A weather advisory issued by the National Weather Service which alerts that a tornado has actually been sighted in the area or has been detected by radar.

tornado watch

A weather advisory issued by the National Weather Service which alerts to the possibility that tornadoes could develop in the designated watch area.

travelers' advisory

A weather advisory issued by the National Weather Service to warn that falling, blowing, or drifting snow, freezing rain or drizzle, sleet, or strong winds may make driving difficult.

tropical storm warnings

A weather advisory issued by the National Weather Service which warns listeners that an area may receive gale-force winds in excess of 40 mph.

warm site

An alternate facility that is partially equipped to resume critical business functions.

winter storm warning

Warns listeners that severe winter weather conditions are imminent.

winter storm watch

Warns listeners that severe winter weather conditions may affect their area. These conditions, which may include freezing rain, sleet, or heavy snow, could occur either separately or in combination.

Index

N

O

P

R

S